Gore Vidal was born in 1925 at the United States Military Academy at West Point. He was brought up in Washington, D.C. He enlisted in the army at the age of seventeen and served as first mate on an army ship in the Bering Sea, where he wrote his first book, *Williwaw*. In the sixties, three widely praised novels established Vidal's reputation as a bestselling author: *Julian* (1964); *Washington, D.C.* (1967); and *Myra Breckinridge* (1968). His collected essays, *United States,* won the National Book Award in 1993. In 1995 he published a memoir, *Palimpsest,* which the *Sunday Times* called 'one of the best first-person accounts of this century we are likely to get'.

Also by GORE VIDAL

NOVELS

Narratives of Empire
Burr
Lincoln
1876
Empire
Hollywood
Washington, D.C.
The Golden Age
Williwaw
In a Yellow Wood
The City and the Pillar
The Season of Comfort
A Search for the King
Dark Green, Bright Red
The Judgment of Paris
Messiah
Julian
Myra Breckinridge
Two Sisters
Myron
Kalki
Creation
Duluth
Live from Golgotha
The Smithsonian
Institution

SHORT STORIES

A Thirsty Evil

PLAYS

An Evening with
Richard Nixon
Weekend
Romulus
The Best Man
Visit to a Small Planet

ESSAYS

Rocking the Boat
Reflections upon a
Sinking Ship
Homage to Daniel Shays
Matters of Fact and of Fiction
Pink Triangle and Yellow Star
Armageddon?
At Home
Screening History
A View from the Diners Club
United States:
Essays 1952–1992
Palimpsest: A Memoir
Virgin Islands
The Essential Gore Vidal

The Last Empire

ESSAYS 1992–2001

GORE VIDAL

An *Abacus* Book

First published in Great Britain by Abacus in 2002
Reprinted 2002

A CIP catalogue record for this book
is available from the British Library.

ISBN 0 349 11528 1

Typeset in Adobe Garamond by M Rules
Printed and bound in Great Britain by Clays Ltd, St Ives plc

Abacus
An imprint of
Time Warner Books UK
Brettenham House
Lancaster Place
London WC2E 7EN

www.TimeWarnerBooks.co.uk

Contents

Lost New York   1

Reply to a Critic   19

Twain's Letters   24

Lindbergh: The Eagle is Grounded   29

Sinatra   51

C. P. Cavafy   56

Amistad   63

Wiretapping the Oval Office   78

Clare Boothe Lace   91

Hersh's JFK   108

Honorable Albert A. Gore, Junior   128

Bad History   149

Blair   159

The Last Empire   164

Shredding the Bill of Rights   188
The New Theocrats   214
Coup de Starr   220
Starr Conspiracy   223
Birds and Bees and Clinton   229
A Letter to Be Delivered   234
Democratic Vistas   243
Three Lies to Rule By   248
Japanese Intentions in the Second World War   259
The Meaning of Timothy McVeigh   270
Black Tuesday   303

Lost New York

By 1946 I had spent three years in the army, where the name of the daily *New York Times* book reviewer, Orville Prescott, struck not a bell, while, to the few who were literary-minded, Edmund Wilson meant everything. Wilson was The American Critic whose praise – or even attention – in *The New Yorker* meant earthly glory for a writer. When my first novel was published, I realized that he no longer bothered much with current novels or new writers. Although politely loyal to commercialite friends like Charles Jackson and Edwin O'Connor, he was now working up large subjects – most lately the suppurating wound of Philoctetes, the necessary archer. Also, he was known to have a not-so-secret passion for beautiful young women who wrote beautiful young prose that he might nurture with his generous praise and gentle advice ('"i" before "e" except after "c," dearest') and, indeed, if he could hack it, actual presence in their lives should the dice so fall. Even so, one still hoped. In my case, in vain – snake eyes.

It was the prissy Orville Prescott who praised me while Mr.

Wilson astonished everyone that season with a Pythian ode to a beautiful young woman called Isabel Bolton, whose first book, *Do I Wake or Sleep*, he hailed as 'school of Henry James . . . the device of the sensitive observer who stands at the center of the action and through the filter of whose consciousness alone the happenings of the story reach us . . . a voice that combines, in a peculiar way, the lyric with the dry; and is exquisitely perfect in accent; every syllable falls as it should . . .' A star was born.

A comic legend was also born. Wilson, ravished by the beauty of Bolton's prose, hoped that its creator was equally beautiful and so . . . Well, Wilson was very much school of Montaigne. Like Montaigne, he was not exactly misogynistic but he felt that the challenge of another male mind was the highest sort of human exchange while possession of a beautiful woman was also of intense importance to him. Could the two ever be combined – the ultimate soulmate? Montaigne thought that if women endured the same education and general experience as men they would probably be no different and so intellectual equality might be achieved. But he gave no examples. By Wilson's time, many women had been similarly educated and luminous feminine minds – chock-a-block with *pensées* – were very much out there. But what about . . . well, to be blunt, Beauty? Could Mind as well as Beauty be found in one person?

Wilson's lifelong quest led him into some strange culs-de-sac. The strangest of all must have been when he discovered that Isabel Bolton – name deliberately reminiscent of Isabel Archer? – was, in reality, a majestic granddame of sixty-three, born Mary Britton Miller in 1883 at New London, Connecticut.

Only five minutes, so legend goes, after my sister. This participation in identical twinship is the most valuable experience of my life . . . Both of my parents died of

pneumonia and within an hour of each other in the fourth
year of my life . . . In my fourteenth year my twin sister
was drowned. After this there seems to be a kind of
blotting out of life – everything became dim, unreal,
artificial.

Perfunctory attendance at a boarding school. A well-off family
made travels in Europe possible. 'Three years in Italy were of profound importance. In 1911 New York became my permanent
home.'

As Miller, she published a half-dozen unmemorable works.
Then, in 1946, she recreated herself under another name; and
entered her kingdom. Wilson's was the first fanfare for a woman
who was to write a half-dozen more novels of which two are as distinguished as her 'first' (the three are now collected in *New York
Mosaic*). Bolton died in 1979 at ninety-two, productive almost to
the end. As practically nothing is now known of her, editor Doris
Grumbach does her best with the odd facts: Bolton came from a
'good' family; had two close lady friends; lived in pre-1914 Europe
and then Manhattan. Attended the Writers' Colony at Yaddo.
Died in Greenwich Village at 81 Barrow Street, not far from where
Wilson's jolliest muse, Dawn Powell, lived. The rest is, so far,
silence, secret – Sapphic?

So little is known of Bolton that one does not know if she and
Wilson ever met. But I am fairly certain he saw to it that they did.
A meeting only the prose of Henry James could have risen to,
unlike the equally great Edith Wharton, who might have fallen
upon it with terrible rending eagle's swoop:

There had been – one wondered not so idly why – no
photograph or other rendering of likeness or, even,

dislikeness, on the homely paper 'jacket' that embraced the
ever, to Wilson, with each passing day, more precious
volume, the distilled essence of all feminine beauty and
sensibility, quite overpowering in its effect upon his
perhaps too febrile adhesive system for which the names so
boldly yet, by some magical art, demurely printed on this
very same 'jacket' convey to him the physical beauty of the
divine girl who had 'cut to roundness and smoothed to
convexity a little crystal of literary form that concentrates
the light like a burning glass' – his very own words in his
devoir for *The New Yorker*, written with so much pounding
of the heart as, to put it in a plain and vulgar fashion, a cry
from that never *not* susceptible heart – in short, a love
letter to the unknown girl – surely, a girl of genius rather
than a woman like his handsome, brilliant, but – well,
incendiary (literally) wife, Mary McCarthy, who had
recently, when he had withdrawn to his study and locked
the door, slipped under that same door a single sheet of
paper deliberately set aflame in order to smoke him, as it
were, from his lair, all the while shouting in a powerful
voice, not so much golden as a reverberating cymbal of
purest brass, 'Fuck you.' The plangent voice resounded
even now, unpleasantly, in his mind, as he rang the
doorbell to a Greenwich Village residence set in a quarter
not too – nor less than – fashionable.

The door opened. 'Mr. Wilson.' The voice was neither
golden nor bronze but of another quality and substance
entirely – honey from Hymettus, collected from blue and
white Attic flowers – perhaps those very same asphodels
which adorn the hill at Marathon that looks upon the sea,
wine-dark sea like the eyes of Isabel Bolton into which he
now so intensely gazed that he let fall the cluster of white

violets he was holding and they scattered, as offering, at her shapely feet encased in crimson velvet with the sort of high instep that caused his heart to beat even more wildly than before. 'Do forgive me,' he said, collecting the fallen blossoms as the divine girl, all willowy with golden hair – no sign of chemical artifice in *those* massed curls – and the small exquisite poitrine like – what was it? gazelles? He must really get around to learning Hebrew one day.

Wilson's praise of the perfect book came in bursts of sound between articulated wheezes of emotion as he drank the perfectly made martini – plainly, there was to be no end to her genius – and his heart, that metaphor as well as vulnerable organ, rattled in his bosom like the unfortunate occupant in the fabled ferrous mask. Here, at last, she was. So entirely *there*, so real – man-brain in girl-shape. She was tantalizingly silent. So must Moira – Fate for the ancient Greeks – have appeared upon first encounter with a mere mortal.

An inner door of the tastefully decorated – all Englishy and yet impeccable – chamber opened, revealing a tall woman, old but majestic, with the creased brow of Juno beneath white hair parted in the middle. As the ancient Norn strode into the room, Wilson rose from his chair, saying to the perfect girl, 'This then is your mother?' The powerful old lady smiled and held out her hand.

'No, Mr. Wilson. I am the Isabel Bolton you have lately written so amiably of in the popular press. This . . .' she indicated the girl of what had been his best dream, ever, 'is my ward, Cherry.' With that, Bolton shook Wilson's hand while her other arm enfolded lovingly, possessively, the narrow waist of the perfect girl.

As Wilson made his all too slow, it seemed to him,

descent to the – yes, entirely clear at last, figure in the Persian carpet, he heard, from far-off, Bolton's voice – could it have been one of brass like Mary's? 'I fear that Mr. Wilson has fainted. But then he is very stout. It is not uncommon at our age. Bring smelling salts.' The last thing he saw were the heavy leather boots of the old lady, with their – what else? fallen insteps.

Needless to say, I have invented Cherry, yet there is often a Sapphic glow to Bolton's exchanges between women. In *Do I Wake or Sleep* the relationship between the exquisite Bridget (for whom Wilson fell as Bolton's surrogate) and the rough-hewn Millicent is lover-like in the teasing French manner rather than today's klutzy American style where each would have had to wear an auctorial label and, if sympathetic, behave correctly according to rules laid down by the heirs and heiresses of Cotton Mather. Happily, for Bolton, the amatory simply is; and, in general, gaiety (old meaning) rules and no one is assigned a label much less sold off in midseason to a team. In this, she is as alien to us as Ovid, and I suspect only a very few rare spirits ever took to her even when the books first came out in post-Hitler days, a time of stern *Julius Caesar* rather than her own *Midsummer Night's Dream*.

To read Bolton's three novels in sequence is to relive the three major moments of the American half century as observed by an unusual writer located aboard what Dawn Powell called 'the happy island,' Manhattan. The first novel takes place in 1939. War is wending its way toward the United States and the protagonist, the enchanting Bridget St. Dennis, is lunching blithely in the French Pavilion at Flushing Meadow's World's Fair. Although the chef, Henri Soulé, would later open what was regarded for many years as New York's best restaurant, it is a part of Bolton's magic that not only do you get quite a few good meals in her books but you get subtle distinctions as well. She shared everyone's delight in Le Pavillon's transfer from Flushing to Manhattan. But Bolton herself opts for the magical Chambord in Third Avenue where, as the cartoon used to say, the elite meet to eat or, as someone said to an ancient bon viveur who was recently extolling the long-vanished Chambord, 'You are living in the past,' to which the old man replied, 'Where else can you get a decent meal?'

Bolton belongs to the James–Wharton school of transatlantic fiction or, perhaps, a new category should be invented – of *mid*-Atlantic literature that flourished, to put arbitrary dates like bookends to its history, from Hawthorne's *Our Old Home* (1863) to T. S. Eliot's *Four Quartets*, published in 1943. It was a long and lively run and brought out the best in two literatures never destined to be one but each able to complement the other while even those professionally committed to the American side, like Twain and Howells, touched base regularly with their common old home. For a writer born in 1883, with sufficient family money but no Jamesian fortune, Europe would be as much a part of her life as Brookline, Massachusetts, where the last of Bolton's protagonists hails from: a world of numerous servants, of courses at dinner, of changes of clothes, presumably to give the servants more than enough to do in the pre-1914 world when Bolton was already a grown woman. As it turned out, pre-1914 continued well into the modern age of cocktails and movie stars – one of Edith Wharton's least-known novels, *Twilight Sleep*, deals with a Hollywood movie star in a way that must make the Collins sisters, the Bel-Air Brontës, quite nervous at how well the stately Mrs. Wharton depicts the life of one who lives on the screen everywhere on earth but nowhere at all in the flesh at home. Then, with Depression and Second War the old world expired. Good riddance, the modern thought. Bolton is of two minds. She is conscious of the *douceur de la vie* of the old time; also of the narrow callow brazen world that that time was rendering all gold, or trying to.

Wilson gets quite right Bolton's 'Jamesian technique in *Do I Wake or Sleep*: the single consciousness that observes all.' I missed it in the first chapter, which is all Bridget, lovingly observed, I thought, by author-god. Then, gradually, one realizes that it is the other woman at the table whose mind we've entered.

Plot: *Do I Wake or Sleep*. Bridget is having lunch at the French Pavilion with a besotted (by her) popular novelist, Percy Jones, equally besotted by martinis, and one Millicent, 'a writer of witty articles and famous tales – beloved of Hollywood.' A character perhaps influenced by Dorothy Parker and from whose point of view the story is told.

Bridget enchants at lunch; and her creator convinces us that she does so by what she says, not often quoted, and by the way that she includes everyone in a kind of vital intimacy. But she is unexpectedly evasive on the subject of her child, Beatrice. We learn that Bridget was born Rosenbaum; married Eric von Mandestadt, 'an Aryan (she'd used the ridiculous word as though it had been incorporated into all the European tongues).' Percy is very much on the case: Beatrice is in Vienna with her paternal grandmother; the Nazis are there, too. Percy feels that it is urgent that the child be got out but Bridget ignores the subject. The first chapter is a very special example of the storyteller's art. It seems to be told in standard third person. But, gradually, with an aside here, a parenthesis there, one realizes that the consciousness taking all this in is the near-silent Millicent, who, in the next chapter, takes shape and autonomy. It is an elegant trick of narrative.

At lunch, Millicent observes and records Bridget as she hovers like a bright blur-winged hummingbird over many subjects. Wilson and Grumbach find much of James, Woolf, and the

Elizabeth Bowen of *The Death of the Heart* in the prose but Bridget herself finesses that essential trio:

> She had been in her brief existence two distinctly different
> beings, and one of these was the creature she was before
> and the other she had become after reading the works of
> Marcel Proust. No, really, she wasn't joking. From the
> experience she'd emerged with all manner of extensions,
> reinforcements, renewals of her entire nervous system –
> indeed, she might say that she'd been endowed with a
> perfectly new apparatus for apprehending the vibration of
> other people's souls . . . We were forced to take about with
> us wherever we went this extraordinary apparatus,
> recording accurately a thousand little matters of which we
> had not formerly been aware, and whether she was glad or
> sorry to be in possession of so delicate and precise an
> instrument, she had never been able to determine.

There is something to be said for putting off one's official first novel until the age of sixty-three. Certainly Bolton is not in the least diffident when it comes to putting the homegrown American product in its place, which is way out yonder in those amber fields of grain:

> Did [Percy] really believe that American novelists were
> ready to accept, to celebrate the same creature, the same
> human heart? It seemed to her that they were always trying
> to reshape, to remold the creature according to some
> pattern they desperately yearned to have it conform
> to – . . . would he agree with her that American novels
> seldom went deep into the realities of character – weren't
> they dealing more with circumstances, places – epochs,

environments? They came boiling up out of the decades –
out of the twenties, out of the thirties – out of
Pittsburgh . . .

Poor novelist Percy is reeling by now. Yes, he is inclined to agree
with her that American novelists are moralists but . . . Henry
James, he makes the great name toll over the guinea hen. Bridget
counterattacks – Dostoyevsky. 'Who could really call Henry James
in comparison a good psychologist? . . . matchless brilliance and
probity . . . innocent, indignant and upright response to the
vulgar, the brutal, the material aspects of society . . . But if you
tried to compare him with Dostoyevsky, he was a child, a holy
innocent. [Dostoyevsky] was the traveler in the desert of the soul.'

Fast forward, another restaurant: 'I believe,' said the head
waiter, benignly, 'this is Mr. Michael Korda's table. There's been
some mistake. I do apologize. He is with,' a conspiratorial whisper,
'Mr. Stephen King.'

Yes, to this day, the Four Seasons still echoes with that never-
ending literary debate as the waiter shows them to their table in a
shallow pool of water. 'Mr. Kissinger's favorite table. But as it's
Tuesday, he's lunching in Beijing.'

The plot is simply the next day. Lunch again with Percy and
Millicent. Percy obsessed by the child as putative victim of the
Nazis. Bridget evasive. They meet at the Algonquin. Go on to
Chambord. Dover sole newly arrived in brine aboard the
Normandie. Later, to a cocktail party – *the* New York cocktail
party of the Forties where the currently celebrated and fashionable
mill about, grist for Millicent's eye and ear ever grinding them all
up, finer and finer. Percy, drunk, misbehaves: gets knocked out.
Doctor comes. No, he is not dead. The party ends – the denoue-
ment is that the child is somehow defective – the word 'cretin' is
used, rather than 'challenged' as they now say at the Four Seasons:

in fact, a sort of monster. Then we learn that Bridget's evasiveness is due to the fact that she is currently penniless; even so, she will bring the child home.

What strikes one most is Millicent's deep-seated passion for America in general and for New York City in particular, understandable in the case of a provincial like Thomas Wolfe come wide-eyed to the web and the rock but odd in a partly Europeanized woman of her age. There has been a definite shift in mood since the generation before her: Mrs. Wharton shuddered at the sound of American voices and Henry James gave a murderously deadpan description of 'American City' somewhere or other out there in the flat empty regions where the states are simply drawn on the national map with a ruler, and the buffalo roam.

Millicent contrasts New York with European cities: 'Here you walked in a vacuum. There were no echoes, no reverberations.' She looks at the Empire State Building.

It was one of the wonders of the world. Nevertheless she
didn't (and how many people she wondered did) even
know the name of its architect. It rose above you,
innocent of fame or fable . . . What a strange, what a
fantastic city: and yet, and yet; there was something here
that one experienced nowhere else on earth. Something
one loved intensely. What was it? Crossing the streets –
standing on the street corners with the crowds: what was it
that induced this special climate of the nerves? . . . There
was something – a peculiar sense of intimacy, friendliness,
being here with all these people and in this strange
place . . . They touched your heart with tenderness
and you felt yourself a part of the real flight and

flutter-searching their faces, speculating about their dooms and destinies.

She has a sudden vision of Apocalypse. War. Towers crashing yet 'an unchallenged faith and love and generosity, which . . . still lay deep-rooted in the American psyche to deliver us from death – remembering the Fair at the Flushing Meadow, the Futurama (sponsored by General Motors and displaying with such naive assurance the chart and prospect of these United States).' There is a kind of patrician Whitman at work here and one wonders does anyone now, nearly sixty years later, feel so intimately about Manhattan, the American fact?

In *The Christmas Tree*, Bolton has moved on to 1945. Mrs. Danforth wants her six-year-old grandson, Henry, to have a proper old-fashioned Christmas tree while all that he wants is to play with his bomber and fighter planes. She lives in a sky-scraper overlooking the East River but a part of her is still anchored in the brownstone world of her youth, 'the days when people really believed in their wealth and special privilege . . . the days of elegance, of arrogance, of ignorance and what a rashly planned security.' Today Christmas is vast and mass-pro-duced on every side unlike the days of her youth. She broods on her son Larry, father to Henry. He lives now in Washington with a male lover while Anne, his ex-wife, is en route to New York for Christmas, accompanied by her new husband, Captain Fletcher, an army air force wing commander. (Bolton errs on this one: he would have been at least a full colonel if not brigadier general.) Mrs. Danforth admires Anne's resilience: the coolness with which she accepts the fact that she is often drawn to 'the invert, the schizophrene, the artist. Men like that were never normal sexually.'

Mrs. Danforth is sufficiently in the grip of the Freudians of the Forties – never again, happily, to be so ubiquitous or so serenely off-base – to wonder if she had loved her son too much when they lived in Paris and it was quite clear to her that, at fifteen, he was having an affair with a French boy a year or two older. 'She'd felt no censure of the boys, she had no inclination to reproach them. She'd only felt an immense love, an overwhelming pity for them. And oh, she questioned passionately, how much could she herself be held responsible for Larry's inclinations? How much had she been implicated?' This was the era of the Oedipus Complex (something Oedipus himself did not suffer from since he didn't know that it was Mom he had married after killing what he hadn't known was Dad); also, of the era of popular books with titles like *Generation of Vipers* – denouncing the American Mom for castrating her sons. Although Proust must have taught Bolton a lot more than Mrs. Danforth would ever learn, it is probably true to the time that Mother would blame herself for her son's unorthodox sexual appetites.

Grumbach likes this the best of Bolton's novels. It is certainly the most tightly plotted; it would make a solid old-fashioned drawing-room comedy with a melodramatic twist. Unfortunately, Bolton's scenes between Larry and his lover are not quite all there on the page and what *is* there doesn't have the reverberation that a memory, say, of Mrs. Danforth's youth sets off in other pages. Bolton also makes the narrative more difficult for herself by shifting points of 'view.' Mrs. Danforth gives way to Larry, preparing to break up with a lover while brooding upon his Parisian past; finally, should he join his ex-wife Anne and her new husband beneath his mother's Christmas tree? We next shift to Anne on her way from Reno with her American husband; she is nostalgic for Larry,

an exceptional human being, she sometimes suspected that
he'd given very little to anyone and that, as a matter of fact,
he'd taken from others even less. It was in his enormous
concern for the general human plight that his affections
were the most implicated; his love of humanity in the large
impersonal sense was profound . . . He was at the mercy of
certain tricks and habits of bad behavior – nervous reflexes
which apparently he could not control . . .

There the fatal flaw is named and prepares us for what is to come.

Anne and her manly captain make up the family scene with the
child and Mrs. Danforth. Larry's presence is a dissonant note made
worse by the arrival of his lover. Despite good manners all around,
the collision between Larry and the captain takes place over the
child, who tells Larry that he hates him. The child prefers the war
hero who has brought him numerous toy planes. The captain then
launches what is currently known as a 'homophobic' rage at Larry,
who tells him to get out. But instead they go out onto the terrace,
sixteen stories above the street. The ladies hear loud voices, terrible
epithets; silence. Larry comes back into the room, alone. He says
that he has killed the captain; pushed him over the railing. No, it
was not an accident.

The others are willing to perjure themselves to save Larry.
But he will not allow it; he rings the police; he confesses. '*Au
revoir, Maman*,' he says, when they come to take him away.
Mother and son have now reverted to their earlier happier
selves . . .

With what pride, with what great pride she had watched
him go!
    There was a flickering, a brightness, somewhere in the
room. She turned; she lifted her eyes. The light was

smiting the silver angel on top of Henry's Christmas tree, poised and trembling, with its wings and herald trumpet shining brightly, there it hung above the guttered candles and the general disarray.

'Pardon us our iniquities, forgive us our transgressions – have mercy on the world,' she prayed.

The Christmas Tree was published one year after the Kinsey Report furrowed a peasant nation's brow. The melodramatic ending meant that Bolton was responding, as so many of us did, to the fierce Zeitgeist. But her general coolness in dealing with the taboo probably accounts for the almost instant obscurity of her work amongst the apple-knockers.

Many Mansions was published when Bolton was close to seventy. She writes of Miss Sylvester, who is recreating her own past by reading a memoir-like novel she had written years earlier. It is February 1, 1950, her birthday: she is eighty-four and Harry Truman's birthday present for her is to give the order to build the hydrogen bomb.

She broods upon her great age:

The life of the aged was a constant maneuvering to appease and assuage the poor decrepit body. Why, most of the time she was nothing more than a nurse attending to its every need. As for the greater part of the night one's position was positively disreputable, all alone and clothed in ugly withering flesh – fully conscious of the ugliness, the ignominy – having to wait upon oneself with such menial devotion – here now, if you think you've got to get up mind you don't fall, put on the slippers, don't trip on the rug.

The body is now a perpetual sly nemesis, waiting to strike its mortal blow.

Meanwhile, Miss Sylvester has taken to pursuing lost time, that long-ago time when the body was a partner in a grand exercise known as life. She also frets about money. Has she enough if she should live to be ninety? Should she die soon, what about leaving her small fortune to the young Adam Stone whom 'she had picked up in a restaurant . . . the only person in her life for whom she felt genuine concern'? Adam had been in the Second War; emerged bitter; devoured books 'ravenously'; was at work upon a novel: 'He had cast off his family. He had cast off one girl after another, or very likely one girl after another had cast him off.' Miss Sylvester had spoken to him in an Armenian restaurant on Fourth Avenue. 'I see you're reading Dante,' was her opening gambit. She knows Italian and he does not; this proves to be an icebreaker though hardly a matchmaker.

Now she turns to her long-abandoned manuscript. Two families. Great houses. And the old century was still a splendid all-golden present for the rich. Seasons now come back to her. 'Summer was that high field on the high shelf above the ocean . . . the surf strong, the waves breaking. Something pretty terrible about it – getting, in one fell swoop, the fury of the breakers carried back to crack and echo in the dunes . . . the wild cold smell of the salt spray inducing mania excitement.' One suspects that Bolton is actually writing of her fourteen-year-old twin who drowned, but Miss Sylvester, her present alter ego, is single and singular and in wild nature more natural.

As an adolescent she lives among numerous grand relatives; but always set apart. Her father was an 'Italian musician,' a 'Dago organ-grinder,' she comes to believe, as the subject is unmentionable. Then, on a memorable Easter Sunday dinner, her grandfather makes a toast, 'Let us drink to the burial of the feud.' The organ-grinder, her father, Sylvester, is dead in southern Italy. He had been paid by the family to go away, leaving behind his daughter as a sort of boarder in their great houses.

Then, almost idly, she falls in love with a married relative; becomes pregnant. The resourceful family assigns yet another relative to her, Cecilia, who takes her to Europe, to fateful Italy, where she is treated as a respectable married woman in an interesting condition. The child, a boy, is born in Fiesole; but she never sees him; her positively Napoleonic family has promptly passed him on to an elegant childless New York couple who whisk him away to a new life, under a name that she will never learn. Cecilia raves about the anonymous couple's charm; their wealth; the guaranteed happiness of the boy's life. Grimly, the mother murmurs the phrase '"tabula rasa," . . . as though she'd coined it.' She would now begin again as if nothing had ever happened.

The old lady finished her reading: 'If her book should fall into the hands of others addicted as she was to the habitual reading of novels, what exactly would their feelings be?' One wonders – is there such a thing now as *a habitual reader* of novels? Even the ambitious, the ravenously literary young Adam seems to have a suspicion that he may have got himself into the stained-glass-window trade.

With a sufficient income, Miss Sylvester moves to New York. She becomes involved with another young woman, Mary (they live in a gentle ladies' pension near Fifth Avenue, presided over by yet another of the multitudinous cousins). 'How passionately Mary loved the world and with what eagerness she dedicated herself to reforming it . . .' The two young women study to be opera singers; but they have no talent. Then Mary involves them in settlement work and organizing women workers – it is the era of the young Eleanor Roosevelt, and Miss Sylvester realizes in old age that 'with all the central founts of love – sexual passion and maternity – so disastrously cut off, had not this deep, this steadfast friendship for Mary been the one human relationship where love had never failed to nourish and replenish her?' But she loses Mary to marriage; then to death, which also claims, at Okinawa, Mary's son.

Miss Sylvester has a long relationship with a Jewish intellectual, Felix; but feels she is too old to marry him; then he announces that he is to marry his secretary, who has been his mistress for ten years: Miss Sylvester's decade of intimacy. They part fondly, for good.

She takes in, as a boarder, a young novelist. Son of a fashionable boring couple she once knew. Bolton is too elegant a novelist to reveal him as the old lady's son but sufficiently mischievous to find him, despite great charm, of indifferent character, even flawed.

The book concludes with Miss Sylvester in her flat, collecting some much needed cash for Adam, who is waiting for her at the Armenian restaurant. But even as he is telephoning, she is felled by a stroke. Angrily, Adam leaves the telephone booth 'to go back in the dining-room to wait for his old lady, under the impression that she is on her way.'

What then was the figure in the carpet that my highly imagined Edmund Wilson made out on his stately way to the floor? As I emerge from Bolton's world, I am sure that what he saw was the fourteen-year-old twin sister brought back from full fathom five – with pearls for eyes – by a great act of will and considerable art to replace the mediocre Mary Britton Miller with a magically alive writer whom she chose to call Isabel Bolton, for our delight.

The New York Review of Books
18 December 1997

Reply to a Critic

While writing about Mark Twain's views on imperialism, I checked some recent 'scholarly' works to see how his reputation is bearing up under the great fiery cross of political correctness. We were all astonished, some years ago, when a squad of sharp-eyed textual investigators discovered, to their manifest surprise and horror, that the noblest character in Twain's fiction was called 'Nigger' Jim. There was an understandable outcry from some blacks; there was also a totally incomprehensible howl from a number of fevered white males, many of them professors emeritus and so, to strike the tautological note, career-minded conservatives unused to manning barricades.

In an apparently vain effort at comprehension, I quoted a number of malicious and, worse, foolish things that these silly-billies are writing about Twain. Thanks to an editorial quirk, one hothead was mentioned by *name*, for which I apologize. I always try to shield the infamous from their folly in the hope that they may, one day, straighten up and fly right. But a single name *was* mentioned and now we have its owner's letter at hand. For serene duplicity and snappy illogic it compares favorably to some of the screeds, I believe they are called, from my pen pals in the Lincoln priesthood.

Although my new pen pal does acknowledge that I am report-ing the views of other critics on Twain's impotence, sexual infantilism, fondness for small girls, he declares mysteriously that this is 'not what I say.' But it is what he says and presumably means. The Jesuits like to say: 'The wise man never lies.' But in the army of my day, any soldier (or indeed discomfited general) who spent too much time twisting about the language of regulations in his own favor was called a guardhouse lawyer. I now put the case on the evidence at hand, that we have here a compulsive guard-house lawyer or quibbler. Straight sentences must be bent like pretzels to change meanings to score points. But then much of what passes for literary discourse in these states is simply hustling words to get them to mean what they don't. 'That Clemens dreamed of little girls is well known.' Thus Quibbler wrote but now he has – tangential? – second thoughts. Actually who knows what Twain's dreams were. But let us agree that he doted on the company of Dodgsonesque girls and so may well have dreamed . . . fantasized about them in a sexual way. Why not? But Quibbler is getting a bit edgy. He thinks, too, that I have given him a splendid chance to open the guardhouse door. Now we improvise: 'that his dreams and reveries were pederastic is not said in my book by me or by anyone else.' But, of course, that's what the professor (and presumably, those whom he adverts to) means in the course of a chapter entitled 'Impotence and Pedophilia.'

But Quibbler has leaped at the adjective 'pederastic.' Like so many Greekless Americans with pretensions, he thinks that the word means a liking for boys by men with buggery on their mind. But I had gone back to the original noun root, *paid*, from which comes pederasty, pedophilia, etc.; and *paid* means not boy but child. A quibble can be made that, as vulgar usage associates the word with boys, that's what I mean but, as context makes clear, it is Lolita-*paid* – not Ganymede-*paid* – that Twain *may* be dreaming of. So this quibble is meaningless.

'The idea of impotence excited Clemens's anxious interest: apparently he suffered from erectile dysfunction at about the age of fifty.' I noted in my review that 'so do many men over fifty who drink as much Scotch whisky as Twain did.' Next: 'Psychoanalysts have noted many cases in which diminished sexual capacity . . . has been related to a constellation of psychic problems like those which affected Clemens.' All right. Which psychoanalysts? Did any know him? As for his psychic problems, did he really have a constellation's worth? 'Evidence that he became impotent ranges from the filmy to the relatively firm' – I had some fun with those two loony adjectives. 'Likelihood is high that diminished capacity may be inferred . . .' All these 'apparentlys,' 'likelihoods,' 'inferreds' as well as filmy to firm 'evidence' appear in one short paragraph.

What we have here is not a serious literary – or even, God help us, psychoanalytic – view of Twain's sex life as imagined by a politically correct schoolteacher but what I take to be outright character assassination of a great man who happens to be one of the handful – small hand, too – of good writers our flimsy culture has produced. ('Filmy,' of course, may be the *mot juste* if we count the movies.) At one point, in the midst of a prurient flow of nonsense, the professor suddenly concedes, 'We do not know the intimate details of Clemens's life very well . . .' I'll say we don't, so why go to such imaginative length to turn him into an impotent pederast, or pedophile?

Point two. Here we get the denial-of-meaning quibble based on Absence of Quotation Marks. I remark on Twain's having, sickeningly, in the professor's view, '*married above his station* in order to advance himself socially.' Blandly, the professor quibbles that he never used the italicized words. Yet they are an exact paraphrase of how he interprets Twain's marriage to Olivia Langdon. Quibbler has reinvented his own text. Actually, it is his view that Twain did not marry above his station in any but the economic sense, although 'like the most bourgeois of the bourgeois he delighted in money, and high living, and he fervently wished to become a member of the eastern establishment.' Surely, to get from Hannibal, Missouri, to the Gold Coast of Hartford was going to take a bit of social climbing, which he did by marrying into the Langdon family.

'Clemens was what Freud would call a narcissistic suitor.' Quibbler acts as if he is quoting some sort of authority in these matters. Ward McAllister might have been more to his point on American social climbing. '[Clemens] ardently wished to marry a woman who typified not what he was but what he wished to be – rich and possessed of status, a member of the eastern social order.' So, as I said in a phrase to which Quibbler objects, for no clear reason, 'he married above his station.' (I'm surprised he does not make the point that Grand Central *Station* was not in use that hymenal year.) My use of the adverb 'sickeningly' was meant to be ironic, something to which the teaching of school tends to make impervious even the brightest and the best. Anyway, Twain's hypergamous marriage was a happy one, so what's the big deal?

A lust for money that is banal anal (as opposed to floral oral) is simply a verbally symmetrical way of setting up Freud's notion of money as 'faeces.' How did I happen to get this juxtaposition in my head? At one point, our author suddenly quibbles that Twain didn't marry Olivia for her money, at least 'not in any banal sense of the phrase; but he very much wanted to be rich.' As I read the word 'banal,' I knew that Freud's theory of anality was coming up. I turned the page. There it was. 'Freud stresses the anal character of money and equates money and feces: it means power, vitality, potency.' The one good thing about bad writing is that one is never surprised by any turn an argument, much less a cliché, may take.

Let me now indulge in quibbler creativity. Freud would never have characterized Twain as narcissistic – an adjective currently used to describe anyone better-looking than oneself. As performer-writer Twain took by storm Vienna in general and Freud in particular. Freud was also something of a connoisseur of jokes and he enjoyed Mark Twain in person and on the page quite as much as he would have reveled in the letter of Professor Emeritus Guy Cardwell. *Ich kann nicht anders,* I can hear Sigmund chuckle through his cigar smoke. (Cf. *The Strange Case of Dr. Luther Adler* by an Unknown Actress – op. cit. Just about anywhere.)

The New York Review of Books
19 September 1996

Twain's Letters

Reporting for the BBC during the election campaign, I stood in front of the Albert Hall, the voice of the crown in Parliament incarnate, John Major, still ringing in my ears as, inside, a recording of Elgar caused a thousand gorges to rise, including that little part of me which is forever Dimbleby. I faced the BBC cameras. A *petit* mini-mini-documentary was in progress. 'Here,' I said, head empty of all but emotion, 'is the proof that only through England's glorious past can a bright future be secured for this land of Drake and Nelson, of Clive – and Crippen.'

The BBC crew was ecstatic: like television crews everywhere, nobody ever listens to what the talking head is actually saying. What had come over me? What on earth was I doing? Well, like most American writers at one time or another, I was playing Mark Twain. The deadpan sonorous delivery. Then the careful dropping of the one fatal name. With Twain's description of the Albert Hall flashing in my head, 'a dome atop a gasometer,' I dimbled on to the safe ground of the understated cliché.

Mark Twain is our greatest . . . Mark Twain. He is not, properly speaking, a novelist nor 'just' a journalist nor polemicist. He is simply a voice like no other. The only mystery to him is this: was he a great comic actor who could also write much as he acted, or was he a great writer who could also act, like Dickens? Some evidence of how he did both is now at hand in the form of the 309 letters that he wrote in the years 1872–3, when he first visited England and took the country by storm as a performer (the books *Innocents Abroad* and *Roughing It* had already, despite – or because of – their Americanness, been popular). England also took hugely to the thirty-six-year-old Twain (a.k.a. Samuel Clemens of Hannibal, Mo., and Hartford, Conn.). To his wife, Olivia, he wrote, after six months' residence in the Langham Hotel (later to contain the BBC's secret abattoir), 'I would rather live in England than America – which is treason.' The fact of the matter is that he was having a wonderful time being lionized by London's tamers, ever on the lookout for a good joke. But then, as he himself put it, he was 'by long odds the most widely known and popular American author among the English.' This was true too.

On Twain's first trip he did not lecture. On his second, accompanied by wife and daughter, he filled halls with a lecture on the Sandwich Islands, which he eventually tired of and replaced with one on his early days in Nevada, based on *Roughing It.*

The liking for a country not one's own (or for a celebrity not one's own) is usually based on serious misunderstandings all around. Twain's comedy was based on a Manichaean view of life. But neither audiences nor readers suspected the darkness that was at the core of his curious sensibility. As for Twain himself, in England he was very much the passionate pilgrim, to appropriate Henry James's phrase (it can safely be said that the two writers could not abide each other). Each in his own way had found American society a bit on the thin side. But where James was after very big game indeed, psychologically, Twain simply preferred local color, while reveling in a sense of the past that often came rather too close to ye olde. 'Spent all day yesterday driving about Warwickshire in an open barouche. We visited Kenilworth ruins, Warwick Castle (pronounce it Warrick) and the Shakespeare celebrities in and about Stratford-on-Avon (pronounce that 'a' just as you would in Kate).' All in all, 'I would rather live here if I could get the rest of you over.' As it turned out, by the end of his life he had lived seventeen years abroad, much of the time in England.

But there are some marked oddities in these love letters to England. For one thing there are hardly any people in them, any English people, that is. Trollope had him to dinner at the Garrick, but he gives no description of this occasion even when writing to his bookish mother. He met Browning: no serious mention. He does ask the poet laureate to one of his lectures and, thoughtfully, sends along a ticket. Return post: 'Dear Sir, I saw some of your countrymen last Sunday who spoke so highly of your Lectures that I longed to come and hear you; but whether I come or not I am equally beholden to you for your kindness. Yours with all thanks, A. Tennyson.' Not quite in the class of Disraeli, thanking an author for sending him a book 'which I shall waste no time in reading.'

Where are the London hostesses of the day? Did they pursue him? He hated staying in other people's houses so there are no descriptions of Bitter Homes and Gardens. For someone who had just finished a political satire, *The Gilded Age* (a 'partnership' novel, he called it, with Charles Dudley Warner), he does not seem to have met any politicians other than the MP Douglas Straight, whose family was soon to be transatlantic. He does not mention what, if anything, he is reading. During his first London seasons he is simply absorbing color and drawing strength from the great crowds that come to hear him; first in Hanover Square and, later, around England.

These are very much the letters and thoughts of a businessman-actor-writer with a gift for comedy. He is, in short, a star on tour as well as a writer with an ever-alert eye for incidents to be used in such later books as *A Connecticut Yankee* and *The Prince and the Pauper*. Current productions by others (Samuel Butler's *Erewhon*, Thomas Hardy's *Under the Greenwood Tree*, and John Stuart Mill's *Autobiography*) go unremarked.

So what then did British audiences actually see and hear? London *Daily News*: 'Mr. Twain is a comparatively young man, small in form and feature, dark-haired and dark complexioned.' Actually, he was ginger-haired with a ruddy face. 'He has a good deal of the nasal tone of some portion of the Americans.' London *Examiner*: 'His dry manner, his admirable self-possession, and perfectly grave counten-ance formed a background that made the humorous portion of the lecture irresistible.' Often with no more than a carefully positioned pause, he would set up his joke, let the audience do the rest. 'A smile never appears on his lips and he makes the most startling remarks as if he were uttering merest commonplace.'

But a predictably sour note was struck by the expatriate secetary to the American legation: 'He [Twain] is a wiry man, with brown, crisp, wiry hair: a narrow forehead, Roman nose and sinister expression, and does not seem to know as much as would hurt him.' The secretary had once had literary longings.

Mark Twain's Letters covers two years in 691 pages, of which one is blank except for the ominous phrase 'Editorial Apparatus.' To come? One trembles. This is hardly a labor of love for the common reader. There are footnotes upon footnotes. Nothing is not explained. Twain meets a gentleman who affects a Plantagenet connection. The irrelevant history of that broomish family is flung at the reader.

American scholarship is now a sort of huge make-work program for the conventionally educated. In a case like this, scholar squirrels gather up every scrap of writing they can find and stuff these bits into volume after volume, with metastasizing footnotes. The arrangements that Mr. and Mrs. Clemens made to have their laundry and dry-cleaning done by mail (no, I won't explain how that worked) is a joy for those of us who revel in dry-cleaning, but what of the unkempt many who sit in darkness? No matter. We are dealing here with ruthless collectors. To them, one 'fact' is equal to any other. I accept this thoroughness. But is it necessary to note every phrase – indeed every letter of the alphabet that Twain and his various correspondents saw fit to cross out? ~~Like this~~. No.

The Sunday Times
11 May 1997

Lindbergh: The Eagle Is Grounded

On May 20–21, 1927, in thirty-three and a half hours, Charles A. Lindbergh, Jr., flew nonstop from New York City to Paris's Le Bourget airport. At the age of twenty-five, Slim, as he was known to associates, became the most famous person in the world, and so he remained for much of a life that ended in 1974. As is usual with heroes, his popularity waxed and waned; also, as is not usual with ordinary heroes, he was much more than just the one adventure. He was also an engineering genius with a mystical bent that, by the time of his death, had made him regret the world he had helped create – *Modern Times* (starring the world's second most recognized man, Charlie Chaplin). Slim was drawn more and more to Thoreau and to primal nature as well as to Lao Tzu, who saw essential change in those waters and tides that are able to wear down rock surfaces, no matter how adamantine, in order to make a new world. Finally, he turned himself into a good writer; school of Julius Caesar, yes, but Caesar crossed with Lucretius' sense of the beauty of 'things' and their arrangement, precisely described.

Lindbergh was a very strange sort of American for the first part of the century now ending. He is practically incomprehensible today.

A. Scott Berg has produced a characteristically workmanlike survey of the many things that Lindbergh did, and of some of the things that he was. Aside from the creation of airlines in the 1930s, he invented a 'perfusion pump,' variations of which now keep alive bodily organs until they are ready to be transplanted. Also, as early as 1929, the prescient Lindbergh befriended Robert Goddard, whose rocket research could have given the United States the unmanned missile long before Hitler's V-2, which nearly won the war for the Nazis.

In 1932, when the Lindberghs' two-year-old son was kidnapped and killed, fearful for their growing family and hounded by a press every bit as dreadful then as now, Lindbergh and his wife, Anne Morrow, moved to Europe, where they stayed for three years.

At the request of the American military, Lindbergh checked out the German Luftwaffe, which he found alarmingly advanced in both design and production, while the French and British air forces combined were not in the same league. In 1939 Lindbergh came home to call for 'an impregnable system of defense.' Also, between 1939 and 1941, he was the chief voice raised against U.S. intervention in the Second World War. In a notorious speech at Des Moines in 1941, he identified America's three interventionist groups: the Roosevelt administration, the Jews, and the British. Although the country was deeply isolationist, the interventionists were very resourceful, and Lindbergh was promptly attacked as a pro-Nazi anti-Semite when he was no more than a classic Midwestern isolationist, reflective of a majority of the country. But along with such noble isolationists as Norman Thomas and Burton K. Wheeler, not to mention Lindbergh's friend Harry Guggenheim's foundation, the 'America First' movement, as it was called, did attract some genuine homegrown fascists who would have been amazed to learn that there was never a 'Jewish plot' to get the United States into the Second World War. Quite the contrary. Before Pearl Harbor, as Berg notes, 'though most of the American motion-picture studios were owned by Jews, most were virtually paranoid about keeping pro-Jewish sentiment off the screen.' Also, Arthur Hayes Sulzberger, publisher of *The New York Times*, confided as late as September 1941 to the British Special Operations Executive agent Valentine Williams 'that for the first time in his life he regretted being a Jew because, with the tide of anti-Semitism rising, he was unable to champion the anti-Hitler policy of the administration as vigorously and as universally as he would like, as his sponsorship would be attributed to Jewish influence by isolationists and thus lose something of its force.'

It was not until November 25, 1996, that an American academic, Thomas E. Mahl, researching Britain's various Secret Service archives, came across the Williams file. He has now published *Desperate Deception*, as full a story as we are ever apt to get of 'British Covert Operations in the United States 1939–44.' Although media and schools condition Americans to start giggling at the mention of the word 'conspiracy,' there are, at any moment, all sorts of conspiracies crisscrossing our spacious skies and amber fields of grain, and of them all in this century; the largest, most intricate and finally most successful was that of the British to get us into the Second World War. Mahl shows us just how busy their operatives were, from Ronald Colman starring in pro-British films and the Korda brothers making them, to Walter Winchell reading on his Sunday broadcast pro-British messages written for him by Ernest Cuneo, who also ghosted pro-British newspaper columns for Drew Pearson. There was indeed a vast conspiracy to maneuver an essentially isolationist country into war. There was also a dedicated conspiracy to destroy Lindbergh's reputation as hero.

Meanwhile, just who was the hero? In 1932 the rococo English journalist Beverly Nichols met Lindbergh. 'What is all this fuss about flying the Atlantic?' Nichols later marveled. 'Isn't that just the sort of thing a bore like that *would* do? Now if Noel or I had flown, you would have a real story!' So one would. But Slim did fly, alone, and thereby hangs a century's great story, The Lone Eagle.

Lindbergh's daughter, Reeve, has now written a charming memoir of her father and mother, *Under a Wing*. She sets out to place her father in his native country, specifically, at Little Falls, above the Mississippi River in northern Minnesota. For reasons that have to do with the nature of the sky in the upper Midwest, a great many of the early – I almost wrote *real* – fliers came from that part of the world: from the Ohio Wright brothers, who pretty much started it all at the turn of the century, to Minnesota Lindbergh and Kansas Earhart to my South Dakota father, an army flier since 1917 and from 1927 to 1930 general manager of Transcontinental Air Transport (TAT, later TWA), for which Lindbergh acted as consultant and general publicist.

On my one visit to South Dakota, as I drove from Madison to Sioux Falls, I was conscious of an all-enveloping bowl of light, as if one were at the bottom of a vast goldfish bowl; odder still, the light also seemed to be coming as much from below as from above. Then I noticed how flat the plain was that I was crossing, how tall sky and low horizon made a luminous globe. In such a landscape, aerial flight seems, somehow, inevitable. So Lindbergh must have felt of his native country over which he was to fly for much of his youth as one of the first airmail carriers.

Earthly geography aimed him for the sky. Family, too. A paternal grandfather left Sweden during a political-financial scandal that Berg handles the best of anyone I've read. Ola Mansson was a farmer with a large family. Elected to the Swedish Parliament in

1847, he had an illegitimate child by a Stockholm waitress. Thanks to a scandal that involved the king, he fled Sweden, leaving behind his first family but taking with him the mother of his young son, Karl August. By 1859 he had changed his name to August Lindbergh; he had also become a farmer near Sauk Center, Minnesota, where Sinclair Lewis would be born in 1895. A politician in the old country, August became something of one in the new, but it was his eldest son, now called Charles August, who was to rise in that line of work. C.A. became a lawyer, married and had two children. After the death of his wife, he married a doctor's daughter. Evangeline Land was twenty-four; C.A. was forty. They were considered the best-looking couple in the heart of the heart of the country.

Enter American literature. Evangeline was a schoolteacher, well educated for the time, with fanciful artistic leanings. She loved amateur theatricals. Beauty, too. She wanted to 'be an inspiration. I suppose I'd better become a teacher then . . . I'll make 'em put in a village green, and darling cottages . . .' Thus speaks Carol Kennicott, heroine of Sinclair Lewis's *Main Street*. Thus spake, it would appear, Evangeline Lindbergh, on whom Carol appears to be based. Most intriguingly, Lewis wrote his novel seven years before Carol Evangeline's son became world-famous.

Although Lindbergh (born 1902) was to remain as close to his mother as two cool Scandinavians could ever be (or so she termed them when they refused to embrace for the press as he left for Paris), she was never to be the influence that his father was. In 1906, C.A. was elected to the House of Representatives as a Progressive on the Republican ticket, very much in the Robert LaFollette populist isolationist tradition.

To understand the son's politics – or, perhaps, tropisms, reflexes to the public business – one must understand C.A. and his world.

Although Berg's book is well assembled and full of new detail,

Loss of Eden by Joyce Milton is still, perhaps, the liveliest biography in the sense that she manages to bring alive her cast in a way not usual in contemporary biographies. But finally, it is Lindbergh himself, particularly in his posthumous *Autobiography of Values*, who bears the most interesting witness to a life so extraordinary that it becomes, paradoxically, emblematic of the American character at its most fulfilled.

Of his childhood, Lindbergh wrote:

My father grew up on the frontier. His parents had
brought him there from Sweden when he was six years old.
They staked out a homestead and from it axed a clearing
and plowed a field. His early boyhood had been spent in
constant fear of Indians and reliance upon soldiers. On one
occasion when the Sioux had taken the warpath, my
grandfather abandoned his homestead and with his family
fled by ox-cart to the fort at St. Cloud. A massacre of
settlers took place in a village to the south and reasonable
security was not regained until soldiers came with their
rifles . . . During the early years of my life, I lived under
the influence of three environments: our farm and town,
my grandfather's Detroit laboratory (Dr. Land invented the
porcelain tooth), and the city of Washington, D.C., where
my father served for ten years in Congress and where I
attended school. My interests were divided between the
farm and the laboratory, for I disliked school and had little
curiosity about the politics of Washington.

It is hard to think of the boy Lindbergh serving two years at Friends School, where so many of us were to do time in later years, including Mrs. Ronald Reagan.

In Congress, C.A. was the people's man or, as Milton puts it:

If there was a single event that symbolized for the Progressives all that was wrong with unfettered capitalism, it was a meeting held in the library of the Madison Avenue home of New York financier J. P. Morgan in December 1890. At that conference Morgan had convinced the presidents of seven major railroads to call a halt to their cutthroat competition and form a cartel. The meeting marked the beginning of the era of the trusts, and during the next fifteen years Morgan would personally preside over the organization of more than a half-dozen mega-corporations – among them United States Steel, the Guggenheim copper trust, etc.

Most Progressives glumly accepted things as they were, but C.A. declared war on what he called the Money Trust, centered on the house of Morgan. Needless to say, the Money Trust survived his attacks but his marriage did not. C.A. and Evangeline separated. By 1907, she and Charles were in Detroit with her parents. Dr. Land was, like so many of the livelier figures of that age, an inventor. Charles would also become an inventor, a natural sort of activity at the dawn of the age of technology, whose presiding genius was Henry Ford.

In the end, Evangeline agreed to live in Washington, but not with C.A. At the age of eleven, Charles mastered Ford's invention and drove C.A. about his Minnesota district. Although more interested in the combustion engine than C.A.'s attacks on the Money Trust, Charles was bound to absorb a good deal of the populist faith. C.A. blasted the gold standard, the 'subsidized press,' the 'anglophiles' who, by 1914, were eager for us to enter the European war, aided and abetted by J. P. Morgan, who supported the British and French currencies while supplying the Allies with arms. During all this, President Wilson was quietly maneuvering the United States into the war while running for reelection in 1916, using Senator T. P. Gore's slogan, 'He kept us out of war.' Representative Lindbergh and Senator Gore were not only allies in this, but each admired LaFollette, who also opposed, along with a majority of the American people, foreign entanglements and adventures. But the bankers' war, as the isolationists thought of it, was inevitable. The subsidized press that would later so damage Charles's reputation beat the drums for war, and, according to C.A.'s hyperbole, 'at no period in the world's history has deceit been so bold and aggressive as now [*sic*] attempting to engulf all humanity in a maelstrom of hell.' Little did the apolitical, science-loving Charles suspect that a generation later he would be making the same sort of speeches in the face of a conspiracy that neither he, nor anyone else much, understood at the time.

Berg is at his best with the two great news stories of Lindbergh's life – the 1927 flight to Paris and subsequent fame; and the 1932 kidnapping and killing of his two-year-old son and the chaotic search for the murderer, a German immigrant called Bruno Richard Hauptmann. (These sections read most excitingly, and despite the work of the inevitable revisionists, it seems more than ever clear that Hauptmann was indeed the kidnapper.) Berg dutifully notes that the first question King George V asked Lindbergh after his Atlantic flight was, 'How did you pee?' Lindbergh was already used to the question. He had used paper cups. My father, Gene Vidal, his colleague, was more probing. 'How did you . . .?' Lindbergh laughed. 'Well,' he said, 'I sort of felt sorry for those Frenchmen who were carrying me on their shoulders.'

Neither Berg nor Milton is particularly good on the early days of aviation, a period awaiting its historian. By 1928, Lindbergh and Gene were involved in the first transcontinental airline, which took two days to cross the country (no night flying) by rail and air, landing at Glendale. The company's name, TAT, was an acronym, according to cynics, for Take A Train. Since Lindbergh virtuously refused to capitalize on his name (he rejected the fortune that William Randolph Hearst offered him to appear in a movie about his life), he settled for being a publicist for commercial aviation in general and TAT in particular.

'But what did he do?' I once asked my father. 'He let us use his name. The Lindbergh line we called ourselves. Then he visited all around the country, sometimes checking out sites for landing fields. But then we all . . . those of us who were pilots . . . did that. We'd also taken on Amelia Earhart. We called her Assistant Traffic Manager. But, basically, it was all public relations. Everyone in the world wanted to look at those two. Amelia's main function for us was to convince women that it was safe to fly.' 'You mean you wanted more women pilots?' Gene was amused. 'No. We were trying to get the women to let the men – their husbands, relatives, friends – fly. Amelia had such a cool and serene disposition that she really put people at ease, and so made the whole thing look a lot safer than it really was.'

Milton is amusing about the somewhat edgy relations between the god of flight and, as of 1928, the goddess of flight. Much was made of the physical resemblance between Charles and Amelia. Milton seems to think that publisher-publicist George Palmer Putnam had 'plucked her from obscurity . . . impressed by her striking resemblance to the hero of 1927 and promoted her as "Lady Lindy."' It was always my impression that she had plucked herself from obscurity by becoming a flier and that Putnam proceeded to commercialize her. Amelia was very much a proto-feminist whose Bible was Virginia Woolf's A *Room of One's Own*. Anne Morrow, Lindbergh's new wife, was also an enthusiast of Woolf, but Anne disappointed Amelia by insisting that she was not 'a modern career woman but rather the wife of a modern man.'

According to Milton, while the two women were first bonding at a kitchen table, the practical joker Slim sneaked up behind his wife and began to dribble water on her silk dress. Amelia was delighted when Anne turned around and threw a glass of butter-milk in his face. But there was always a certain edginess between the Yin and Yang of flight. As Gene once said, tactfully, 'Amelia was not a natural seat-of-the-pants flier like Slim.' While Berg tells a joke that I'd not heard before. After Amelia soloed to Ireland in 1932, Lindbergh is supposed to have said, 'I hear that Amelia made a good landing – once.'

Berg gives almost equal space to Anne Morrow, as does Milton. Anne was born into the enemy camp. She was the daughter of a wealthy Morgan partner, Dwight Morrow, who was serving as his friend President Coolidge's ambassador to Mexico, where she first got to know her husband from the sky. Anne had graduated from Smith; published poetry; despite shyness, she enjoyed social life. Farm boy and society girl ought not to have got on at all, and, in a sense, the marriage was unbalanced, but she had wanted to marry a hero, and that meant accommodating herself to a hero's person-ality, Swedish division. As it was, she never ceased to admire him, something of a record in any marriage. They were to have six chil-dren.

In many ways, the marriage was a successful partnership; he taught her to fly, to be a navigator, while she encouraged him to become a serious writer. It is hard now to realize that, for years, each was one of the most popular writers in the world, a world that they saw from so far above that they were a bit like observant gods, hovering over all our seas and lands and noticing what the earthbound do not, the unity of things. They also raised a family, which their youngest daughter, Reeve, now describes in *Under a Wing*. The ethereal but tough Anne needed someone perhaps more sensitive to her moods – not to mention, more often at home; Slim was forever in motion. Later, Anne seems to have found a soulmate, first, briefly and intensely, in another poet-flier, Antoine de Saint-Exupéry, and, later, in her doctor. Interestingly, the twenty-seven-year-old Charles and the twenty-three-year-old Anne appear to have been virgins at the time of their wedding. We learn from Milton that, before the Paris flight, Slim had never attended a dinner party, never learned to dance, never gone out with a girl – because he'd had no time to learn what he regarded as the separate language of women. From the photographs, his love life seems to have involved a series of dogs, by no means an affective deprivation.

In 1933, Gene Vidal became Roosevelt's director of air commerce, and for four years he systematized commercial aviation, issuing the first pilot's licenses (thoughtfully giving himself number one); he standardized the national system of airports. He also worked closely with his former colleague at TAT, now a consultant to Juan Trippe's Pan American Airways. During this period, the Lindberghs moved to Europe – but not before the opening gun in what would prove to be the most significant *mano a mano* duel of the hero's life.

It was the not unnatural view of Franklin Delano Roosevelt that in a time of crisis there could not be two heroes in the United States at the same time. As a mere governor, he had asked Slim for an autographed picture. But in 1932, when the mandate of heaven was bestowed upon FDR, he became the embodiment of a nation's fears and hopes. He was alone . . . well, almost. Unfortunately, the Lone Eagle could always draw a bigger crowd. Fortunately, for FDR, Lindbergh genuinely hated the limelight, and after the death of his child, he vanished as much as he could within the New York laboratory of Dr. Alexis Carrel, where he worked on the perfusion pump, far from the rabid eyes of the press. With hindsight, one now sees how dramatically inevitable it was that the two largest figures on the national stage must eventually confront each other. To that end, the great dramaturge in the sky carefully set the scene, using Gene, at times, as third character.

The Hoover administration had awarded airmail contracts in a somewhat questionable manner, favoring rich conglomerates over independent airlines. When Gene Vidal's Ludington airline was passed over in favor of a conglomerate, Gene went public to denounce 'Hoover socialism,' something truly new under the sun. Once in office, FDR saw a neat way of scoring points off the Republican Party. He got the postmaster general to accuse his predecessor of 'conspiracy and collusion' in the awarding of contracts, then, on February 9, 1934, by executive order, FDR canceled all airmail contracts. The army had flown the mail in 1918; they would do so again. The director of air commerce objected. Army pilots did not have the wildcat skills of mail pilots. Gene knew. He was an army pilot. But FDR would not budge. I've always suspected that Gene got secretly to Lindbergh, who was both an army pilot and an ex-mail pilot, and urged him to speak out before things got even worse – if that was possible: by the end of the first week, five army pilots were dead, six critically injured, eight planes totaled. Meanwhile, airlines without mail contracts faced abrupt ruin.

Lindbergh sent off a 275-word telegram to the President while, simultaneously, releasing a copy to the press. This was *lèse majesté*. The White House attacked Lindbergh. The Senate called him before one of its committees. The hero was accused of publicity-seeking. This occasioned the only genuine laugh in the whole mess. Privately, Gene observed that FDR's state of denial over his blunder now required that Lindbergh be made the villain of the piece. In this the President was aided by another paladin of air, General Billy Mitchell, the apostle of military air power. Mitchell thought FDR should have taken over TWA to fly the mail until new – 'honest' – contracts had been awarded. Meanwhile, Mitchell smeared Lindbergh as 'a front of the Air Trust' and, worse, identified him as 'that son-in-law of Dwight Morrow.' So C.A., enemy for life of the Money Trust and the House of Morgan, now had a son said to be in thrall to the moneyed powers of darkness. Luckily, C.A. had died before his son married Anne Morrow.

As army pilots kept falling from the skies, Roosevelt backed down. The mail, he declared, would be flown by any commercial airline that had not benefited from the previous regime. The old TAT, now Transcontinental and Western Air, became Trans World Airlines. Lindbergh found this semantic solution 'reminiscent of something to be found in *Alice in Wonderland*.'

The obligatory Schilleresque scene between the antagonists did not take place until April 1939. Lindbergh had been impressed – hoodwinked, some thought – by the German air forces. He had also, for the American military, gone to the Soviet Union, where he was appalled by the general military incompetence; and depressed by the political system. Like so many American conservatives of the day, he feared 'Asian' Communism more than he did Nazi efficiency. In any case, after nearly four years of exile, he came home to ask for a military buildup by the United States, just in case; he had also come home to preach against involvement in the approaching European war. On the buildup, as the two heroes were wary allies, they met for the first and last time.

From Lindbergh's diary:

I went to see the President about 12:45 . . . He was seated at his desk at one end of a large room. There were several model ships around the walls. He leaned forward from his chair to meet me as I entered, and it is only now that I stop to think that he is crippled. I did not notice it and had not thought of it during our meeting. He immediately asked me how Anne was and mentioned the fact that she knew his daughter in school. He is an accomplished, suave, interesting conversationalist. I liked him and feel that I could get along with him well. Acquaintanceship would be pleasant and interesting.

But there was something about him I did not trust, something a little too suave, too pleasant, too easy. Still, he is our President, and there is no reason for any antagonism between us in the work I am now doing. The airmail situation is past – one of the worst political maneuvers I know of, and unfair in the extreme, to say the least. But nothing constructive will be gained by bringing it up again at this time.

Roosevelt gave me the impression of being a very tired man, but with enough energy left to carry on for a long time. I doubt that he realizes how tired he is. His face has that gray look of an over-worked businessman. And his voice has that even, routine tone that one seemed to get when the mind is dulled by too much and too frequent conversation. It has that dull quality that comes to any one of the senses when it is overused: taste, with too much of the same food day after day; hearing, when the music never changes; touch, when one's hand is never lifted.

Roosevelt judges his man quickly and plays him cleverly. He is mostly politician, and I think we would never get along on many fundamentals. But there are things about him I like, and why worry about the others unless and until they necessitate consideration. It is better to work

together as long as we can; yet somehow I have a feeling
that it may not be for long.

Thus the great dramaturge keeps the plot aboil. Also,
Lindbergh's impressions are as interesting and 'accurate' a take on
FDR as anything written by a contemporary. Certainly, it is
unique in Lindbergh's diary because he – who was observed constantly by everyone else – seldom observes anyone, not so much
due to lack of interest but of opportunity. Happily, for gossips, he
did note how astonishingly boring the Duke of Windsor was at
dinner when he discussed at length how much higher the Etoile
was than the Place de la Concorde, plainly an all-time room-
emptier.

The truce with FDR was short. That summer, Lindbergh worked
with the Commanding General of the army air force, H. H.
Arnold; research and development was the Lindbergh assignment.
On September 1, the Germans invaded Poland. The European
war had begun. On September 15, Lindbergh took to the air-
waves to speak on 'America and the European Wars.' Of this, he
writes, 'An interesting incident relating to the address had occurred
earlier in the day.' A colonel had been sent to him to say 'the
Administration was very much worried by my intention of speaking over the radio and opposing actively this country's entry into
a European war. [He] said that if I did not do this, a secretaryship
of air would be created in the Cabinet and given to me! . . . This
offer on Roosevelt's part does not surprise me after what I have
learned about his Administration. It does surprise me, though,
that he still thinks I might be influenced by such an offer. It is a
great mistake for him to let the Army know that he deals in such
a way.'

This is very prim indeed, but Lindbergh knew that, from

Arnold on down, the President had been told Lindbergh wouldn't accept. 'Regardless of the fact that [FDR] had publicly advocated a policy of neutrality for the United States, it seemed to me apparent that he intended to lead our country into the war. The powers he influenced and controlled were great. Opposing them would require planning, political skill, and organization. For me, this meant entering a new framework of life.'

For nearly three years, the son of C.A. galvanized the country with his speeches and rallies. The first and, thus far, last great debate of the 'American Century' was now engaged. Although Lindbergh had many formidable allies, the President had not only great skills and powers, he had, as we now know, the British Secret Services at work throughout the land, and their first task was the deconstruction of a hero.

To swing American opinion toward war, the British knew that they could count on the wily Roosevelt only up to a point. He had a third term to win in 1940; he also had a country with an isolationist majority, and a Lone Eagle pecking away at him. He could still launch trial balloons like his 1937 'Quarantine the Aggressors' speech, which was, according to Canada's Governor-General, Lord Tweedsmuir, 'the culmination of a long conspiracy between us (this must be kept secret)!' Unfortunately, that balloon burst and FDR retreated, for the moment. He always had the same advice for enthusiasts whose aims he shared but dared not support openly in the absence of a political majority. 'You must *force* me to act,' he would say blithely. When a denunciation of his inaction was being prepared by the interventionists, he suggested 'pusillanimous' as a nice word to describe his cautious public policies.

C.A.'s son was now beginning to see, if not the covert hand of the British in our affairs, the overt hand of the House of Morgan, not to mention his own father-in-law, Dwight Morrow. Lindbergh had never much minded the Money Trust that had so incensed his father. He had gone from being a farm boy, to stunt flier, to army flier and then to world hero. Social injustice seemed never to have concerned him. After all, he had looked after himself and everything had turned out rather more than well. He had allowed himself to be taken up by Dwight Morrow and the Morgan partners who invested his money for him and made him rich without ever commercializing his name. Incidentally, Berg made a gentlemanly treaty with Anne Morrow Lindbergh (still alive in her nineties) to use her diaries and correspondence. One *quid* for this *quo* is that Berg never mentions the fact that the brilliant, self-made Morrow was an alcoholic. It is here that Milton is much more interesting than Berg about the family that Lindbergh married into.

One fact of the national condition that can never be discussed with candor is the class system. At the peak of the American pyramid – the one with that awful unblinking eye in it – is the WASP eastern establishment. Mahl notes that C. Wright Mills took considerable flak when

> he identified [it] in his book *The Power Elite* (1956). The
> United States, wrote Mills, was controlled not by the mass
> of its citizens as described by democratic theory, but by a
> wealthy Anglo-Saxon Protestant elite from Ivy League
> schools. In a flurry of caustic reviews, critics, often Cold
> War liberals, heatedly denied that there was such an elite.
> That debate now seems over, as Douglas Little noted in a
> recent review article in *Diplomatic History*. 'Far from
> rejecting the idea of a power elite . . . [the books under
> review] celebrate its short lived Periclean age during the
> quarter century after 1945 . . .'

The British had never displayed any similar doubts about the existence of an American 'power elite.' As early as 1917, Lord

Robert Cecil in Cabinet noted that 'though the American people are very largely foreign, both in origin and modes of thought, their rulers are almost exclusively Anglo-Saxons, and share our political ideals.'

The Swedish Lindberghs were as foreign to this establishment as the Sulzbergers. But in the instance of war or peace the Sulzbergers sided with the WASP elite, while Charles Lindbergh missed the point which Anne swiftly got the moment he showed her the medal that Goering had unexpectedly handed him at dinner in Berlin. 'Your albatross,' she said. Lindbergh seems never to have got it.

Meanwhile, between WASP elite and British agents, the United States was being totally transformed. From President Washington's day to Pearl Harbor, isolationism was the honorable, if sometimes opportunistically ignored, national creed. But by 1940, one of the two leading isolationist senators, Arthur Vandenberg, had been converted to war and, later, to global hegemony, by three enchanting ladies in the pay of the British. Mahl gives names, addresses. One of them, wife to a British diplomat, code name 'Cynthia,' was the heroine of an eponymous study by H. Montgomery Hyde in 1965. Finally, just in case FDR was defeated in 1940, the other great isolationist, Senator Robert A. Taft, was overwhelmed at the Republican convention by the British candidate, the previously unknown Wendell Willkie.

After Pearl Harbor, Lindbergh offered his services to the air force. FDR, never one to forgo an enmity, took pleasure in turning him down, despite the *New York Times* editorial to the effect that he should be used as 'he is a superb air man, and this is primarily and essentially an air war.' But Roosevelt could not allow his competition to regain hero status, which, indeed, despite the best efforts of many interested parties, he never did lose for most of the people. Lone Eagles tend to outsoar presidents, no matter how bad the weather. As it was, Lindbergh got to the South Pacific, where he flew clandestine combat missions with men half his age. As he was only an observer, this was illegal, but commanders in the field were delighted to have so consummate and useful an airman in their midst.

Once the war was over, Lindbergh continued his travels with Anne; they also raised their five surviving children. It appears that Lindbergh was a conscientious father, with a tendency to reinvent the wheel when there was something to be explained. He was also a bit of a martinet with checklists (yes, he invented that pilot's routine) for each child. He was alert to the utility of things. Reeve records a hilarious (to read, that is) lecture on 'punk design':

He also had a normal-looking flashlight with an ugly hexagonal head, to which feature he drew our attention every time he put the flashlight down on a flat surface.

'You see that?' He would point. 'It doesn't move.' We saw. The flashlight lay there on the shelf, or the table, or the floor, exactly as he had placed it. It didn't move a bit. Nor did we, as he fixed us with his penetrating, instructive blue eyes.

'It doesn't roll off the table,' he would say, looking at us searchingly, challenging someone to contradict him. Nobody did.

'Why aren't all flashlights made like this one?' he wondered aloud. None of us would hazard a guess.

'Cylinders!' He explained irritably. 'You buy a flashlight, nine times out of ten it comes in a cylindrical shape. Now, a cylinder will always roll. A cylinder was made to roll. And rolling is fine, for a rolling pin. But you put down a cylindrical flashlight in the dark, near a place where you're working, so you can use two hands, and what's it going to do? It's going to roll away from you, of course! Off the shelf, under the car, what good is that?'

No good at all, we knew. And we knew what he would say next, too.

'All they would have to do is change the shape of the head. Not the whole flashlight, just the head. The whole problem would be solved. What's the matter with these people? Pentagonal, hexagonal, even a square, for heaven's sake. Just the head . . .'

As one surveys his life, one sees him move from phase to phase, much as the human race itself has done. The boy on the farm, fascinated by husbandry. By eugenics, a pseudoscience of the day. By nature. By medical science to improve life. By machinery. By flight. By the next step after the propeller, jet propulsion – as early as the late 1920s. Fascinated by the old civilizations that he had flown over throughout his life, he now saw how precarious they were in the face of the instrument that he had helped perfect, the aircraft. He saw the necessity for the avoidance of war, while establishing an equilibrium between the planet's resources and human population. By the need to understand ancient tribal patterns, in order to undo or mitigate what science is doing to modern man. He lived among primitive tribes; tried to understand their ancient adaptabilities. He literally thought himself, doggedly, from one level to the next.

Toward the end, he had come to dislike the world that he had done so much to create. First, he noticed the standardization of air bases everywhere. The sameness of food, even landscape. The boredom of air travel in jet liners. The fun was gone. A key word in his early works was 'adventure.' He stops using it. Finally, there is his lifelong vein of mysticism. Many of the early fliers had a curious sense of hyperreality when contemplating their own relationship with earth and sky, not to mention with the tiny human beings whom they passed over, swiftly, like gods. Much of the magic of air power at the beginning was the image of a silver ship-bird coming out of the blue, like a sky-god returning to the ground people.

The early fliers were literally extraterrestrial as they came in for their landings, for their rebirth as earthlings. On this subject, Lindbergh was amused by the great myth-maker himself, Carl Jung. The Lindberghs sat with the 'old wizard' on the Zurichsee's north bank. 'Conversation turned to "flying saucers." Jung had written a book about them . . . I had expected him to discuss the psychological and psychiatric aspects of people's fantasizing . . . I was amazed to find that he believed in their reality . . . When I mentioned a discussion I had had with General Carl Spaatz, the chief of staff of the Air Force . . . Jung said, "There are many things taking place upon earth that you and General Spaatz do not know about."' Lindbergh reflects upon superstition as a constant in human affairs:

I know myself as mortal, but this raises the question 'What is I?' Am I an individual, or am I an evolving life stream composed of countless selves? . . . As one identity, I was born in A.D. 1902. But as twentieth-century man, I am billions of years old. The life I consider as myself has existed through past eons with unbroken continuity. Individuals are custodians of the life stream – temporal manifestations of far greater being, forming from and returning to their essence like so many dreams . . . I recall standing on the edge of a deep valley in the Hawaiian island of Maui, thinking that a life stream is like a mountain river – springing from hidden sources, born out

of the earth, touched by stars, merging, blending, evolving
in the shape momentarily seen.

By thinking ahead from what he had observed, Lindbergh had
been able to think himself back to Lucretius: *Nil posse creari de
nilo*, 'Nothing can be created out of nothing.' Or, 'The sum of
things is ever being replenished and mortals live one and all by give
and take. Some races wax and others wane, and in a short space the
tribes of living things are changed, and like runners hand on the
torch of life.' Lindbergh sums up: 'I am form and I am formless. I
am life and I am matter, mortal and immortal. I am one and
many – myself and humanity in flux . . . After my death, the mol-
ecules of my being will return to the earth and sky. They came
from the stars. I am of the stars.'

Disraeli, born a Jew, christened an Anglican, avoided church. A
character in one of his novels was asked what his religion was. The
character responded, 'All wise men have the same religion.' When
asked what that was, he said, 'Wise men never say.' It is the most
perfect irony that Roosevelt and Lindbergh, heroic antagonists,
shared, at the end, the same religion. Each wanted to be buried so
that his atoms would get back into circulation as quickly as possible, one with a missing side to his coffin in a rose garden, the
other in a biodegradable wooden box on a Pacific island. Thus,
each meant to rejoin the life stream, and the genitive stars.
Meanwhile, it might be a pleasant gift to the new century and the
new millennium to replace the pejorative 1812 caricature of a sly
treacherous Uncle Sam with that of Lindbergh, the best that we are
ever apt to produce in the hero line, American style.

The Times Literary Supplement
30 October 1998

Sinatra

At least two generations of Americans were conceived to the sound of Sinatra's voice on record or radio. Conception in cinema houses was not unknown but considered flashy. There were several Sinatras in the six or seven decades of his career. There was the wartime idol of the young. He was skinny, gaunt-faced with a floppy bow tie and a left profile like that of a Donatello bronze. At New York's Paramount Theater pubescent girls howled like Bacchae at the sight and sound of him and fainted like dowagers in tight stays.

I met him first while I was in the army, just before going overseas. We were at a Hollywood party where everyone was a star and I was a private to whom no one spoke except Sinatra, who singled me out and charmed me for life. In person and in art. That was the hero Sinatra whose populism was to bring him soon to ruin.

The story, a selective part of it, is well known. Born in New Jersey, Francis Sinatra had a formidable mother, active in Democratic city ward politics. He knew at first hand the politics of immigrant Italians, of the urban working class. He was one of them.

He began his career singing wherever he could; he became famous singing with the big bands of the day. 'His grace notes are like Bach,' said Virgil Thomson, our leading music critic. Everyone thought Virgil was joking but he wasn't. Sinatra's voice was like no other. But I leave that to music critics. What interests me is the rise and fall of a political hero whose apotheosis, or, to be precise, hell, was to become a neutered creature of the American right wing, crooning in Nancy Reagan's ear at the White House. An Italo-American Faust.

At the height of Sinatra's popular fame as a singer he made a short documentary called *The House I Live In*. This was 1947; he won an Academy Award for the song, whose lyrics – The people that I work with. The workers that I meet . . . The right to speak my mind. That is America to me – were a straightforward plea for tolerance that neither cloyed nor bored.

Jon Wiener in *Professors, Politics and Pop* (Verso) has given a moving account of how Sinatra then fell foul of the FBI and the professional patriots and the then powerful Hearst press. In the course of the next eight years, Congress's Un-American Activities Committee, in its *Index* 'of Communists,' named *The House I Live In* twelve times while *The New York Times*, forever up to no good, in its *Index* for 1949 published a cross-reference: 'Sinatra, Frank: See U.S. – Espionage.' That was all the news fit to print about our greatest popular singer.

To add to the demonization, one Harry Anslinger, head of the Federal Narcotics Bureau, and the FBI's ineffable J. Edgar Hoover (who lived long enough to keep a file on the subversions and perversions of John Lennon), were out to get Sinatra not only as a crypto-Communist but as a mafioso. Since any night-club singer must work in a nightclub or a casino and since the mob controlled these glittering venues, every entertainer was obliged to traffic with them.

In 1947 Sinatra was smeared as a mafioso by a right-wing Hearst columnist, Lee Mortimer. Sinatra, notoriously short-tempered and not unfamiliar with fiery waters, knocked Mortimer down in a nightclub. Press ink flowed like Niagara Falls. Sinatra was transformed by the right-wing press 'overnight,' as Wiener wrote, 'from the crooning idol of bobby-soxers into violent, left-wing mafioso.'

Roman Catholic organs, respectful of their co-religionist's fame, tried to downplay the attacks, maintaining he was a mere 'pawn.' But he wasn't. Sinatra had indeed been active in left-wing (by American standards) activities. In 1946 he blasted Franco, a favorite of America's High Command. That same year he became vice president of the Hollywood Independent Citizens Committee of the Arts, Sciences and Professions, along with many other stars and Thomas Mann.

In 1948 he supported Henry Wallace for President against the proto-McCarthyite Harry S. Truman. Undeterred by the harm to his career, Sinatra wrote an open letter to the then liberal *New Republic* imploring Henry Wallace, as heir to Roosevelt, 'to take up the fight we like to think of as ours – the fight for tolerance, which is the basis of any fight for peace.' Wiener reports that three months later he was publicly branded a Communist and sacked from his radio show; by 1949 Columbia Records had broken with him and by 1950 MGM dismissed him from his film contract. A has-been at thirty-four.

After a time of trouble with his wife, Ava Gardner, and the loss of his voice due to alcohol and stress, he made his astonishing comeback in the film *From Here to Eternity*, for which he was obliged to take a minimal salary. He also developed a brand-new voice, grace notes like Mabel Mercer.

By 1960 Sinatra was again political. He had been a playmate of Jack Kennedy in his senatorial days; he was also gung-ho to help out his conservative but attractive Catholic friend. But some Kennedy advisers thought the Red Mafioso should be avoided at all costs; others wanted to use him for a voter drive in Harlem 'where he is recognised as a hero of the cause of the Negro,' something that Kennedy was not, to say the least.

Although, at times, Sinatra seemed to be ranging between megalomania and just plain hard drinking, he was still a major singer, also a movie star, famous for doing scenes in only one take – known in the trade as 'walking through.' Kennedy's candidacy revved him up. But for those who have wondered what dinner might have been like for Falstaff when Prince Hal – now King – snubbed him, I can report that after Kennedy was nominated in Los Angeles at the convention where I was a delegate, Tony Curtis and Janet Lee gave a movie-star party for the nominee. I was placed, along with Sinatra, at the table where Kennedy would sit. We waited. And waited. Sinatra looked edgy; started to drink heavily. Dinner began. Then one of the toothy sisters of the nominee said, casually, 'Oh, Jack's sorry. He can't come. He's gone to the movies.' Opposite me, Falstaff deflated and spoke no more that evening.

Once Kennedy was elected, Sinatra organized the inaugural ball. But the President's father and brother Robert said no more Sinatra and there was no more Sinatra.

When President Kennedy came to stay in Palm Springs, he stayed not with Sinatra, as announced, but with his rival Bing Crosby. Insult to injury. From then on, in public and private, he often behaved boorishly (to riot in understatement).

In due course, he was called before a congressional committee on the Mafia. They got nowhere. Nowhere to go. Nowhere for him, either. He became a Reagan Republican. But then no

Democratic president asked him to perform at the White House. It was sly old Nixon, whose House committee had smeared him, who asked Sinatra to sing *The House I Live In*.

'At the end of the program,' Wiener writes, 'for the first time in his public career, Sinatra was in tears.' It is not easy to be good, much less a tribune of the people, in the land of milk and money once your house is gone.

The Observer
17 May 1998

C. P. Cavafy

Forty years ago, in a more than usually run-down quarter of Athens, there was a bar called the Nea Zoe. The brightly lit raw-wood interior smelled of pinecones and liquorice – retsina wine and ouzo. A jukebox played Greek music – minor key with a strong martial beat – to which soldiers from a nearby barracks gravely danced with one another or in groups or alone. Women were not encouraged to join in. The Nea Zoe was a sanctuary where Greek men performed pre-Christian dances taught them by their fathers, who in turn had learned them from their fathers all the way back to the start of history if not before. The dances celebrated the deeds of gods and heroes. I recall one astonishing – dizzying – solo where a soldier arrived on the dance floor with a great leap and then began a series of rapid turns while striking the floor with the flat of his hand.

'He is doing the dance of Antaeus,' said the old Greek colonel who had brought me to the bar. 'Antaeus was son of the sea god Poseidon out of Gaia, mother earth. Antaeus is the world's strongest wrestler but he can only remain strong by touching earth, his mother.' The colonel knew all the ancient dances and he could tell from the way a boy danced where he came from: the islands, the Peloponnese, Thessaly. 'There used to be a dozen of these places here in Athens but since that movie . . .' He sighed. *That* movie was the recently released *Never on Sunday*; it had charmed the world but it had also inspired many American tourists to come to places like the Nea Zoe to laugh at the fairies dancing. Since ancient Greek has no word for such a made-up category as fairy, the soldiers were at first bewildered by so much weird attention. Then, when they realized how insulting the fat Americans were, they would gravely take them outside and beat them up. Unfortunately, tourism is more important to governments than two-thousand-year-old dances; the bars were shut down.

Nea Zoe means new life. 'That was also the name of the magazine where Cavafy published many of his best poems.' I should note that my first visit to Athens took place in 1961, the year that *The Complete Poems of C.P. Cavafy* was published by the Hogarth Press with an introduction by W. H. Auden. We were all reading Cavafy that season, in Rae Dalven's translation from the Greek. Now, forty years on, Theoharis Constantine Theoharis has given us what is, at last, all the poems that he could find.

Constantine P. Cavafy was born at Constantinople, April 17, 1863, not too long after Walt Whitman added 'Calamus' to *Leaves of Grass*. Constantinople had been built to be the capital of the Eastern – and largely Greek – Roman empire. For several generations the Cavafys were successful manufacturers and exporters. But by the time of the death of Cavafy's father, there was almost no money left. After a time in London, the widow Cavafy and six sons moved on to the other ancient Greek city, Alexandria, in Egypt. Although Cavafy's formal education was classical, he was a bookish young man who largely educated himself while being supported by a family network until, on March 1, 1892, not quite twenty-nine – a shadow-line for the young men he writes of in his poems – he became provisional clerk in the Ministry of Irrigation. Since he had chosen to be a Greek citizen, he remained for thirty years 'provisional,' a permanently temporary clerk of the Egyptian government. Thanks to his knowledge of English, French, Italian, Greek, and Arabic, he sometimes moonlighted as a broker. In 1895 he acquired a civilized friend, Pericles Anastasiades, who would be for him the other self that Etienne de la Boëtie had been for Montaigne. This was also the year Cavafy began to write 'seriously.' By 1903 he was being published in the Athenian magazine *Panatheneum.* A year later he published his first book, containing fourteen poems; he was now forty-one. From 1908 to 1918 he published frequently in *Nea Zoe*; he became known throughout the Greek world: then came translations in English, French, Italian. From 1908 to 1933 – the year of his death – Cavafy lived alone at 10 Lepsius Street, Alexandria, today a modest shrine. There is a long hallway lined with books and a living room that contains a large sofa and what is described as 'Arab furniture'; his study was also his bedroom.

E. M. Forster famously described him at the time of the First War: '. . . A Greek gentleman in a straw hat standing absolutely motionless at a slight angle to the universe. His arms are extended, possibly. "Oh, Cavafy . . .!" Yes, it is Mr. Cavafy, and he is going either from his flat to the office, or from his office to the flat. If the former, he vanishes when seen, with a slight gesture of despair. If the latter, he may be prevailed upon to begin a sentence – an immense complicated yet shapely sentence, full of parentheses that never get mixed and of reservations that really do reserve; a sentence that moves with logic to its foreseen end, yet to an end that is always more vivid and thrilling than one foresaw. And despite its intellectual richness and human outlook, despite the matured charity of its judgments, one feels that it too stands at a slight angle to the universe.'

Although Cavafy himself appears to have been a conventional Greek Orthodox Christian, as poet he inhabits the pagan Greco-Roman world of legend as well as the everyday world of Alexandria in which he might be called the Pindar of the one-night stand between males. A troubled, sometime Christian puritan, W. H. Auden suspects that the passionate encounters he describes are largely one-sided because the poet no doubt paid: It is true that the grave soldiers at the Nea Zoe expected a small payment for their company but the business transacted was always mutual and the double nimbus of accomplished lust can be spectacularly bright in a shadowy room full of Arabian furniture not to mention ghosts and even gods.

Yes, the gods themselves, always youthful, eternal, still appear to men. 'When an August morning dawns over you, / your scented space gleams with their life; / and sometimes a young man's ethe-rial [*sic*] form, / vanishing, passing quickly, crosses the tops of your hills.' In *One of Their Gods,* Cavafy observes: 'When one of them passed through Selefkia's market, / at the hour when darkness first comes on, / as would a tall, and consummately handsome youth / with the joy of invulnerability in his eyes . . . headed for the quarter that only lives at night, with orgies and debaucheries / with every type of frenzy and abandon, / they speculated about which of Them he was, and for which of his suspicious entertain-ments / he'd descended to the streets of Selefkia / from his Worshipped, his most Venerated Halls.'

Here is a standard exercise given students in classical times: imagine that you are Julius Caesar, you have just crossed the river Rubicon; you are at war with your own republic. Now, as Caesar, write what you are thinking and feeling. A canny exercise because to put yourself in the place of another encourages empathy and understanding. J. G. Herder even invented the German word *Einfühlen* to describe those, like Cavafy, who have the capacity to enter and inhabit other-time. Some of his best poems are soliloquies that he invents for those who once lived and died in history or, more intimately, for those whom he has known and loved in his own story.

The history that he most draws upon is the world of Alexander the Great, whose heirs created Greek kingdoms in Egypt and Asia Minor, sovereignties that, in less than three centuries, were powerless Roman dependencies. Marc Antony's loss of the Roman world to Octavian Augustus particularly fascinates him. 'Suddenly, at midnight, when an invisible troupe / is heard passing, / with exquisite players, with voices – / do not lament your luck, now utterly exhausted / your acts that failed . . . / listen, taking your final pleasure, / to the sounds, to that mystic troupe's rare playing, / and say your last farewell to her, to that Alexandria you are losing.' For Cavafy, Alexandria, not Cleopatra, is the heroine of the hero's tragedy.

Despite Cavafy's sense that the old gods have never forsaken us, he shows no sympathy at all for the Emperor Julian, who, vainly, tried to restore the worship of the gods in the fourth century. Admittedly, Julian could be a grinding bore, but even so, the essentially pagan Cavafy should have admired him. But he doesn't. Why not? I think one pronoun shows us what Cavafy is up to. 'In Antioch we were perplexed on hearing / about Julian's latest behavior.' There it is. *We.* Cavafy is writing as a Christian citizen of Antioch, a city which disdained the emperor and all his works. *Einfühlen* at work. Cavafy is like an actor here, in character – or like Shakespeare when he imagines himself heir to a murdered king even though, according to one of Cavafy's most ingenious poems, it is Claudius who is the good king and Hamlet, the student prince, the villain, the youth, 'was nervous in the extreme, / while he was studying in Wittenberg many of his fellow students thought him a maniac.'

Cavafy once analyzed his own temperament and talent. 'To me, the immediate impression is never a starting point for work. The impression has got to age, has got to falsify itself with time, without my having to falsify it.

'I have two capacities: to write Poetry or to write History. I haven't written history and it's too late now. Now, you'll say, how do I know that I could write History? I feel it. I make the experiment, and ask myself: Cavafy, could you write fiction? Ten voices cry No. I ask the question again: Cavafy, could you write a play? Twenty-five voices again cry No. Then I ask again: Cavafy, could you write History? A hundred and twenty-five voices tell me you could.' The critic Robert Liddell thought Cavafy could have been a master of historical fiction. Luckily, he chose to be himself, a unique poet at an odd angle to our culture.

It was noted at the death of America's tragic twentieth-century empress – the one who died with a Greek name as well as fate – that her favorite poem was Cavafy's 'Ithaca'. One can see why. Cavafy has gone back to Homer: the origin of Greek narrative. Odysseus, returning from Troy to his home island of Ithaca, is endlessly delayed by the malice of the sea god Poseidon. Cavafy appears to be addressing Odysseus himself but it could be anyone on a life's journey. 'As you set out toward Ithaca, / hope the way is long, full of reversals, full of knowing.' He advises the traveler not to brood too much on the malice of those who want to destroy him, to keep him from his goal. If you don't take them to heart, they cannot defeat you. The poet also advises the traveler to enjoy the exotic cities along the way; he even favors selective shopping, something that also appealed to our nineteenth-century tragic empress, Mrs. Abraham Lincoln. Why not take advantage of a visit to Egypt for wisdom? 'Keep Ithaca always in your mind. / Arriving there is what has been ordained for you. / But do not hurry the journey at all. Better if it lasts many years: and you dock an old man on the island, rich with all that you have gained on the way, not expecting Ithaca to give you wealth / Ithaca gave you the beautiful journey. / Without her you would not have set out. / She has nothing more to give you.' Then the final insight; acceptance of a life now lived. 'And if you find her poor, Ithaca has not fooled you. / Having become so wise, with so much experience, / you will have understood, by then, what these Ithacas mean.' One does not need to be a tragic empress to be impressed by Cavafy's practical wisdom.

Amistad

In December, coming to a theater near you: Steven Spielberg's *Amistad*. The explicator of the Holocaust turns his compassionate gaze upon the peculiar institution of slavery, deferring yet again the high hopes of Armenians that their tragic story will be screened by the *conscience de nos jours*. Meanwhile, a press release from the Lyric Opera of Chicago tells us that, 'by remarkable coincidence,' November 29 will see the world première of an opera, *Amistad*, by Anthony Davis, with libretto by Thulani Davis. What, then, is the *Amistad* affair that we now have so much of it?

In early 1839, Portuguese slavers kidnapped several hundred West Africans for shipment to the slave markets of Cuba. Among them was twenty-five-year-old Joseph Cinqué, from Sierra Leone, a British colony where slavery had been abolished. Cinqué's wife and three children had no idea what happened to him: he simply vanished one day from the rice fields where he worked. During the two months that it took for the slave ship to sail to Cuba, a third of the captives died. But Cinqué survived the trip, with every intention of freeing himself or dying in the attempt.

Although the Spanish King had outlawed the slave trade in 1817, his Cuban governors continued to sell the services of Africans to local planters, while a mere ninety miles to the north of Cuba slavery was not only legal but a triumphant way of life in the Southern states of a republic whose most eloquent founder had proclaimed that 'all men are created equal' – except, as is so often the case in an imperfect world, those who are not. But by 1839 organized opposition to slavery was mounting in the North of the United States, to such an extent that, in twenty years, there would be a fiery disunion of South from North, and civil war. The case of the young rice farmer from Sierra Leone proved to be the first significant shot in that war.

In Havana, two Spaniards, José Ruiz and Pedro Montes, bought fifty-three slaves, paying four hundred and fifty dollars apiece for the adult males, among them Cinqué. The captives were then herded aboard the schooner *Amistad* to be transported to Puerto Príncipe, the Cuban town where they would be sold. Below deck, Cinqué found a nail and broke the lock on his iron collar. Then he freed the others. Mutiny on the *Amistad* had begun. Captain and cook were killed, and two sailors leaped overboard. Ruiz and Montes were taken captive. Cinqué spoke no Spanish; he also knew nothing about navigation. But he did know that when they came from Africa they had sailed into the setting sun, so now, to return home, he wanted the course set into the rising sun. Through sign language, he instructed Montes, who took the helm. But Montes tricked him. In the daytime, he would let the sails flap, making little headway; then, at night, he headed north to the Mecca of slavery, the United States. After two months, the ship ran out of food and water off the coast of Long Island.

When Cinqué and several men went ashore to forage, they

were met by the local inhabitants. Once Cinqué was convinced that these white men were not Spaniards, he offered them doubloons to take them all home to Sierra Leone. But by then an American man-of-war was on the scene, and the *Amistad*, with its human cargo, was taken not to a port in New York, where slavery had been abolished, but to New London, Connecticut, where slavery was still legal.

At first, Cinqué and his comrades got a predictably bad press. They were pirates – *black* pirates – who had murdered captain and crew. (Happily, personality and appearance have always meant more to Americans than deeds, good or bad, and Cinqué was unmistakably handsome, 'son of an African chief,' the press sighed – a young Sidney Poitier.) A Connecticut judge promptly put the new arrivals in the clink and bound them over to the next grand jury of Hartford's United States Circuit Court.

At this point I said to Jean-Jacques Annaud, the director with whom I was discussing how to film *Mutiny on the Amistad*, in 1993, 'What do we do with the dialogue? For almost half the picture Cinqué and the Africans don't talk in English, while Montes and Ruiz speak Spanish. That means an awful lot of subtitles.' He was unperturbed. As it turned out, Annaud and I did not make the picture, but now Spielberg has, and I'm curious to see how he handles dialogue in the 'action' sequences. The opera in Chicago, one reads in the press release, will be 'sung in English with projected English titles,' a somewhat inspired solution.

It was the last half of the *Amistad* story that most intrigued me, although the sympathetic Cinqué hasn't much to do at this point. The story turns into a titanic legal struggle at whose heart is the explosive question: Can slavery be permissible in a nation ostensibly founded on the notion that all men are created equal? More to the point, the United States was the last among civilized 'white' nations to maintain the institution rightly called peculiar. That is the real story back of the *Mutiny on the 'Amistad,'* the title of a first-rate study by Howard Jones (Oxford, 1987). Coincidentally, I should mention that there is also a new book called *Amistad*, the work of a journalist named David Pesci (Marlowe, $22.95). The publishers refer to it as 'a page-turning novel,' a true novelty for the Internet's jaded readers; and it comes to us with high praise from one Roberta Flack, the 'singer, songwriter, and entertainer.' Apparently, Spielberg has not used Mr. Pesci's book as a source for his movie.

Why bother now with this long-forgotten incident? Because it shows a black man who wins – a rarity in the age of slavery. Cinqué gets to go home, as he intended all along. He outsmarts the government of the United States, and in this enterprise he is aided by one of the most remarkable men in our history, the sixth President, John Quincy Adams. After one unhappy term (1824–28), Adams was defeated by Andrew Jackson, who is best remembered for driving Eastern Indian tribes to 'reservations' west of the Mississippi and for his wild destruction of the Bank of the United States, which led to several years of financial chaos. But Adams was destined for greater things than the presidency. He became the permanent scourge of what he called the 'slaveocracy.'

Of all our forgotten presidents . . . As I write that line, I recall what the wife of a film director once said to a journalist who was writing yet another in-shallow study of the late Grace Kelly. Inevitable question: 'How many of her leading men did she go to bed with?' Gracious response: 'It might save us both time if I were simply to skip to the ones that she did *not*.' Now, in a somewhat similar context, when I speak of forgotten presidents I refer to just about the whole line. Although the names of the four on Mount Rushmore are not entirely unknown to Anglophone

Americans, the rest of the cavalcade is very dim indeed. At the time of John F. Kennedy's assassination, it was discovered that 10 percent of the American people had never heard of him. It was not until the televising of his proto-Dianesque funeral that they were put, at last, in the picture. Of course, we're now up to forty-two presidents, and more than two centuries have passed since the first one. Even an attentive, politically minded person would have trouble keeping them all straight. Nevertheless, with a history as murderously fascinating as ours, it is truly a marvel that, year after year, history is found to be the least popular subject taught in high schools. Certainly, it is the least well absorbed.

Adams. *Amistad.* Spielberg. If the film – an action thriller, I suspect – works, people will, for a few months, learn of J. Q. Adams and his fierce brilliance in the matter of race. Since there is no longer any possibility of actual American history ever being taught in the public schools – and not all that much penetrates the private ones – the only way our history will get to us is through movies and television. Unfortunately, on the rare occasion filmmakers put a horny Jurassic toe, as it were, into controversial waters, the result is muddied. Some years ago, television made a fine mess of the Adams family, turning four generations of our most interesting family into costumed dummies. Lately, the estimable Ken Burns turned his attention to the mind and landscape of Thomas Jefferson. Despite the presence of several fine historians onscreen, the result was chloroform. Any attempts (at least mine) to note significant flaws and contradictions in Jefferson's character were carefully removed. In regard to Jefferson, J. Q. Adams himself might have been called as witness. He found dining with Jefferson exasperating, because of what Adams called his 'prodigies,' a polite word for lies of a Munchausen splendor. When Jefferson was in France, he claimed that the thermometer remained below zero for six weeks; then he shyly confided that on a trip to Europe he had taught himself Spanish. 'He knows better,' J.Q.A. groaned, 'but he wants to excite wonder.' And admiration, something no Puritan Adams could ever do.

Currently, *John Quincy Adams: A Public Life, a Private Life,* by Paul C. Nagel (Knopf, $30), is being published – the first biography of J.Q.A. in a quarter-century, according to the publisher, and the first 'that draws upon Adams' massive manuscript diary.' That journal is now available on microfilm; it is unlikely ever to be published in its entirety. But then four generations of the Adams family probably produced more words than any other family in American history, starting in 1755, when John Adams began *his* diary, and ending only with the death, in 1927, of his great-grandson Brooks, whose sketch of the intellectual tradition of the Adams family forms a preface to his late brother Henry's *The Degradation of the Democratic Dogma* (1919) – a title that suggests a not entirely sanguine view of our national development. Mr. Nagel feels that there is a mystery at the core of J.Q.A.'s life. It is true that family and contemporaries found him 'enigmatic,' a necessity for a hard-minded politician not about to give away the game. He was often accused of 'disagreeableness.' But *anyone* who takes on unpopular causes is bound not to agree with those millions who supported slavery, say, or who find risible the spending of government money to educate the people; Adams was much mocked by congressional yahoos when he called for astronomical observatories, which he poetically called 'lighthouses of the sky.'

Adams was the first president to be photographed – fourteen years after he left office. He was five feet seven, bald and stout, like most of his family – his father, John, the second president, was known as His Rotundity. Now I read that Adams is to be impersonated in *Amistad* by Anthony Hopkins, a solid, workmanlike English repertory actor, often excellent with a good English script like *The Remains of the Day*, often not so good if miscast, as in *Nixon*. But then it is always dispiriting that whenever a somewhat tony highbrow sort is to be impersonated, American producers, as vague about American class accents as about English ones, seize on British actors. I am sure that there are American actors more than capable of recreating that sharp-tongued total New Englander J.Q.A. As Joe Pesci said when I joined the cast of a picture in which he starred, 'I saw this list of all these English actors for the part of this Harvard professor you're playing and I said, "Why do we always have to take an English asshole when we have one of our own?"'

Although the occasional screening of our history is probably the last chance we shall ever have to know something about who we were, a moving picture, because it moves, is the one form of narrative that cannot convey an idea of any kind, as opposed to a generalized emotion. Mary McCarthy used to counter dedicated *cinéastes* with 'All right. In *Battleship Potemkin*, what does that abandoned baby carriage bouncing down the steps *mean*?'

Worse, our writers and directors tend to know as little about the country's history as the audience, so when they set a story in the past the characters are just like us except they're in costume. But the past is another country, and to bring it to some sort of dramatic life takes a capacity for which there is no English word. It was not until the eighteenth century that a German, J. G. Herder, coined *Einfühlen* – the act of feeling one's way into the past not by holding up a mirror but by stepping *through* the mirror into the alien world.

For instance, we keep death out of sight, and out of mind, too. But the world of the Adamses was saturated with death: infants dead at birth; their mothers, too. Plagues took off whole families – memento mori on every side gave a dark resonance to their days.

Words were also different for them. They looked upon words as deeds. Words defined the republic that the Adamses helped create. Words defined the role that the Adams family wanted our Union to play in the world. But convincing words are the one commodity that Hollywood cannot supply our predecessors, as American vocabularies shrink with each generation. 'I don't do grammar,' an expensive screenwriter said to a director friend of mine who had suggested that perhaps a highly educated English teacher in a film wouldn't keep saying 'between you and I.' Now that the action film's clattering machinery and vivid flames have crowded so much else off the screen, dialogue is more and more used as captions to pictures, to explain to slow members of the audience what they are looking at. Yet spoken language is not only the sum of a dramatized character; it is just as much action as a car crash.

John Quincy Adams spoke as follows on the Fourth of July, 1821: the true America 'goes not abroad in search of monsters to destroy . . . She well knows that by once enlisting under other banners than her own, were they even the banners of foreign independence, she would involve herself, beyond the powers of extrication, in all the wars of interest and intrigue, of individual avarice, envy, and ambition which assume the colors and usurp the standard of freedom . . . She might become the dictatress of the world; she would no longer be the ruler of her own spirit.' This is a terrible truth that can still, I think, rock an American soul – if such there be, of course. It is also language that, chauvinistically, I would rather hear from Newman or Pacino or Hoffman than from an actor, no matter how gifted, not implicated in our curious enterprise.

The standard life of J.Q.A. remains that of Samuel Flagg Bemis (personally I prefer Marie B. Hecht's *John Quincy Adams*, 1972). Mr. Nagel now gives us the inner man, based on the diaries that J.Q.A.'s son Charles Francis once cut down and edited to twelve volumes. Of his father, he said, wearily, 'He took to diary writing early, and he took to it bad.'

J.Q.A. was always something of a prodigy with words and ideas and concepts. When John Adams was made American minister to France, and then Holland, he took his son with him. An aptitude for languages combined with a natural eloquence made J.Q.A. a formidable diplomat. At fourteen, he was sent to St. Petersburg as secretary to an American diplomat. After John Adams was posted to England, in 1785, J.Q.A. glumly gave up his exciting life to enter Harvard and prepare to be a lawyer. Even before we had a country, we had lawyers, who, in due course, gave us the Revolution and the Constitution, under which, in succession to George Washington, John Adams became president and moved to the village in the Southern wilderness named after his predecessor, where he and his wife, Abigail, camped out in the unfinished White House.

Although J.Q.A.'s mother is one of the first brilliant women recorded in our history, she was not at her best as a mother. She was cold, domineering, and insensitive. J.Q.A. had a good deal to put up with. She also proved to be the carrier of an alcoholic gene: J.Q.A.'s two brothers and, later, his two sons were all to die of acute alcoholism. J.Q.A. himself often confided to his diary that he had talked 'overmuch' the night before and felt somewhat despondent the next day. Much of his famous depression (Nagel's 'Rosebud' is that J.Q.A.'s irritable nature was due to manic depression) sounds to me like serial hangovers. Luckily, Adams married Louisa Johnson, a woman as intelligent as Abigail and far more amiable.

After Harvard, J.Q.A. listlessly tried the law. But he found his true métier as a polemicist. Under various newspaper pseudonyms, he supported George Washington's general policy of neutrality in regard to other nations. Washington's celebrated – and long

ignored – farewell to the nation, warning against passionate friend-
ships and enmities with foreign powers, was influenced by letters
that he (and Alexander Hamilton) had read from J.Q.A., whom he
had made minister to The Hague.

In 1802, J.Q.A. was elected to the Massachusetts legislature,
and then to the United States Senate, where he proved to be disastrously independent. Though President Jefferson's personality
got on his nerves – throughout Jefferson's career, Adams found his
perfidy 'worthy of Tiberius Caesar' – Adams supported Jefferson
whenever he thought him right, particularly in regard to the 1807
embargo on American products to England and France, a retaliation for their wartime restrictions on United States trade. Since
New England lived by trade with Europe, J.Q.A.'s support of the
embargo so infuriated Massachusetts that he was forced out of
the Senate before his term was up. But Jefferson's successor,
Madison, made him the first U.S. minister to Russia, and then
sent him to Ghent to negotiate the end of the War of 1812, and on
to London as minister, where he stayed until he became secretary
of state to the new president, Monroe, for whom he drafted what
is still known (even if it is no longer in force) as the Monroe
Doctrine.

In those days, secretaries of state tended to succeed their presidents, and so J.Q.A. made, many thought, 'a corrupt bargain' with
Henry Clay. Although Andrew Jackson had got the most votes for
president in 1824, he failed of a majority, and the election was
decided in the House of Representatives, where the Speaker, Clay,
gave Adams his votes. J.Q.A. began his presidency under a cloud
that got even darker when he made Clay secretary of state. Four
years later, when Adams was thoroughly defeated by the triumphant Jackson, he claimed to see a silver lining to this darkest
cloud: at last he could go home, write poetry, plant trees, be a wise
essayist, like Cicero. Instead, after a year of retirement he was so

bored that he did what no other former president had – or has – done: he was elected to Congress. It was Ralph Waldo Emerson who got his number when he wrote: 'Mr. Adams chose wisely and according to his constitution, when, on leaving the presidency, he went into Congress. He is no literary old gentleman, but a bruiser, and he loves the *mêlée* . . . He is an old roué who cannot live on slops, but must have sulphuric acid in his tea.'

Paradoxically, as a lowly member of the House, J.Q.A. had now entered upon the major phase of his political career: ineffectual president became impassioned tribune of the people. To make sure that slavery could not be debated, the Southern members had put in place a so-called 'gag rule.' For eight years, J.Q.A. fought the rule with all his wit and eloquence. Finally, in 1844, he got the House to rescind the gag rule. Of Jackson's 1837 removal of the Indians to the West, he noted, 'We have done more harm to the Indians since our Revolution than had been done to them by the French and English nations before . . . These are crying sins for which we are answerable before a higher Jurisdiction.' As for slavery, he thought it 'an outrage upon the goodness of God.' One difference between then – so foreign to us – and now is the extent to which Christians actually believed in the Christian God. Where our politicians oscillate between hypocrisy and bigoted religiosity, they had, for better or worse, religion, something that takes a lot of *Einfühlen* for us to grasp. Needless to say, in 1846 J.Q.A. found morally reprehensible the American invasion of Mexico that would give us the Southwest and California.

Finally, the mutiny on the *Amistad*. The noble Lewis Tappan, a founder of the American Anti-Slavery Society, persuaded J.Q.A. to join forces with the lawyer Roger S. Baldwin to defend the by now thirty-nine Africans before the Supreme Court. A federal judge had agreed that the Africans were not slaves; rather, they were free men who had been kidnapped in order to be turned into slaves by Spanish Cubans, and their mutiny had forestalled enslavement. Thus far, the case was clear-cut. But, as so often happens in our affairs, a presidential election had intervened, and Jackson's heir, Martin Van Buren, a smooth New Yorker who was eager to be reelected with Southern votes, filled the air with arcane talk of laws of the sea and the complexities of international treaties, effectively stalling the release of the Africans. He also came up with a plan that would have sent them to Cuba for trial. What pleasure this might have given the voters of the South was insufficient to reelect Matty Van, as he was known; he went down to defeat in November 1840.

In February 1841, the Supreme Court met to decide what should be done with the mutineers from the *Amistad*. J.Q.A. had not appeared before the Court in many years; had not, indeed, appeared in courts at all during his long periods of public service. He was nervous. He was also less and less master of a temper that was growing more terrible with age as he denounced equally intemperate Southerners in the House. Many thought his eruptions were not so much righteous as mad; and he himself prayed, in his diary, for 'firmness to rule my own spirit.'

Baldwin opened for the defense. The next day, a somewhat jittery J.Q.A. closed the defense. Over the years, despite a shrill voice, he had become a great orator; thousands came to hear him wherever he spoke – for seldom less than three hours. Now, in the dank subterranean Supreme Court, beneath the Capitol's Senate chamber, he faced a packed house, always an encouragement to a performer.

Five members of the Court, including Chief Justice Roger B. Taney, were Southerners. It was thought that they were inclined to send the Africans back to Cuba, in their double capacity as merchandise and murderers. Happily, one Southerner was too ill to sit upon the case and another died of a heart attack the evening of the day J.Q.A. finished his four-and-a-half-hour defense. Baldwin had already questioned the jurisdiction of the Court in determining the fate of men who, even had they been slaves, were free in New York State; also, had not our finest and greatest Chief Justice, John Marshall, ruled at the beginning of the Republic, 'The Courts of no country execute the penal laws of another'? One wonders if Noriega's American lawyer quoted Marshall in that travesty of a trial where, after murdering a number of Panamanians in Panama during peacetime, George Bush ordered the kidnapping of the Panamanian leader, Noriega, so that he could be tried in an American court, which had no jurisdiction over him, on charges that should have been brought, if at all, in Panama, an allegedly foreign nation.

J.Q.A. took much the same tack as Baldwin, but he was out for blood, specifically that of former President Van Buren, whose interference in the case he found intolerable. On March 9, Associate Justice Joseph Story, of Massachusetts, gave the majority opinion. Apropos J.Q.A.'s defense, he wrote his wife that it was an 'extraordinary argument . . . extraordinary . . . for its power, for its bitter sarcasm, and its dealing with topics far beyond the record and points of discussion.' Wisely, Story ignored the possible culpability of Van Buren and kept to the issue: Were these free men who had been unlawfully seized and, in self-defense, had freed themselves, a natural right, 'the ultimate right of all human beings in extreme cases: to resist oppression, and to apply force against ruinous injustice'? Since it seemed unlikely to the Court that they had intended 'to import themselves here as slaves, or for sale as slaves,' the mutineers were declared free to go home to Sierra Leone. And so, nearly three years after Cinqué left Africa, he finally achieved this season's wonderful TV word, 'closure,' which is so akin to death. And now, a hundred and fifty-five years later, he is enjoying posthumous closure, so like resurrection, The Movie.

John Quincy Adams ended his days as a beloved national hero. The son of a Founding Father, he must have seemed to his contemporaries as an ever-bright link to the first days of the Republic. He loved a good fight and fought the noblest one on offer in his time, earning himself what he regarded as the supreme accolade from a Virginia congressman, who found him 'the acutest, the astutest, the archest enemy of Southern slavery.'

Adams's last days were very much like the last days of anyone old. He suffered a stroke. He weakened. But he continued to go to the House. On February 21, 1848, he cast his last vote, a 'no' in regard to the war upon Mexico. He motioned to the chair that he would like to speak. As he rose, he staggered. Another member caught him before he hit the floor. He was carried into the Speaker's private chamber. For two days, he drifted in and out of consciousness. Then, on February 23: 'This is the last of earth,' he was heard to murmur. 'I am composed.' Final words. Articulate to the end.

There is, of course, no place for such a man in American politics today – and only through the exercise of a powerful will did Adams make himself so high a place in his own time. Nevertheless, instead of today's whites emptily apologizing for their ancestors' enslavement of the ancestors of black Americans, Congress would be better advised to hire some sculptors with sandblasters and let them loose on Mount Rushmore so that they can turn the likeness of the war lover Theodore Roosevelt into that of a true hero, John Quincy Adams. The only American historian of the last half-century who can safely be called great, William Appleman Williams, particularly revered Adams because, among other things, 'he challenged America to become truly unique by mastering its fears. It was Jefferson and his followers who did not face up to the tension that freedom involved. They denied it was possible to be free *and* disciplined. Adams insisted that was the only meaningful definition of freedom . . . "The great object of civil government," Adams declared in his first annual message to the Congress, "is the improvement of the conditions of those who are parties to the social compact.'"

The New Yorker
10 November 1997

Wiretapping the
Oval Office

It all began in the heat of the summer of 1940. Hitler was at his peak in Europe. France had been defeated. Operation Sealion, the invasion of Britain, would be launched once the aerial bombardment of England had, presumably, broken the spirit of the island's residents. Although Franklin Delano Roosevelt, twice elected President of the United States, was doing his best to aid the British, who were flat broke, 88 percent of the American people wanted no part of a war in Europe, while the isolationists in Congress were uncommonly eloquent. But Roosevelt was a sly and devious man (and I mean those adjectives, as Nixon once said when applying them to Eisenhower, 'in the best sense of those words'). Some time that summer, probably in June, FDR decided to run for a third term, something no president had done before. But slyness and deviousness were very much the order of the day, particularly when, after a closed session with congressional leaders, FDR was promptly quoted as having said that the border of the United States was the Rhine River; this was a dangerous misquotation. What to do?

Into history strode one Henry Kannee – a mere walk-on, an under-five-lines player, as they say in movies. But remember that name. This under-five changed history, permanently. Why not, he said, bug the Oval Office? FDR was delighted. David Sarnoff, the head of RCA, was sent for, presumably with his drills and wires and toolbox, as well as a Kiel Sound Recorder, the ancestor of today's tape recorder.

William Doyle has written *Inside the Oval Office*, an entertaining study of 'The White House Tapes from FDR to Clinton.' This subtitle is something of a misnomer, since not all the presidents taped themselves and their visitors. Ronald Reagan, as befitted a bona fide movie star, was not about to be demoted to what, in effect, was a mere radio performer. He occasionally called in video recorders to show him in full majestic crisis-control as well as in full color to emphasize those curious bright red clown spots on his cheekbones. (It should be noted that Doyle is partial to our very conservative presidents, as opposed to the standard conservative models we are usually permitted.)

In 1988 Doyle made a fascinating documentary for television. Apparently, from August to November 1940, FDR was haphazardly taped (the microphone was in his desk lamp). The tapes were not discovered until 1978. One FDR admirer has remarked how similar his private speaking voice was to his high ecclesiastical speechifying. What is fascinating is how *un*-bishoplike the New York politician is in private. The voice is dry; vowels short; consonants clipped at the end like every other farmer in the Dutchess County of those days. He was something of a chatterbox and often filibustered to make sure that he wasn't told what he didn't want to hear. He also, as Harry Truman sternly noted, 'lies.' Associates of Truman have noted the same thing of Truman and, indeed, shocking though it must be to contemporary members of the House of Representatives, presidents, when not outright telling lies, feel obliged to shade the truth most of the time. This is called politics; when a president lies successfully, he is called a statesman.

FDR's tapes provide little of interest. He does wonder how best to smear his opponent in the 1940 election, Wendell Willkie, who was having a fairly open affair with 'the gal,' Irita Van Doren, editor of *The New York Herald Tribune Book Review* (imagine George W. Bush even knowing the name of Michiko Kakutani). They were intellectual giants then. FDR tells civil rights leaders that he's been integrating blacks into the armed services; this is a real whopper. When challenged, he forlornly notes that the innate musicality of Negroes might pep up the military bands and so could lead, with luck, to an indigo band leader. Doyle affects shock that FDR refers to black men as 'boys,' particularly in front of black civil rights leaders. It is sickening, of course, to be exposed even fifty-nine years after the fact to such a horror at a time when our sensibilities have never been so delicately attuned to the feelings of others. But I suppose this is a small flaw in the man who gave us the entire world. Doyle sadly quotes Dean Acheson, an assistant secretary of state at the time, on how FDR 'condescended [to people] . . . it was patronizing and humiliating.' Doyle neglects to note that Acheson was bounced by FDR in 1933 only to be rehired in a lesser capacity eight years later. I don't think Doyle likes FDR; if he does, why does he note gratuitously that FDR 'laughed at his own jokes'?

Potentially, the most interesting tape is the Cabinet meeting after our fleet was sunk at Pearl Harbor. Although FDR knew that his ultimatum of November 26, 1941, would oblige the Japanese to attack us somewhere, it now seems clear that, thanks to our breaking of many of the twenty-nine Japanese naval codes the previous year, we had at least several days' warning that Pearl Harbor would be hit; yet, mysteriously, the American commanders in Hawaii were given no alert. It was commented upon at the time that the President was less astonished than others by what had happened; in any case, it would be interesting to reinterpret the talk in the Oval Office on December 8, in light of the revelations about to be made in *Day of Deceit* (The Free Press, December), where Robert Stinnett, after years of studying those coded naval intercepts, shows that FDR was complicitous in the attack since, otherwise, he could not have got the American people into the virtuous war against Hitler. With this latest information, one might be able to . . . well, *de*code the cryptic White House conversations about the – expected? – attack that brought us into the Second World War.

Except for a brief tryout of FDR's recording apparatus, Harry Truman did not record himself or others for history or even blackmail. Doyle is now obliged to slog his way through the management styles of various presidents. While Truman presented us with a militarized economy and government, Eisenhower brought the skills of a military politician to the Oval Office. He regarded the taping of conversations as a 'management tool,' and in his memoir *Crusade in Europe* he duly notes that he was a recorder of talk from early days. Of course, 'I made it a habit to inform visitors of the system that we used so that each would understand its purpose was merely to facilitate the execution of business.' This shows a noble concern but such candor was not, perhaps, the best way to get interesting information out of people who didn't want their secrets put on the record.

Most presidents tend to have a low view of their immediate predecessors. Eisenhower, the methodical staff officer executive, disliked FDR's chaotic, secretive style, and he was disgusted by

Truman's use of cronies. It was Ike who switched off the British empire for good at the time of Suez. In 'secret,' Britain, France, and Israel attacked Egypt, ostensibly to recover the Suez Canal, which Nasser had rudely seized. Ike and Prime Minister Anthony Eden (recorded by a 'dead key' – someone listening in on the telephone) provided a poignant last post for Eden, Suez and the ghost of the Raj. The beginning of their talk is superb and sets the tone. Eisenhower: 'This is a very clear connection.' Eden: 'I can just hear you.' Was it not ever thus between slave and master? Ike has ordered a cease-fire at Suez. An edgy Eden sounds as if he has to go to the bathroom; actually, he is due in 'my' Parliament in five minutes. Eden takes down his orders; then Ike says, 'Now that we know connections are so good, you can call me anytime you please.' Eden: 'If I survive here tonight I will call you tomorrow.' Three months later Eden was, as they say nowadays, toast.

Kennedy was the least prepared of the presidents whom Doyle deals with. He quickly demonstrated his inability to execute a coherent policy at the Bay of Pigs, a misadventure cooked up by his predecessor that he had then made his very own, with disastrous results. Although Kennedy had a sharp mind, he was not used to hard work of any sort other than the haphazard barnstorming of politics. After the Cuban disaster, McGeorge Bundy wrote him a memo, placing the blame firmly, if tactfully, on Kennedy's management style, to the extent that he could be said to have one. 'We can't get you to sit still . . . Truman and Eisenhower did their daily dozen in foreign affairs the first thing in the morning, and a couple of weeks ago you asked me to begin to meet you on this basis. I have succeeded in catching you on three mornings, for a total of about eight minutes, and I conclude this is not really how you like to begin the day.' Although the

Kennedy promiscuity has been much discussed, far more important for the state was his bad health. He was in bed a good deal of
the time, and the cortisone injections he was obliged to take did
not concentrate his mind.

In the summer of 1962 Kennedy installed the most thorough recording system of all, wiring the Oval Office, Cabinet
room, parts of the living quarters. In his office, a button controlled the recording switch. When it was on, others did most of
the talking while the self-conscious President was laconic, grave,
noncommittal. Doyle gives us the dialogue with the Governor
of Mississippi when the university was being integrated and
civil war seemed a possibility, at least in Oxford, Mississippi.
Kennedy expertly maneuvers the Governor into place. He's
learning.

On October 16, 1962, McGeorge Bundy informs the President
that the Soviets have placed missiles in Cuba. Crucially, military
intelligence is certain that the missiles do *not* have nuclear warheads. Oddly, no one really questions the absolute certainty of the
team that brought us the Bay of Pigs. It was only a few years ago
that we learned that the missiles were indeed so equipped and that
if Cuba was attacked, the Russians were willing to take out a
number of American cities as far north as Seattle. The dialogue is
chilling in light of what we now know. Shall the missiles be taken
out with an airstrike, promptly followed by invasion? General
Taylor notes that the United States is vulnerable from the south.
Ambassador Thompson comes up with a compromise – a blockade. But air force chief of staff Curtis LeMay ('Bomb 'em back to
the Stone Age') is all for some serious bombing. It has been
reported that LeMay's presence at any meeting with Kennedy was
sufficient to give the President 'fits.' LeMay is ready for an all-out
war over Cuba; Berlin, too, if we're not chicken. This does not

play well in the Oval Office. In the end, Kennedy's political instinct was classic: When in doubt, *do nothing*, particularly if the something that you do could end life on the planet. When Khrushchev helped Kennedy end the crisis, JFK was heard to say: 'If they want this job, fuck 'em. They can have it – it's no great joy to me.'

President Johnson started installing recording devices his first day in office. Johnson is perhaps the only great comic figure to have occupied the White House. He was not only a master of Lincolnian outhouse humor but he was a deadly mimic. He recorded, between November 1963 and 1968, some 700 hours of White House meetings and phone calls: well worth a CD of his very own. When Johnson names the venerable Senator Richard Russell to the Warren Commission investigating Kennedy's murder, they meet. Russell is furious.

Russell: Well, Mr. President, you ought to have told me you were going to name me.

LBJ: I told you. I told you the other day I was going to name the chief justice. I called you.

Russell: You did not. You talked about getting somebody from Supreme Court. You didn't tell me you were going to name [both Warren and me] . . . Mr. President, please now . . .

LBJ: I just want to counsel with you and I just want your judgment and your wisdom, 'cause I haven't got any Daddy and you're going to be it . . .

Russell: Well, I'm not going to say anything more, Mr. President. I'm at your command.

LBJ: You damned sure going to be at my command. You're going to be at my command as long as I'm here.

The most startling revelation is how clearly – and early – LBJ understood that the Vietnam War was unwinnable. As of 1964, he is again confiding in Russell.

LBJ: What do you think of this Vietnam thing?
Russell: I don't see how we're ever going to get out of it, without getting in a major war with the Chinese and all of them down there in those rice paddies and jungles. I just don't see it. It's – I – I – just don't know what to do.
LBJ: Well, that's the way I've been feeling for six months . . . I spend all my days with Rusk and McNamara and Bundy and Harriman and Vance and all those folks that are dealing with it and I would say that it pretty well adds up to them now that we've got to show some force . . . I don't think that the American people are for it . . . You don't have any doubt that if we go in there, and get them up against a wall, the Chinese Communists are going to come in?
Russell: No doubt at all.
LBJ: That's my judgment, and my people don't think so . . .
Russell: I guess going in there with all the troops, I tell you it'll be the most expensive adventure that this country ever went into.

Doyle quotes C. Douglas Dillon to the effect that LBJ so frightened everybody that no one dared tell him the truth about the extent of defeats until the Tet Offensive. But it is clear from what's on record that he had a perfectly clear view of how he had been trapped by his inherited Kennedy advisers, to a man vain and blinkered, and by his own innate cowardice, which allowed him to be turned into a disastrous war-president instead of what he was born to be, the completer of the New Deal.

Where Kennedy never forgot that he was being recorded, Nixon seems never to have remembered. He is being immortalized. Despite intermittent political skills, Nixon seems, on the evidence of the tapes, to have had no conscious mind. He is all flowing unconscious. Remembered slights, grudges, conspiracies. 'We are surrounded by enemies,' he declared after his reelection by one of the greatest majorities in history. Two years into his first term Nixon joined the taping club. Along with the normal presidential desire to get something on others before they get it on him, Nixon had Kissinger. Nixon knew, everyone knew, that Kissinger would say one thing to the President and then just the opposite to journalists in order to build himself up in the eyes of the public. All in all, it would have been cheaper – and less bloody – for Nixon to have got a new foreign policy adviser, but, as Dick liked to say, jowls aquiver, that would be the *easy* way. Along with tracking enemies, Nixon used the tapes simply to rant against the Ivy League, Georgetown set as well as Jews, the Pentagon, the CIA. Regularly, he ordered crimes to be committed that his staff promptly forgot about. Doyle quotes Bob Haldeman as observing, 'Nixon was the weirdest man ever to live in the White House.' The great Gen. Alexander Haig said, 'My God, if I had done everything Richard Nixon told me to do, I'd probably be in Leavenworth today!' In any case, at the end, Nixon's own talk did him in. He obstructed justice, suborned witnesses, and, most horrifying, talked dirty and even *blasphemed* in the Oval Office, the pure heart of our empire. So – California, here I come.

Doyle accepts the generous view that Nixon was a master of foreign affairs who brought to an end the Vietnam War. That is one way of looking at it. But the war that he pretended to have a plan to end in 1968 kept right on going through 1972 and almost up to his own political end.

Nixon's appointed vice president, Gerald Ford, vowed that he would not record. Doyle has found an authorized telephone tape between Ford and Kissinger. They appear to think the world of each other. Doyle also pads things out with the minutes of the tense national security meetings over the seizure of an American merchant ship by the Cambodian Khmer Rouge Communists. Thus Gerald Ford underwent *his* baptism of fire as, yet again, the resolve and will and credibility of the United States, the earth's only *good* nation, were being tested by crafty Asian Communists. One senses the tension in those meetings. Also the playacting. Even Doyle recognizes that the 'participants seem to be as concerned with bellicose posturing and inflicting punitive damage on Cambodia as much as with the actual rescue. Kissinger advised: "Let's look ferocious."' The United States has now entered its Cowardly Lion phase. The appointed vice president, Nelson Rockefeller, has a presentiment of what is to come when he warns: 'Many are watching us, in Korea and elsewhere. The big question is whether or not we look silly.'

Carter did not record. He was also ill suited for the presidency because his virtues – an engineer's convergent mind – were of no use in a job that requires almost surreal divergency. Engineers want to connect everything up and make sense. Politicians – and artists – realize that nothing really makes sense and nothing ever hooks up. As Carter's vice president, Walter Mondale, sadly noted, 'Carter thought politics was sinful.' Happily, he was born to be a *former* president, a phantom office that he has since enhanced. Two years after Ronald Reagan replaced Carter, he too was faced with a crisis. The free world was at risk, yet again, thanks to ruthless Commies at work on the small island of Grenada, where 1,000

Americans, many of them medical students, might possibly be at
risk from a Mr. Bishop, the local point man for the evil men in the
Kremlin. Well, Ron stood tall; he hit his mark. An actor's got to do
what an actor's got to do – so we invaded, 'cause if we hadn't we'd
reveal to the world 'that when the chips were down, we backed
away.' This is a great scenario only slightly spoiled by mean old
General Haig, who observed that 'the Provincetown police force
could have conquered Grenada.'

I feel that Doyle is somewhat dazzled by the Great
Communicator, who slept more on the job than any other president since his idol Calvin Coolidge, who wisely stayed in bed
every chance he got. Reagan did attend to his occasional acting
chores but, as in his movie career, he almost never had a good
script. Sample: Reagan is being videotaped as he tries to sell some
senators on his pro-*contra* line: 'I think what is at issue today is
whether we're voting for or against a plan, we're really voting are
we going to have another Cuba, a Marxist-Leninist totalitarian
country as we have now in Nicaragua, on the mainland of the
Americas, or are we going to hold out for people who want democracy.' Well, it probably played better than it reads. It was Reagan's
astonishing luck to have, in Gorbachev, a Soviet leader who was
willing to switch off the cold war (and the Soviet Union in the
process, presumably by accident), and a wife, Nancy, who finally
took U.S. policy in hand and made peace with the Russians while
not missing a single lunch with Betsy Bloomingdale. Tapes of *their*
telephone conversations would indeed be the stuff of history.

On to Bush. We are faced by even more Enemy of the Month
Club choices now that the Soviet Union is flying apart. Qaddafi,
Noriega (invasion of Panama, hooray!), Saddam Hussein (light
show over Baghdad!). Next – Clinton. Bit soon for a useful sum-
ming up. Doyle does think that the White House should be wired

for the record, but with the tapes sealed for twenty years unless otherwise needed. He seems aware of the dangers of absolute surveillance over everyone, today's trend. He quotes Frank Church's warning of a quarter-century ago. The senator realized how, with modern technology, we now have the capacity 'to make tyranny total in America, and we must see to it that this agency [the National Security Agency] and all agencies that possess this technology operate within the law and under proper supervision, so that we can never cross over that abyss. That is the abyss from which there is no return.'

Doyle seems to think that there is nothing wrong with the American political system that a few honest guys and gals in high office couldn't cure. But to obtain high office those guys and gals have to raise millions and millions of dollars first and this can only be done dishonestly, even by our Rube Goldberg rules, the ever-shifting campaign-financing laws. As for intellectual honesty, the consumer society in which we glory is based on advertising which is at best hype and at worst plain lying. Thus even the most virtuous candidate is sold, with a merry spin. It has been a long time since any public figure has openly said anything useful, much less true, even in the relative privacy of the Oval Office. Up to a point, this is the nature of our society and kind of fun. When the wise Frank Church heard the virtuous Jimmy Carter promise the American people that he would never lie to them if elected president, Church said, with morose delight, 'He would deny the very nature of politics.' But when, as must happen, all sense of social reality is lost, the rulers and the ruled then plunge into the churchly abyss where nothing at all is ever real again and even the ghost of the Republic is gone while the first, and probably last, global *nuclear* empire reels from crisis to crisis, involving ever weaker enemies, led by ever more off-the-wall rulers.

The overall impression that *Inside the Oval Office* gives is that the Second Law of Thermodynamics is now in serious play: Everything is running down. From our Augustus, FDR, who never worried about his place in history because he knew that he was supremely history, to the present day one notes the increasing second-rateness of our Oval Ones. I suggest that this has nothing to do so much with the caliber of the individuals as it does with an overextended military industrial political complex that wrings tax money from Congress to fight drugs, terrorism and bad guys who use eyeliner like Qaddafi. Money for 'defense' (*sic*) should be spent repairing our rotted home base. But it won't be. Meanwhile, the Ovoids do their best to please the corporations that house them so nicely. They also talk, as politicians always have, in code. FDR was accused of making different agreements with different people. Wearily, Eleanor Roosevelt, if she remembered, would warn those about to approach FDR in his office: 'When Franklin says yes, yes, yes, he isn't agreeing with you. He's just listening to you.' So when polls show that the American people over a weekend rate highly this or that president, they are really only saying yes, yes, yes because there's not much point in saying no, no, no until we can find a new way of selecting what, after all, are essentially powerless figureheads – except in wartime, which is why . . . You complete the sentence. I feel their pain.

The Nation
27 September 1999

Clare Boothe Luce

In the summer of 1967, I wrote my father from Venice about a ball given at the Palazzo Rezzonico. Guests arrived by gondola. Hundreds of torches lit up the facade of the palace on the Grand Canal, while inside thousands of candles burned in the great chandeliers as liveried footmen offered champagne to what looked to be every Perhapsburg in Europe. I had arrived with my assigned date, Clare Boothe Luce, the recent widow of the founder of *Time*, in whose giggly pages both my father and I had so often been fictionalized. *Time* was founded as a news magazine in 1923; actually it was an opinion magazine that presented real people as if they were characters in an ongoing melodrama where Christ and Capitalism were forever at risk. *Time* set, alas, the tone for most journalism since. The malice was unremitting, the humor merry as an open grave.

As our gilded barge docked, Clare and I stood, rather like Antony – well, Octavian – and Cleopatra, while the flashbulbs of paparazzi douched us in that blinding icy white light – limelight –

each found so nourishing. At the ball, by candlelight, the sixty-four-year-old Clare was a perfect silvery moon set among the zircon stars.

I had known her slightly most of my life. Our relationship is pretty much summed up in the note I sent to my father:

> I said I felt novels were finished. She said, 'Yes, but there's still a kind of fiction people love!' 'Yes,' I said, '*Time* magazine.' 'No,' she said, 'I meant fiction.' 'I know,' I said, 'I meant *Time*.' 'Don't be naughty,' she said. 'I meant detective stories.' Then she insisted we be photographed in the room where Browning died (enclosed).

The picture is lost. But I recall that as we stood beside a round table (that he wrote at?) Clare, in a melting voice, misquoted 'My Last Duchess.' Gently, I corrected her. Then I misquoted Elizabeth Barrett Browning's 'I shall but love thee better after death' sonnet, and she radiantly corrected me. One-upmanship was how we passed the rare times we saw each other.

The last time I saw Clare Boothe Luce was in 1985, on her final trip to Rome, where, from 1953 to 1956, she had been Eisenhower's turbulent ambassador, single-handedly saving Italy from Communism, blissfully unaware that Italian Communists had little interest in leveling the classes – her great fear – and little sympathy for the *ci-devant* Soviet Union. No matter. Clare was a fierce professional warrior for God and the deserving rich and, at one point, for Trieste to rejoin Italy – or was it the other way around?

The American ambassador gave a dinner for her, which Imelda Marcos excitingly crashed. A ten-year-old godchild of mine was put next to Clare. She spent most of her time at table amusing the wide-eyed girl, who could not believe that an interesting and witty grown-up would want to talk to her when there were so many fascinating folk at hand to dazzle. Clare was endlessly seductive. She was also a great many other things, as Sylvia Jukes Morris points out in *Rage for Fame: The Ascent of Clare Boothe Luce* (Random House, $30), which takes her life up to 1942, when, after three hit plays on Broadway and the power marriage to Henry R. Luce, she got elected to Congress from Connecticut; here Morris ends her first volume.

This is a biography of the sort that only real writers – as opposed, say, to professional scholars or journalists – can write. Morris has done serious research; yet she writes in short, sharp, dramatic bursts. Like her subject, she has a gift for aphorism: Clare became, in later life, 'more conservative now that she had so much to conserve.'

This sort of book does make one wonder what will become of the mallsters' novelists. Clare's life has every staple of pop fiction: illegitimacy (hers), poverty, a mother who advanced from lowly call girl to kept woman; then Clare's marriage to and divorce from a rich alcoholic by whom she had a daughter, later tragically killed. Once divorced, she goes to work, rises from caption writer at *Vogue* to managing editor of *Vanity Fair* while being herself somewhat kept by that busy financier and world-class bore, Bernard Baruch. Then on to the heights: the marriage to Luce in 1935; the hit plays; the elections won . . . The Collins sisters are left far behind in the gold dust of fact.

Everyone turns up in Clare's story, in or out of bed. One can only hope that Morris does not belong to the coitus-interruptus school of biography so starkly personified by her husband, Edmund Morris (after a splendid first volume on Theodore Roosevelt's life, he has kept us waiting for eighteen years for the next shoe to drop) and by sly Arthur Schlesinger, Jr., who put aside *in medias res* his distinguished multivolume life of FDR to grind out fictional narratives about the wayward residents of Riverdale, New York's, house of Atreus.

What was Clare like to know? I've used the word 'seductive.' Most people do. She was five feet five and slender, and she was often compared to a Dresden doll because of her yellow hair, blue eyes, and chiseled features – chiseled first by Noguchi in marble and then by a plastic surgeon, obliging Clare to call Noguchi in for an emergency session to make her marble nose conform to 'Nature.' Noguchi denies that he made the change, but he did. In any case, 'Dresden doll' suggests a delicate figurine easily broken. Clare was not breakable. In her senior years, she swam, snorkeled, water-skied; and outlived most of her detractors, while occasionally dropping a bit of acid.

The day after the embassy party, we had lunch at Vecchia Roma, near my apartment in Largo Argentina. Clare was accompanied by her biographer, Ms. Morris. I remember wondering, How is *this* going to turn out? Because if they become friends . . .? A further complication for an honest biographer: Clare enjoyed lying about herself. But then there had been a great deal for her to lie about, starting with a failed-musician father, who never married her mother; and a mother who married a country doctor but was kept to the end by one Joel Jacobs (she wouldn't marry *him* because he was a Jew); and, finally, Clare's syphilitic brother, who failed at everything, including embezzlement (he got caught).

But I did note, at lunch, that she was being candid about most things. Also, for once, she and I did not row about politics. Instead memory lane beckoned. My stepfather, Hugh D. Auchincloss (known as Hughdie), awash with Standard Oil money, befriended an impoverished Yale classmate, one Harry Luce, son of a missionary in China, awash with Jesus and raw ambition. Hughdie paid for Harry's first trip to Europe. In reflective mood, Hughdie would observe, 'You know, wherever we went in Europe, Harry managed to make new enemies for the United States.' Later, Hughdie put up a part of the eighty-six thousand dollars with which Harry started *Time*; when the magazine was profitable, he was repaid, without interest. Later still, Harry, no doubt in senti-mental mood, tried to take Hughdie's wife away from him. I think that is why my mother was one of the few women of Clare's gen-eration who did not hate her on principle. After all, she could afford to be generous: she had, as they used to say, put the horns on Clare. 'Poor Clare,' she would sigh, after she turned down Harry's offer of marriage in the spring of 1942. (I was in the next room and heard him say, 'Clare doesn't understand me. We don't share the same interests. We're getting a divorce.') As it turned out, my mother did divorce Hughdie in order to marry not Luce but an air force general, while the Luces, now seriously incorporated as business partners, continued their manifold good works to the end of his life. She had her affairs. He had his. Understanding, finally, had everything to do with it.

At that last lunch, Clare mentioned the one story that most enraged her. A zealous convert to Catholicism, she is supposed to have been observed in the Vatican, haranguing the Pope, who kept saying, over and over again, ever more desperately, 'But, madam, I *am* Catholic.'

'The story was invented by . . .' She named a name I've forgot-ten. 'It's not like me at all, anyway.' But, of course, it was. Once, when we were both going at each other in a political quarrel, she said, grimly, 'I see you have a didactic side, too.'

'Anyway, I had a talk with Punch Sulzberger' – the *Times*' pub-lisher. 'And I said I know that that story is going to be the lead in my obituary and it's absolutely untrue and you must do something about it.'

'Did he?' The *Times*' little treacheries were almost in a class with Harry's own *Time* magazine.

'Well, you'll know before I will.' I did, in 1987. The story was repeated widely.

After Eleanor Roosevelt, Clare was easily the most hated woman of her time – she was too beautiful, too successful in the theater, in politics, in marriage. Feminism as we now know it was a minor eccentricity in those days. Otherwise, she might have been admired as what she was, a very tough woman who had so perfectly made it in a man's world. But then, as one thinks of Hillary Clinton, perhaps not – of course, Hillary-haters are mostly men, and the men of long ago were generally fetched by Clare. It was the women who wanted to do her in. She had her revenge.

Clare had a savage tongue as well as the dangerous gift of phrase. In her ascent from poverty and from a life on the wrong side of just about every track the country had to offer, she educated herself, and became rich through a society marriage to one George Brokaw and then the union with Luce. She also maintained a long relationship with Bernard Baruch, thirty-two years her senior, with whom she had, she records sadly in her diary, 'half-sex.' 'He gave her millions,' my mother would say with wonder. But Clare would say that he only invested money for her, and, as a popular playwright, she earned a great deal.

With Clare's second Broadway play, she let the girls have it. *The Women*, with its all-female cast, was a great success in the theater and on the screen. The women struck back as best they could: Clare could not have written the play all by herself; it was actually the work of George Kaufman and Moss Hart, together or separately. Finally, Kaufman made a public statement: If he had written *The Women*, 'why should I sign it Clare Boothe?' No one seems to have had any more than an editorial hand in a comedy whose bubbling misogyny was Clare at her purest.

But, from that moment on, practically everything she wrote was supposedly the work of a man, including her wartime reportage for *Life*. Rather like Hillary Clinton, today, Clare could not be allowed to win.

At lunch: 'Do you realize that because of Harry I was never on the cover of *Time*?'

'He kept you off?'

'No, *they* kept me off. The editors.' I should note that for almost a half-century to appear on the cover of *Time* meant that its subject was a permanent, for good or ill, member of the world's grandest vanity fair.

Even Dawn Powell, our best mid-century novelist, had it in for Clare. Dawn herself had enjoyed almost no success from her novels and plays; then along comes what she regards as a dilettante beauty who takes Broadway – and all the other ways save the strait and narrow – by the proverbial storm. Dawn parodies the Luces as Julian and Amanda in *A Time to Be Born*. Like everyone else, Dawn takes it for granted that Amanda doesn't bother to do her own writing. Amanda believes that 'the tragedy of the Attic poets, Keats, Shelley, Burns, was not that they died young but that they were obliged by poverty to do all their own writing.'

Dawn also reflects another generally held theory about Clare: that a woman so attractive to men must be, at heart, cold and calculating and . . . yes, the ultimate putdown in sexist times, frigid. 'She knew,' writes Dawn, 'exactly what she wanted from life, which was, in a word, everything . . . She had a genuine distaste for sexual intimacy . . . but there were so many things to be gained by trading on sex and she thought so little of the process that she itched to use it as currency once again.'

Morris has read Clare's diaries; and candid they are. Apparently, she liked sex very much. At eighteen she fell in love with a young army lieutenant who then married an older woman with money, proving to Clare that man is 'only a sublimated anthropoid ape.'

But the iron – or should one say the bright gold? – had entered her soul. 'I'll marry for money,' she confided to a girlfriend. 'Lots of it . . . Damned if I'll ever love any mere man. Money! I need it and the power it brings, and someday you shall hear my name spoken of as famous.' This was fifteen years before Scarlett O'Hara sprang, full-bosomed, from the pages of *Gone With the Wind*.

In 1922, Clare's mother and Clare were taken to Europe by her stepfather, Dr. Austin. In the shabby streets of defeated Berlin, Clare had a vastation. Newspapers were sailing along the side-walk. One wrapped itself around her leg, she told me in 1970 over lunch at her beachside pleasure dome in Hawaii. 'My mother had a sententious side to her – which I've inherited, they tell me.' Clare gave me a quick look to cut me off at the pass. 'Anyway, when she saw that newspaper she said, "This is the sort of thing that happens when a society grows decadent and no longer keeps itself up." I was deeply impressed. Now you ask me why I gave up New York. Well, one day not long after Harry died, I came out of the Sherry Netherland and a newspaper suddenly wrapped itself around my leg. I heard my mother's voice, saw a street even worse than that dusty Berlin street, realized the Weimar Republic had arrived in New York, and so I went off to live in Hawaii, happily beneath the American flag.'

In youth, Clare tried silent-movie acting, without success. Later she worked briefly for that passionate women's rights activist Alva Vanderbilt Belmont. But Clare was not made for distributing pamphlets. She was sexually experienced by the time she married money in the form of George Brokaw, who was an alcoholic then in his mid-forties. Although Clare claimed to have brought a virginal body to the bridal suite at the Plaza Hotel, she also claimed that she wanted to jump out the window on their wedding night. When her new husband didn't simply pass out, the mustard remained largely uncut, or, as she later put it, with hardly a virginal tentativeness, 'The Bill of Fare is neither varied nor sufficient.' Eventually, a daughter was born, followed by a friendly divorce.

The restless Mrs. Brokaw wanted a job at *Vogue*. When nothing seemed available, she simply arrived one day, took over a desk, and soon was put to work writing picture captions. No one ever actually hired her. But everyone was delighted that she was there. She was now twenty-six. What next on the Bill of Fare? Why not Fame? As she wrote in her school yearbook, 'What rage for fame attends both great and small.' This aphorism is perhaps not airtight – the small are too busy trying to survive ever to daydream of a ride in triumph through the streets of Persepolis.

From *Vogue* she moved to Condé Nast's *Vanity Fair*, where she wrote a great deal of lively copy. Condé Nast's wife, Leslie, was a daughter of Bilitis, in those days the most secretive cult in the United States. Clare, ever experimental, allowed Leslie to seduce her, commenting afterward on the prodigious length and sharpness of Leslie's fingernails. But the central affair in Clare's life was with Donald Freeman, a young, brilliant, unbeautiful editor who taught her a good deal about writing. When Freeman killed himself in a car crash, Clare was consoled by the fact that she was his successor as managing editor of *Vanity Fair*; she also got her hands on his journals, and kept them. In his last letter to her he wrote, 'It is only human nature that I should be discarded – what with . . . men of affairs like Mr. Baruch sighing for your time . . . It has been only in the past few days that the cloud of my three years' love for you has been gradually lifting from the brain of one who has almost been a madman for the whole time.' She was now twenty-nine.

Two years later, at a dinner, Fame arrived in the shape of 'a tall sandy-haired man whose copious eyebrows arched over narrow eyes.' Apparently, she teased Henry R. Luce about the flaws in his

latest magazine, *Fortune*, and suggested he publish a picture magazine. (She had given Condé Nast the same advice, but he lacked
the money.) Luce did his usual social number, firing dozens of
questions at her, like a prosecuting attorney; then he looked at his
watch, said he was late, left. Clare thought him the rudest man she
had ever met and was, of course, hooked.

They next met at an Elsa Maxwell ball at the Waldorf-Astoria.
After a drink together, he said that he had something he wanted to
tell her. They found as private a spot as they could. Clare expected
a job offer. Instead she had a Luce offer: 'The French call it *coup de
foudre*. I know you are the one woman in my life.' Clare was astonished: she had been in his life, thus far, less than an hour. Luce also
said, according to Morris, that 'whether or not romance developed
between them . . . he had decided to end his marriage of eleven
years. For at least the last two, he had felt a need for a different
kind of companionship. His wife did not share his interests.' Six
years later, I heard him make the exact same speech to my
mother – only by then Clare was the wife.

In Miami, while the *foudre* was still electrifying him, they
became as one sexually; and this proved to be an ominous failure.
Although no man can become a daughter of Bilitis, Morris tells us
that 'in old age, Clare painfully recalled Harry's strong hands and
long fingers. "If he touched you it was like he was tearing you
apart. I suppose today I would have given him a handbook of sex,
but in those days women were expected to keep quiet."' I must
say it is hard to imagine Clare not lecturing him on the spot, but
then her clumsy partner meant not only money but Fame. He
was, periodically, impotent with Clare, unlike his first wife, with
whom 'he simply did it and then rolled over and thought about
Time.'

Whatever their incompatibilities, each needed the idea of the
other. What failed them in the sack sustained them on the page,

and they wrote each other interesting analyses of themselves. Clare: 'A badly burnt child I am so afraid of happiness, that let a perfect moment begin to unfold like a rose in my hands, and I instantly try to crush it.' Harry: 'Happiness, I thought until recently, had nothing whatever to do with my life . . . Now I think otherwise . . . There are those who can always hear, beneath the rumble of traffic, the stars singing.' One must not forget that he was the indulgent employer of the dread poet Archibald MacLeish. Clare: 'Most everyone that knew me casually preferred to think of me as a cold, remote, shrewd and ambitious woman: I have always contrived to behave so in their company.' Others thought her a sexpot, but, 'until I met you I never knew anyone who challenged enough of the real heart and mind of me, to interrupt me in my emotional juggling.' Thus Lioness to Lion.

The first Mrs. Luce took Harry to the cleaners; as a result, he became a resident of Connecticut, where there was no state income tax. Clare returned to playwriting, but, as Morris points out, 'reluctant to be totally honest about her experiences, she was at the same time so self-obsessed that she was unable to write well about anyone or anything else.' Two days after her play *Abide with Me* failed on Broadway, she married Luce. *Time*'s play reviewer was in a bind. He drafted a favorable review. Luce, in his role as God, said, 'Show isn't that good. Write what you thought.' He did. Later she beat Harry at golf; he never played with her again. Also, her attempts to be helpful with the magazines were sternly rebuffed, particularly when she expected to have a hand in what she always claimed was her original idea, a photo magazine that became the highly popular *Life*. Soon Lion was more or less permanently impotent with Lioness, not perhaps the best situation for a man of a romantic if narrow temperament to find himself in. But they had by then been more or less permanently incorporated, with him as the highly potent senior partner. With no role to play in his magazines, Clare was obliged to make her own fame, in what was then, after movie stardom, the showiest place of all, Broadway.

In three days in 1936 Clare wrote the first draft of *The Women*, par for the Noel Coward course, to which she brought her . . . what is it? a mashie? Anyway, commercially the play was a hole in one, and the all-star film that George Cukor made of it still amuses audiences. At the time, this hymn to misogyny rather shocked the gentlemen while, perversely, the ladies were delighted with Clare's witty send-ups of *other* ladies. Meanwhile, 1936 was also a year of triumph for Harry. *Life* appeared, and was a success. Harry was now having presidential daydreams. Then *The New Yorker*'s Wolcott Gibbs did a profile of him, in which *Time*'s awful phony Homeric style was parodied: 'Prone he to wave aside pleasures . . . argues still that "names make news," that he would not hesitate to print a scandal involving his best friend' – or get off with his wife. When Harry complained to *The New Yorker*'s editor, Harold Ross, he was told that the Luce periodicals had a reputation for 'crassness in description, for cruelty and scandal-mongering and insult.' That was the upside. As for Harry himself, he was held to be 'mean,' even 'scurrilous' at times, and was 'in a hell of a position to ask anything.' What price glory?

In 1938, the Luces decided to check out Hitler's Germany. It was Harry who missed the point, and Clare, possibly because of her long affair with Baruch and her mother's affair with Jacobs, who quickly saw the dangerous rise in anti-Semitism. (Incidentally, it is now the custom to establish that anyone worthy of an 'intimate' biography must be revealed not only as a homosexual but as an anti-Semite: plainly the two most dreadful 'preferences' of all. Clare did have at least one fling with a daughter of Bilitis, but she was no anti-Semite.) Where Harry noted, approvingly, that Hitler had 'suspended the class system,' whatever that meant, Clare saw a close analogy between the Nazis and our own Ku Klux Klan: 'Indeed the swastika never burns more brightly or savagely in the Schwarzwald than the Fiery Cross of the Klan once burned in the bayous and cypress swamps of Dixie.' This was from the introduction to her next Broadway hit, *Kiss the Boys Good-Bye*, set in the South. Meanwhile, her friend Baruch was trying to get Roosevelt to rearm. 'The nation is not ready,' said the President, who, himself, was.

Like so many successful commercialites, Clare had immortal longings. Would she – could she – reach Shaw's level? George Bernard, not Irwin (who had rebuffed her advances). Eleanor Roosevelt wrote that Miss Boothe might indeed be a first-class playwright, 'when the bitterness of the experiences which she has evidently had are completely out of her system.' Clare thanked her for the kind thought but said that the cold 'stupidity' of this world had done her in, she feared, as a potential builder of another, 'sweeter place.'

Back to Europe in the crucial year 1939. Clare flirted with Gertrude Stein. Then, in two weeks, she wrote her anti-Nazi play, *Margin for Error*, a somewhat confused melodrama with quite a few sharp, funny lines: 'The Third Reich allows no margin for error.'

Clare was now turning more and more political. In September 1939, she marched into the office of *Life*'s editor and said that she wanted to be a war correspondent. She was no longer just the boss's interfering wife. She was a famous writer and, as such, she was hired, though Harry worried about their being separated for so long, even though they had not been getting on. So, as was her habit, Clare wrote him a position paper, noting that for him 'to conjure up some dominant discontent or misery out of such good fortune as ours is positively wanton.' Then:

There are times when a man or woman does better to act
with sense than to react with sensibility. This seems to me
to be one of them . . . I would like to show more sympathy
to you in this matter, but . . . if I did, I should not be
acting with as much love as I feel for you. You see, I not
only love you . . . but I like you, and admire you far more
than you think. Indeed, you always seem to be afraid that
if I didn't love you blindly, I would dislike you openly.
That is not the case . . . Now darling, to bed. I do not like
to go to bed without you. But somehow, lately, even when
I'm with you, I seem to go to bed without you.

Had Broadway been less sternly lowbrow, Clare might have been
our Congreve.

Harry's response was hardly in the same class. In short, he said
he feared Time's winged wastebasket. By February 1940, they were
discussing divorce. Meanwhile, war correspondent Clare was
having a splendid time in Europe. Lecherous ambassador to
Britain Joe Kennedy had designs on her as well as a good deal of
pro-Nazi propaganda to pour into her ear. Clare was at the Ritz
Hotel in Paris when the Germans swept through France. She
wanted to stay until the very end, but on May 30 the concierge
told her that she must leave the now deserted hotel, because 'the
Germans are coming.' When Clare asked him how he knew, he
said, 'Because they have reservations.'

Clare's reports were well written and became a successful book,
Europe in the Spring. Dorothy Parker's review was headed 'All Clare
on the Western Front.' 'While it is never said,' Parker notes, 'that
the teller is the bravest of all those present, it comes through.'

Clare and Harry were both interventionists by now, and they
spent a night at the White House, working over President
Roosevelt, who was all smiling amiability. Clare thought he looked

old, with trembling hands. Yet it was fairly certain that in November he would run for a third term – and why not? A fourth one if the country should be at war.

Although politically minded, Clare could not be said to have any proper politics. She was basically a vulgar Darwinist. The rich were better than the poor; otherwise they would not be rich. She could mock the *idle* rich, but the self-made must be untaxed by such do-gooders as the Roosevelts. Harry was much the same, except for one great bee in his bonnet: he believed, fervently, that it was the task of the United States in the twentieth century to Christianize China, the job that his dad, the missionary, had so signally failed to do. The damage that this one bee did to our politics is still with us, as the Christian right now beats its jungle drums in the chigger belt, calling for war with China.

Clare became a kingmaker. She would elect as president Wendell Willkie, Roosevelt's Republican challenger. Morris describes her appearance at Madison Square Garden: 'She wore a plain black dress, and as she stepped forward on the platform, a powerful spotlight beamed down from distant rafters onto her glossy blond hair. The crowd responded with wild enthusiasm even before she opened her mouth. None of her experiences on a movie set or theater stage had equaled this moment. It was the giant arena she had sought since adolescence.' Even H. L. Mencken was impressed. 'Slim, beautiful and charming . . . when she began to unload her speech, it appeared at once that she was also a fluent and effective talker.' *Don't cry for me, Dun & Bradstreet.*

Two years later, she would be elected to Congress from a Connecticut district; she served two terms. The team of Luce would continue until his death, in 1967.

At our last meeting, in my Roman flat, the sirocco was blowing and the shutters were banging. An Italian woman who occasionally did typing for me unexpectedly arrived. When she saw the former ambassador, she nearly fainted. She had worked for Clare at the Embassy. Clare was amiable. The woman left. I think it was Morris who asked what her function had been. 'Actually,' Clare said, 'she worked for my consort. She was traffic coordinator for Harry's countesses.'

Morris heads her long list of acknowledgments with 'Above all, I wish to thank the late Clare Boothe Luce for cooperating with me on this biography during the last six years of her life. From the age of fifteen . . . she had kept letters, diaries, scrapbooks and masses of other documents, all of which she courageously allowed me to see.' Courageously? Oh, dear. Could that knowing smile in the middle distance belong to the inexorable Janet Malcolm, brooding upon yet another example of her iron law, the necessary betrayal of subject by observer-writer?

> She also submitted to countless hours of interviews and let me stay and work with her in her Washington apartments, her Honolulu house, and a rented mansion one summer in Newport. We spent time together in New York City, her birthplace, in Connecticut, her main residence for most of her life, and at Mepkin Abbey, the former Luce plantation in South Carolina, where she would be buried. We traveled to Canada and London for semi-centennial productions of *The Women*, and to Rome to see the villa and embassy where she had lived and worked as United States Ambassador to Italy. The fruits of that last research, as well as details of our complex personal relationship, will appear in the second volume of this biography.

Complex? All about Eve? The Lady or the Tiger? Rosebud?

Whatever wonders are yet to come, Sylvia Jukes Morris has written a model biography of a woman who, if born a man, could easily have been a president, for what that's worth these days: a cool billion, I believe. As it is, if nothing else, Clare Boothe Luce certainly enlivened the dull – when not downright dangerous – century her husband so pompously hailed as 'the American.' Now we are more modest or, as the current president somewhat edgily put it, we are the one 'indispensable' – or was it 'undisposable'? – nation, while *Time* no longer sets the pace for partisan *ad hominem* malice. Although Harry's poisonous gift to American journalism is still widely imitated, the 'fame' of the Luces themselves has been erased as century ends. Of their once proud monuments, nothing beside remains in the lone and level sands except the logo of a dull, incoherent conglomerate, Time Warner.

The New Yorker
26 May 1997

Hersh's JFK

Early spring, 1959. Dutchess County, New York. My telephone rang. 'Senator Kennedy is calling.' It was Evelyn Lincoln, Jack's secretary. (Her employer hadn't yet metamorphosed into the imperial acronym JFK.) Years later, Mrs. Lincoln wrote a fairly unrevealing memoir of her years with Kennedy – a pity, since she knew a great deal about him, including the subject of his call to me. Jack came on the line. No hello. No how are you. 'That friend of yours up there, Dick Rovere. He's writing a piece for *Esquire* about "Kennedy's last chance to be president" or something. Well, it's not true. Get to him. Tell him I don't have Addison's disease. If I did, how could I keep up the schedule I do?' Many more staccato sentences. No time to lose. Primaries were coming up; then the Convention. Before I went down the road to see Rovere, I looked up Addison's disease: a deterioration of the adrenal function that can lead to early death. No wonder Jack was panicky. Even a hint that he was mortally ill . . .

Background: In 1953, Jack married Jacqueline Bouvier, whose

stepfather, H. D. Auchincloss, had been my stepfather until, in a fit of generosity, my mother passed him, like a well-stuffed safety-deposit box, on to Jackie's needy mother. Through Jackie, I got to know Jack; delighted in his darkly sardonic humor, not unlike my own – or Jackie's, for that matter. In due course, I shifted from the noble – that is, Adlai Stevensonian – side of the Democratic Party to the raffish gang of new kids from Massachusetts, by way of Riverdale, N.Y. Then I, too, went into active politics; by 1960 I would be the Democratic-Liberal candidate for Congress from New York's highly conservative Twenty-ninth District, and our party's presidential candidate was a matter of poignant interest to me. When Jack rang me – the first and last time – I was eager for him to be nominated, even though I had already seen a poll that indicated that his Roman Catholicism could cost our district the election. In the end, I was to get 43.3 percent of the vote to his 38 percent; this was very satisfying to me. Unfortunately, the Republican incumbent congressman got 56.7 percent. This was less satisfying. 'Your loss,' Jack grinned afterward, 'was a real tragedy for our nation.' Whatever else, he was funny.

Richard H. Rovere wrote the much read and admired Letter from Washington for *The New Yorker*. 'The Washington Letter as mailed from vital Rhinebeck, New York,' Jack used to chuckle. 'That shows real dedication. Endless tracking down of sources. In-depth analyses on the spot . . .' But Dick was now onto something that could cost Jack the nomination.

Rovere lived in a gingerbread frame house on a tree-lined street in Rhinebeck. He had a large, nearly bald head with patchy red skin and a scarred neck. Jack had asked me if he was a drinker. I said no, I thought it was eczema. Thick glasses so magnified his eyes that he seemed like some rare aquatic specimen peering back at you through aquarium glass. In youth, Rovere had been a Communist. Later, when he saw that the Marxist god had failed, he left the Party; he also must have made some sort of inner vow that never again would he be taken in by anyone or anything that required mindless loyalty. As of spring 1959, Rovere was inclined to support Stevenson, who had not yet made up his mind about running for a third time.

I began, to the point, 'Kennedy does not have Addison's disease.'

Rovere insisted that he did. He had acquired the journalist's habit of always being, no matter what the subject, more knowledgeable than anyone else in the room. I asked him how *he* knew. 'A friend's wife has Addison's, and they took her to the Lahey Clinic in Boston where they have all the latest procedures, including one that was cooked up for Kennedy. They put a pellet under your skin and it's supposed to drip adrenaline into you for a week or so and then you get another pellet.'

I used Jack's arguments. How explain his tremendous energy? How could he have been campaigning so furiously ever since 1956 if he was ill, etc.? Dick was unimpressed. He had the doctor's name; he had a lot of clinical data. He was already writing the piece. *Esquire* had been advertising it. No turning back.

Question for today: Did I suspect that the story was true? I suppose, in court, I'd say I'm not a pathologist and so how could I know? Jack had had, all his life, numerous mysterious illnesses. Four times, he had been given the last rites. The yellow-gold complexion (typical of Addison's) was explained as the result of wartime malaria. I suppose now, with hindsight, I had already made up my mind that if he thought he could survive four years of the presidency 'vigorously' – his key word that season – as well as he had survived four years of campaigning, then whatever was wrong with him was under control. Thus one embraces, so painlessly, falsity.

Dick's piece duly appeared with no mention of Addison's

disease. I did bet him a hundred dollars, even money, that Jack would be nominated and elected. Dick was cheerfully condescending. 'At those odds, I can get you a lot more bets.' In November, he paid off. Oddly – well, not so oddly – Dick and I never again alluded to our business.

Point to story: How easily so many people – best and brightest as well as worst and dullest – got caught up in the Kennedy bandwagon. The amount of lying that went on in that era was, the ineffable Nixon to one side, unique in our homely history.

Three years later, Rovere and I had a row that pretty much put an end to our friendship. Again the subject was Kennedy lying. The Cuban missile crisis of October 1962 was resolved between Kennedy and Khrushchev with a secret deal: we would remove our missiles from Turkey if the Soviets withdrew theirs from Cuba. Neither side would give the game away. No gloating. No publicity. But, as always, there was a leak. To plug it, Jack got his old friend the journalist Charles Bartlett to write a *Saturday Evening Post* article declaring that the bold macho leader of the free world could never have backed down on anything. JFK had simply ordered the Russians off the premises, and they had slunk away. In a fit of thoughtful malice, Jack decided that this would be a good moment to knife his ambassador to the United Nations, Adlai Stevenson, and he added that 'that old woman Adlai' had wanted the President to make a deal. Bartlett wrote that the resolute Jack never made deals with darkness.

I learned what had happened from Bartlett's assistant: my half-sister, Jackie's stepsister, who had heard Bartlett discussing details of the article with Kennedy over the telephone. I repeated the matter to Rovere. 'No!' he said, which was his response to whatever anyone said. Dick got very red. A heavy smoker, he almost vanished in a blue-white cloud. To my amazement, he was, by now, so much a Kennedy loyalist that not only could he not believe so vicious a tale but if it was by any chance even remotely true he was done with Kennedy forever, presumably as he had finished with that other god that failed him.

Now I read in *One Hell of a Gamble*, a fascinatingly detailed narrative of the Cuban missile crisis (by Aleksandr Fursenko and Timothy Naftali; Norton, $27.50), that an aide to McGeorge Bundy was sent round to Bartlett to tell him that Stevenson 'had angered the President by suggesting that the United States pull out its missiles in Turkey in an exchange for the Soviet missiles in Cuba . . . Poor Adlai Stevenson, the two-time failed Democratic Presidential nominee . . . was being hung out to dry.' Later, 'Bartlett had a private dinner with the President. He handed over the draft of the article . . . As Bartlett recalls today, the President "marked it up."'

'I told you so,' I muttered to myself, in lieu of the now dead Rovere, when I read the confirmation of Jack's lively malice.

This is a deliberately roundabout way of getting to Seymour Hersh (*The Dark Side of Camelot*, Little, Brown, $26.95) and his current collision with what I have just been describing: the great disinformation apparatus put in place forty years ago, a monster that even now continues to metastasize within academe and the media to such a degree that myth threatens to overthrow history. Spin is all. Spin of past as well as present.

For some reason, Hersh's 'revelations' are offensive to many journalists, most of whom are quick to assure us that although there is absolutely nothing new in the book (what a lot they've kept to themselves!), Hersh has 'proved' nothing. Of course, there is really no way for anyone ever to prove much of anything, short of having confessions from participants, like the four Secret Service men who told Hersh about getting girls in and out of Jack's bed. But when confronted with these smoking guns the monkeys clap their hands over their eyes and ears and chatter, 'Foul allegations by soreheads.' The responses to Hersh's book made me feel as if I were in a deranged time warp. Since there is not, in any foreseeable future, a Kennedy candidate for president, why is there so much fury and fuss at Hersh's attempt to let daylight in on old, old black magic? Sufficient, surely, to the day is the blessed martyr Paula Jones; small potatoes, perhaps, but our very own tuber rose.

Incidentally, how our masters the synergists must be tied in knots. Remember, back in the Eighties: wouldn't it be wonderful if you could own a network *and* a studio that made films to show on it as well as magazines and newspapers to praise them in *and* a publishing house for source material *and* . . .? Well, now we have the marvelous comedy of Hersh's book being published by Little, Brown, which is owned by Time Warner, and reviewed negatively-nervously, nervously-negatively by *Time* (same owner-ship), while *Newsweek* (owned by the Washington Post Company and still, perhaps, influenced by Kennedy's old friend Ben Bradlee) denounces Hersh, while ABC (owned by Disney) pre-pares a TV documentary that is tied in with . . . Many years ago, there used to be something called 'conflict of interest.' No longer, I'm afraid. Today, we all bathe in the same river. It will be a relief when Bill Gates finally owns everything and there will be just the one story.

Now let me declare my interest. I got a second telephone call thirty-six years after the one from Jack. This was from Seymour Hersh, whom I'd never met. He told me about the book he was writing and why he was ringing me. He had just read my memoirs, *Palimpsest*. 'You have some new stuff on Kennedy in your book,' he said, 'and I wondered why I hadn't heard about it before. I got curious. I got a researcher to check your American reviews, and I found that not one mentioned all the new things you'd come up with. Why did nobody write about you spending a couple days with Kennedy at Hyannis Port during the Berlin crisis and keeping notes?' I gave him my theory. Few American reviewers actually read an entire book, particularly if the author is known to hold opinions that are not those of the conglomerate for which the reviewer is writing. Also, since I'm a novelist, my books are given to English teachers to review, rather than to history teachers, say – which is possibly no great improvement if they serve the empire too well or, worse, grow misty-eyed when they hear 'If Ever I Would Leave You.'

'Well,' said Hersh, 'I'm glad I got to you.' Hersh is brisk and bumptious. 'I got some questions for you. That detail in your book about how he was having sex in the tub with this girl on top of him and then, as he's about to come, he pushes her head underwater. Why?'

Now, I think that I am one of the few Americans who honestly don't want to know about the sex lives of real people as opposed to fictional ones, as in pornography. Like Kennedy, I came out of the Second World War, where a great promiscuous time was had by just about all who could hack it sexually. Most of us were not into warm, mature, meaningful relationships. We were cool, 'immature,' meaningless. Getting laid as often as possible was the name of our game, and I don't regret a moment so spent. Neither, I am sure, does Jack's ghost. But this is hardly the right attitude at century's end, when the dull heirs and heiresses of Cotton Mather are like Seventh-Day Adventists with St. Vitus' dance, darting about with scarlet 'A's in one hand and, in the other, emblematic rosy curved cocks as big around as a – *quarter*?

I explained to Sy that the shock of the head being shoved underwater would cause vaginal contractions, thus increasing the pleasure of a man's own orgasm. 'Crazy,' he said. 'So how do you know this?' I said I'd been told the story years ago by an actress Jack and I both knew. Sy was exuberant. 'Well, I got four retired

Secret Service men – serious guys – and one of them told me how he would bring the President a hooker when he was lying on his back in the tub and then she'd get on top of him and then when he was ready the Secret Service guy standing behind her would shove her head underwater. Well, I couldn't really believe this. But now you tell the same story. You both can't be making it up.' A bit irritated, I said not only did I have no reason to make the story up, I could never have thought it up.

Predictably, the press frenzy over Hersh's book has centered on JFK's promiscuity. This is believed to sell newspapers. But then no other country, save our edgy adjunct the U.K., bothers with the sexual lives of its public men, on the ground that their official lives are sufficiently dispiriting, when not downright dangerous, to occupy what small attention the average citizen of the average country can force himself to give to political figures.

This was the case in the United States before mid-century. Private lives were dealt with by gossip columnists, often in what were called 'blind' items (principals unnamed), while public matters were kept to the news columns. The blurring of the two began when vast amounts of money were suddenly required to fight the Second World War and then, immediately after, to pay for our ever-expanding and still ongoing empire, set in place in 1950. The empire requires huge expenditures for more and more bombers that do not fly in the rain, as well as the maintenance, with secret bribes and threats, of our NATO-ASEAN axis, which girdles the thick rotundity of the globe itself. With that much money being wrung from the taxpayer, the last thing that those who govern us want is any serious discussion of what is actually happening to all 'our' money.

Put bluntly, who collects what money from whom in order to spend on what is all there is to politics, and in a serious country should be the central preoccupation of the media. It is also a very interesting subject, at least to those who pay taxes, which in this country means the folks at home, not the conglomerates that own everything. (Taxes on corporate profits once provided the government with more than 40 percent of its revenues – almost as much as the personal income tax provided – but taxes on corporate profits today contribute barely 12 percent.) During Kennedy's three-year administration, he increased the defense budget of the Eisenhower years by seventeen billion dollars. This was one of the biggest, quickest increases in our history. That was – is – the story that ought to have been covered. Unfortunately, politics is the last thing a government like ours wants us to know about. So how do they divert us from the delicate subject?

Until recently, anyone who questioned the Pentagon budget, say, was apt to be labeled a Communist, and that would be that: he could lose his job; become unemployable. This is diversionary politics at its crudest. When Communism went away, sex came into its lurid own as the diversionary smear of choice – a peculiarly American specialty, by the way. Once the imaginary teams, straight and fag, had been established at the start of our century, the fag smear was an irresistible means of destruction. It was used, unsuccessfully, against Adlai Stevenson, while Jack and Bobby would giggle as they argued over which of them first thought to call James Baldwin 'Martin Luther Queen.'

Basically, misuse of tax money is the interesting scandal. Much of the expensive imperial changeover started by Truman was institutionalized by Kennedy's policy of constant overt and covert foreign confrontation. But Hersh, aware that this is pretty much a nonsubject for mass media and most academics, must first get the folks into his sideshow tent. Hence the highlighting of Jack's sexual shenanigans. Later, Hersh does get around to politics – Cuba, Vietnam – and though he has new insights and information, his critics generally fail to respond coherently. They rehash such weighty matters as whether or not JFK briefly married a Palm Beach girl and did his friend Chuck Spalding remove the records from the Palm Beach courthouse. A Camelot court joke circa 1961: Anyone married in Palm Beach in the year 1947 is now no longer married, since Joe Kennedy, while destroying Jack's records, tore out a whole year's worth of marriage registrations.

Typical of the critics is Evan Thomas, in *Newsweek*, who notes skeptically that Hersh's sources include a 'mob lawyer' who allegedly brokered a meeting in Chicago between Sam Giancana and Joe Kennedy at which Joe is supposed to have enlisted organized-crime support within Chicago's labor unions, providing much of the hundred-and-nineteen-thousand-vote margin by which Jack won the 1960 election. Another Hersh source is 'Tina Sinatra, who says her father Frank acted as a go-between for the Kennedys and Giancana.' Although daughters are not taken too seriously, by and large, in the still sexist shady cellars of public life, let me attest that Tina Sinatra is a most intelligent woman who knows a great deal about what went on in those days. The writer does concede that: 'All [this is] possible – but Hersh never stops to ask why the Kennedys needed Giancana to fix the Chicago election when they had Mayor Richard Daley's machine to stuff the ballot box.' 'What's still missing,' he writes more in anger than in sorrow, 'is the kind of solid proof that would rewrite history.' Well, it would be nice, but where would you find such proof? Truman's National Security State, still in place as of this morning, has seen to it that miles of our history, archives, and 'secrets' have been shredded, deep-sixed, made over into frog princes, for the delectation of the dummies we are, collectively, taken to be.

In the tangled weave of human events, there is no *solid* proof. Particularly when governments, with everything to hide or distort, can do so with electronic ease, scattering their misinformation like confetti all over, as well as under, the Internet. At best, what we get are self-serving tales from survivors, not to mention the odd forger of genius. And spin.

Predictably, one of Hersh's chief attackers is Arthur M. Schlesinger, Jr. (*sic* – the Jr., that is). Ever eager for distinction like that of his father, the historian Arthur Schlesinger, young Arthur bestowed on himself his father's middle name so that he could call himself 'Junior,' thus identifying himself with an already famous brand name in academe. Later, his infatuation with the Kennedys earned him the sobriquet 'the tenth Kennedy,' the brilliant if pudgy child that Joe and Rose Kennedy had never had.

'I *worked* at the White House,' Junior told *The New York Times*. 'No doubt, some things happened, but Hersh's capacity to exaggerate is unparalleled.' This is curiously and carefully phrased. In a sense, as the weight of the evidence mounts, it is already quite plain to all but the most enthralled that Hersh's case, slapdash as it often is, is essentially true, if not Truth. Although 'I worked at the White House' sounds as if Schlesinger were in on everything, he was not; he was neither a policymaker nor an intimate. Kennedy made a cold division between the help and his friends – 'his white-trash friends,' as Schlesinger observed bitterly and, I fear, accurately to me. Schlesinger amused Jack, who liked to call him 'the film critic from *Show* magazine,' his other job. But should Arthur ever say that he had no idea about the Kennedy brothers' dalliance, let us say, with Marilyn Monroe, one has only to look at the photograph from the night of the birthday gala for the President. The two Kennedy lads are leaving Monroe, while off to one side stands swinger Arthur, glass in hand, beaming like Emil Jannings in *The Blue Angel*, only he has two male Marlene Dietrichs, the Kennedy brothers, to be demoralized by.

*

Not all of the press has been trash. In *Slate*, a mysterious apparition of a paper edited by 'On the left, I'm Michael Kinsley,' as he used to say on the wondrously silly program *Crossfire*, Jacob Weisberg zeroes in on one of the most interesting bits of news Hersh has brought us, demonstrating the power – and corruption – of the fabled military-industrial complex that Kennedy did so well by.

In August 1962, the Los Angeles apartment of a beautiful young woman, Judith Campbell Exner, was broken into. She had been having the usual off-and-on couplings with JFK, as well as with Sam Giancana, and there was an FBI stakeout on her apartment. The break-in was observed by the agents on watch, and they identified the perpetrators as the two sons of the head of security for General Dynamics, which a few months later received an 'otherwise inexplicable' six-and-a-half-billion-dollar defense contract. Hersh concludes that General Dynamics used the information about Exner to blackmail Kennedy into giving it the contract. Hersh admits that he can't *prove* this: despite five years' effort, the two intruders into Exner's apartment would not talk to him. Hugh Sidey, once *Time*'s White House correspondent, said on Larry King's television program that Hersh, in effect, is making it all up for his 'evil book.' But then the good Sidey never met a president he couldn't worship. On the other hand, I tend to believe this story. First, it is the way our world works. Second, it is the way the Kennedys operated. Third, defense contractors will do anything when billions of dollars are at stake, and, finally, in a well-run world the president involved should have been found out, impeached, and tried.

Weisberg is confused by 'minor inconsistencies': 'Hersh relates one anecdote about a Secret Service agent having to prevent the first lady from finding out for herself what she suspected was going on in the White House swimming pool. Later in the book,

Hersh describes Jackie Kennedy's strenuous efforts to *avoid* catching JFK in action' (my italics). But this is not a contradiction, only sloppy writing. Jackie knew all about Jack's sex life in the White House and before. What she did not want was any sort of confrontation with his playmates. The Kennedys were an eighteenth-century 'amoral' couple, together for convenience. They would have fitted, with ease, into *Les Liaisons Dangereuses*. I mean this very much as praise, though others affect shock. Paradoxically, toward the end of their marriage they actually established something very like a friendship. She said to me, as early as their first year in the White House, 'We never actually got to know each other before the election. He was always off somewhere campaigning. Then, when we did get to this awful place, there we were, finally, just the two of us.' His sexual partners were to her simply anonymous physical therapists. I suspect that's what they were to him, too.

In December 1959, Jackie asked me to a charity costume ball at the Plaza. 'I'll put you at Jack's table, so he'll have someone to talk to. Just ignore what I'm placing between you. She's very beautiful. Very stupid. She's also just arrived from England, so Jack will have first crack at it.' 'It,' not 'her.'

We sat at a round table with eight or so other guests. Jack's costume was a holster with two six-shooters and a bandanna around his neck. He puffed a cigar and gazed intently at the blond girl between us. She was very beautiful. 'You're in politics, aren't you?' Thus she broke the ice. I was curious to see Jack in action. 'Uh . . . well, yes, I am. I'm . . . uh, running for president.'

'That's so fascinating!' she exclaimed. 'And will you win?'

'Well, it won't be easy . . .'

'Why not?'

'Well, you see, I'm . . . uh, Catholic . . .'

'But what's that got to do with anything?'

'Oh, Gore, *you* tell her.' I did, and then he and I talked politics across her: not a woman's court, Camelot.

To this day, Kennedy loyalists point to the missile crisis as a sign of JFK's superb statesmanship, when it is obvious that even to have got oneself into such a situation was hardly something you'd want to write Mother, much less Rose, about. Certainly you don't prepare invasions of Cuba and repeatedly try to kill Castro without encouraging Castro to egg on the Soviets to what proved to be a mad adventure.

Incidentally, those Kennedy apologists who deny that JFK knew anything about the various CIA-Mafia plots to murder Castro are nicely taken care of by Robert Scheer in *The Los Angeles Times*. 'The entire nefarious business is documented in excruciating detail,' he writes, 'in "Report on Plots to Assassinate Fidel Castro," a 133-page memorandum prepared in 1967 by CIA Inspector General J. S. Earman for Director Richard Helms.' The report was so hot that all copies were destroyed except one 'ribbon copy,' which was declassified in 1993. Scheer also notes 'that Giancana was a key player in the effort to overthrow Castro and that the President's brother, the country's top law-enforcement official, knew all about it.'

The Kennedy brothers put a lot of pressure on the CIA to take care of Castro. When – and how – these callow young men got it into their heads that to them belonged the power of life and death over others is more of a metaphysical than a political question. We all know by heart their story: crook pro-Nazi father makes fortune; drives boys to a political peak unavailable to him. But there was always something curiously brittle about the two murdered sons. They were physically fragile. Hence, the effort of will to drive themselves hard, politically and sexually. As their nonadmirer Eugene McCarthy, former senator and forever poet, observed,

'Isn't it curious that they always played touch football and never football.'

Currently, the heirs to Camelot are pointing to the just released tapes that JFK made of himself during October of 1962. When he was ready to address his council, he would secretly switch on a recording machine. The others did not know they were being immortalized, and the nuke-'em-all military men are chilling. JFK is cautious: on the record. Robert Manning, in the international edition of *Newsweek*, gently made fun of the way the whole situation is now being depicted. 'As one who sat in on some of those White House deliberations in the President's cabinet room, I believe that the case can be made that the dangers of that 13-day interlude in October 1962 have been greatly exaggerated.' Manning was an assistant secretary of state; later the *Atlantic Monthly* editor. His case is simple. Whatever Khrushchev might want to do in extremis, we had five thousand nuclear warheads ready to erase the Soviet Union; and they had only between seventy-five and three hundred. 'All those factors dictated a peaceful settlement.' The Russian general who recently said that Moscow had given the commanders in Cuba permission to use nuclear weapons *at will* 'was a pompous windbag, and his claim proved to be patently untrue.' So much for the iron nerve, cool wisdom of Sidey's hero.

To further undo JFK's delicate physical balance, along with the cortisone that he took regularly, there was his reliance on – addiction to, in fact – the amphetamines that the shady drug dispenser Dr. Max Jacobson regularly injected him with. It was through Chuck Spalding that Max entered JFK's life. Max made more than thirty recorded visits to the White House; traveled with the President; provided him with shots that he could give himself. So, in addition to cortisone, which can have dangerous side effects – a sense of misplaced, as it were, euphoria – the President was now hooked on speed. According to Jacobson's memoirs, Bobby was sufficiently concerned to want the medicine analyzed. "'I don't care if it's horse piss,'" Jacobson quoted Kennedy as saying. "'It's the only thing that works.'" In 1975, Max's license to practice medicine was revoked.

In Hersh's interviews with the Secret Service men, sex and drugs to one side, one is struck by how little actual work Jack got done. There were many days when Kennedy 'didn't work at all. He'd come down late, go to his office. There were meetings – the usual things – and then he had pool time before his nap and lunch . . . We didn't know what to think.' My own impression, reading this, was how lucky we were that he wasn't busy all the time, because when he did set his hand to the plow Cuba got invaded and Castro was set up for assassination, while American troops were sent to fight in Vietnam, and the Diem brothers, our unsatisfactory viceroys in that unhappy country, were put to death in a coup, with White House blessing if not direct connivance.

In a way, the voices of the Secret Service men are the most damning of all, and I was prepared for what I call the Historians' Herndon Maneuver. William Herndon was for seventeen years Lincoln's law partner and shared an office with him. Herndon is the principal historical source for those years, except when Lincoln told Herndon that he had contracted syphilis in youth and had a hard time getting rid of it. Herndon wrote this after the President's death. The Lincoln priesthood's response to the syphilis charge is Pavlovian: Herndon was a disreputable drunk and not to be relied on – except when he is. As I read Hersh, I knew that the Kennedy zealots would say the same about the Secret Service man who mentions Jack's nongonorrheal urethritis and all the rest of it. On *Larry King*, a professor appeared along with Hugh Sidey. He conceded that JFK had a 'squalid covert life.' Then, when one of the

Secret Service men was named, it was Sidey who executed the Herndon Maneuver: the agent later had a problem with 'alcohol.'

I think Hersh comes to some wrong conclusions, inevitable considering his task. Incidentally, it is ridiculous to accuse him of not being a serious, sober historian, careful to footnote his way through a past that very few American academics could even begin to deal with. After all, if they were competent to do the job, what effect would it have on those powerful entities and personages who endow universities? Hersh is an old-style muckraker. The fact that he's found more muck in this particular Augean stable than most people want to acknowledge is hardly his fault.

I don't believe, however, that Lyndon Johnson blackmailed Jack into taking him as vice president, which is what Hersh suspects. Although I certainly was not in the allegedly uncrowded room when the decision was made, I was a member of the New York State delegation, and I was present in Los Angeles as the candidates came around, one by one, to work us over. (Tammany Hall had already committed us to Kennedy – the highest form of democracy.) Johnson entered the room in a blaze of TV lights. He was no more manic than usual. Very tall, with a huge head, and a gift for colorful invective, he had taken to calling Kennedy, more or less in private, 'that spavined hunchback.' He discussed his own recent heart attack – before any of us could. He was good as new now. But in the hospital he *had* wondered if he should go ahead and buy this blue suit he had ordered just before the attack. 'Finally, I told Lady Bird, O.K., go buy it. Either way, I'll be using it.' As he was leaving, he stopped to speak to several delegates. I was too far away to hear him. Later, I was told that he had mentioned something about Jack's 'illness.' He had been vague, but by evening Addison's disease was being talked about. If Johnson had gone there to take second place, he would certainly not have mentioned Jack's health. In any case, none of us could imagine why the omnipotent majority leader of the Senate would want to be a powerless vice president. Certainly, in the normal actuarial course of things, Jack was bound to outlive him. In those matters, it is wise to strop Occam's razor. Jack had to carry Texas to win and with Johnson on the ticket he did, barely.

Finally, a correction for Hersh and his readers: He writes, 'There was some talk from inside the family of having a Kennedy-Kennedy ticket in 1964' – Robert to replace Lyndon as vice president – 'most of it, Gore Vidal told me in an interview, coming from Ethel Kennedy, Bobby's wife.' Actually, it was Hersh who told me this story last year. As for Ethel Kennedy, I've only met her once. She wanted to know if I was writing a new dirty play, like Edward Albee.

Hersh does not take his book where it is logically headed from the beginning, the murder in Dallas, and what looks to be a mob killing. Too many lunatics have already checked in on that subject; and Hersh is wise to leave it alone. But it is also frustrating, since the inventors of our official history are forever fetched by that lone mad killer, eaten up with resentment and envy, the two principal American emotions, if our chroniclers are to be believed. Yet the gunning down in public view with wife to one side and all the panoply of state fore and aft is purest Palermo sendoff. Some years ago, the head of the Italian national police, General dalla Chiesa, was similarly killed – at the center of a cortège of police as he drove triumphantly down the main street of Palermo shortly after taking command of the 'war' against the Sicilian Mafia.

What, then, as movie producers like to say, is the 'take-away' of Hersh's book? This means, what is the audience supposed to think at the end? First, for me, the dangerous inadequacy of the American press. We are seldom, if ever, told what we need to know about how presidents get elected and then, once in office, what they do of a secret and often unconstitutional nature, particularly abroad. That the political system doesn't work is no news. Whoever can raise the most corporate money by providing services once in office will be elected, or at least get to be on offer. Clinton and Dole spent, it is said, more than half a billion dollars on the last presidential election. The press accepts all this as just the way things are. On the rare occasions when a journalist does have a specific smoking-gun complaint, he will find few outlets available to him. Soreheads need not apply for space in the mainline press, much less hope for a moment on the Koppel hour of charm.

In retrospect, it has always been incredible that someone as thoroughly disreputable as Joe Kennedy should have been allowed to buy his sons major political careers. So – could that happen today? Yes. It is even worse now, as anyone can attest who has so much as gazed disbelievingly upon Steve Forbes or Michael Huffington, empty suits with full wallets. We all agree, monotonously, that a change in the campaign-financing laws would be helpful, but no Congress or president elected under the present corrupt system could bear to kick over the ladder that got him and his tools to the second floor.

Quite as serious is the danger of electing someone totally dependent on all sorts of mind-altering drugs to enhance mood, not to mention simply stay alive. Curiously, on April 9, 1961, I published a piece about Jack in the London *Sunday Telegraph*. Rereading it, I can see that, subliminally at least, my knowledge of his Addison's disease was bothering me then, just as not having gone public with it in 1959 bothers me now. I wrote that because of the 'killing' job of the presidency, 'despite his youth, Kennedy may very well not survive.' This is a pretty peculiar thing to write of a 'vigorous' man of forty-three. I go on: 'Like himself, the men Kennedy has chosen to advise him have not reached any great height until *now*. They must prove themselves now. Government service will be the high point of their lives.' Alas, this turned out to be true. Between the second-rate cronies who made up the Irish Mafia – only Larry O'Brien was outstanding – and the 'efficient' managers, like McNamara, with no conception of the world they had been set loose in, one wishes that he had taken on a few more aides and advisers who had made their mark elsewhere. But, as he said, plaintively, at the time, 'I don't know *anybody* except politicians. Who the hell is Dean Rusk?' So it came to pass, and even now the photogenic charm of the couple at the center of so much corruption and incompetence still casts its spell, and no harsh Hersh? light let in upon them can ever quite dissolve their magic until time itself places Jack in history's oubliette, alongside another handsome assassinated President, James Abram Garfield.

The New Yorker
1 December 1997

Honorable Albert A. Gore, Junior

Like so many Southerners or half-Southerners, I have never much cared for the fictions of William Faulkner. But where others find shocking, and I find life-enhancing, his use of that emblematic corncob in *Sanctuary*, I am put off by the *familiarity* of his work. I seem to know all his stories in advance, twice-told tales, you might say. I also dislike the ornate imprecision, to put it mildly, of his style, which involves the misuse of gorgeous-sounding words – 'euphemistic' for 'euphonious' and vice versa, while the Bible's 'Suffer the little children' Faulkner takes to be Bronze Age child abuse and not seventeenth-century 'Allow the little children.' But I am not his editor and stylist, as Suzanne Pleshette so vividly introduced herself to the great American author Youngblood Hawke in that great, eponymous – or was it euphemistic? – film of yesteryear.

But, personally, I liked Faulkner, and we had a true connection. He came from Oxford, Mississippi, and his mythical Yoknapatawpha County takes in parts of Chickasaw and Webster counties, founded by the Gore family, among others, in the 1840s. Faulkner knew many of the Gores of his time and spoke fondly of my great-aunt Mary Gore Wyatt, who taught him – or was it Stark Young? – Latin. In 1954 I adapted two Faulkner short stories for live TV. After *Smoke* and *Barn Burning* were aired, Faulkner congratulated me in the lobby of the Algonquin Hotel. 'I don't have the television,' he said, 'but relations do, and they liked those shows very much.' We chatted about kin. What else sustains individuals in a somewhat wild part of the world, never entirely benign to the human? Hence the importance of kin, family, clan. The clans have always been the integuments that hold together Southern communities. They are often vast in numbers and intricate in their workings.

Once a year, the Gore clan gathers, often in a town like Calhoun City (founded by T. T. Gore, born 1776). In 1990 I attended Gore Day in the town of Houston, not far from Elvis Presley's capital city of Tupelo, where I arrived by plane from New York via Nashville with a BBC TV crew: A documentary was being done on my life and times, and as I had never visited Mississippi, where my mother's father, who had brought me up, was born, it was thought that . . . Well, I'm not sure I had any idea what to expect.

I stayed with a cousin, Dr. Ed Gore, a fourth-generation M.D. who heads a large clinic. He is younger than I, with a grown son by his first wife and a bright blond ten- or eleven-year-old son, Blake, by a second wife. The TV crew noted that Blake looked like me at ten. But then the Gore genes are strong, making for large noses and ears and, in many, chinoiserie-style eyes, more gray than blue. Blake certainly had inherited the Gore sharpness of tongue. When one of my Brit companions made some remark about the recent film *Mississippi Burning*, not the most tactful allusion, the older Gores looked puzzled. Why, no, they hadn't seen it . . . Blake roared with laughter: 'You never heard so much fussin' going on round here as when that picture came out.' If there is an uncomfortable truth to be told, at least one Gore can always be counted on to bear sardonic witness. The clan is far-flung now, from one end of the country to the other. Even so, two or three hundred saw fit to gather together to meet, with wives and kin, on a Sunday in Houston in Chickasaw County, which once belonged (all of it, they claim) to our ancestor T. T. Gore, who had bought a considerable chunk of land from the Chickasaw tribe in the 1840s. Earlier, the Indians had been driven west to Mississippi by Andrew Jackson, and then, later, they would, with a dozen other tribes, be transferred to their own territory in what is now Oklahoma, whose first senator proved to be my grandfather, brought up near Houston in nearby Webster County.

Ironies abound, historical and human, in the story of our clan. One irony is that T. T. Gore, in a sense, dispossessed the Indians of their Mississippi land while his great-grandson, T. P. Gore, by establishing the state of Oklahoma in 1907, confined them to reservations on bad land that, when oil was discovered, inspired the federal government to dispossess them yet again. Late in life, T. P. Gore would try to make amends.

'We pick the cousins we want to acknowledge, and we sort of let the others drop,' a Gore lady confided to me at the reunion. I was borderline acceptable. Word of my atheism (like that of my grandfather) had not spread too far. Many of the Gores I met in Houston are born-again; all are believers. For the most part they belong to the professional classes: lawyers, politicians, preachers, teachers, military men. Curiously, none was in trade. Back of them, of course, were generations of farmers and rude mechanicals from the British Isles who came to Maryland and Virginia in the seventeenth century (a 'Thomas Gore, Gentleman' was a lost colonist at Jamestown). The eighteenth-century Gores, pursuing land, moved on to South Carolina, then to Pickens, Alabama, and, finally, to Mississippi, in the 1840s.

Faulkner, in his novels, dwells lovingly on the class divisions of his not-so-mythical county. There were the aristos, called Sartoris (naturally, he, in his Harris tweed jacket, was a Sartoris), while the educated professional class, the Stevenses, were the Gores. Finally, there was the white trash, the pullulating Snopeses, ever breeding, ever multiplying, ever, ah, inheriting all earth itself, so many little foxes forever chomping on the voluptuous vulpine sour grapes of Sartoris and Stevens. 'Of course,' said one old lady, 'Bill himself wasn't so much. After all, this is redneck country. There aren't – never were – many Negroes and certainly no great plantations like they have – or had – down in the Delta. *Those* were the folks who had the mansions with the columns and all the wealth, most of which got lost in the war. Bourbons, we call them. They ran the state for years through the Democratic Party, which our family started to oppose in the 1880s, when your great-grandfather and his people, over in Emory and Eupora and Walthall, helped organize the Party of the People – populists, they were called – and when T.P. ran for the legislature, he ran as a populist. He was in his early twenties and lost in a dirty election that was the making of him, because he skedaddled out of here for Corsicana, Texas, with his father and brothers, to practice law, and then on to the territories, where, practically single-handed, he invented Oklahoma as a state.' I don't think that Governor 'Alfalfa Bill' Murray would like so much credit to go to Senator Thomas Pryor Gore – but then we are in Gore country now.

When T. P. Gore left Mississippi on the last day of December 1895, he was twenty-five, and he vowed he would never return until he was a U.S. senator. He kept his vow. Eighteen years later, Senator Gore was back in Mississippi, a national figure who had played a considerable part (to his everlasting regret) in the election of Woodrow Wilson as president in 1912 and again in 1916. I should note that due to two separate accidents, he was blind from the age of ten, yet got through law school with a cousin – yet again – who read to him.

Although the Gores have – and had – many of the usual prejudices typical of their time and region, the marked absence of slave owners in the family meant that when the Civil War came, they were what they called 'patriots': They were against secession, as were their cousins across the nearby state line of Tennessee. This presented T.P.'s father, Thomas Madison Gore, age twenty-four in 1861, with a terrible choice. Should he go fight for his state against the union that the Gores had helped create in 1776, or should he turn his back on his immediate kin and go join like-minded cousins in nearby eastern Tennessee, which, most famously, did not secede?

With camera crew, I went to the Webster County courthouse, where Thomas Madison had spent all of one day agonizing on the steps. The building is large and imposing – and practically alone in the wilderness all about it. Nearby is the one-room schoolhouse where my grandfather had learned to read and write until his own light was switched off.

I sat on the steps where Thomas Madison had sat. Described to the camera how one can be torn between duty to the clan and to the nation. Described how, in the end, the clan usually wins. He chose to fight with his two brothers for Mississippi. One brother was killed, and Thomas Madison was wounded and taken captive not far from home at Shiloh. 'As far as I know,' he would say years later, when he had settled in as chancery clerk of Webster County (in the same building on whose steps he had agonized as a youth), 'I am the only Confederate soldier who never rose above the rank of corporal. Somehow the others all got to be majors and colonels.' It should be noted that one of his brothers, too young to fight, was

Albert Cox Gore, who after the war graduated from the Memphis Medical College in Tennessee.

I have been told so many times how Thomas Pryor Gore and Albert Arnold Gore, Sr., are related that I have permanently forgotten and must again ask the cousinage or check various biographies (fifth cousins, I have just been told again). T. P. Gore was the clan's great man for the first half of the twentieth century. We never claimed our Tennessee relations as kin because we had hardly heard of them until Albert Sr. came to the House of Representatives in 1939, age thirty-one. He had been born in 1907, the year T. P. Gore came to the Senate, age thirty-seven. I remember sometime around 1940 my grandfather's telling me that he had been sitting in the Senate cloakroom 'and this young man comes up to me and says, "You know, you look just like my father."' It was the new congressman from Tennessee – and they did look alike. They also knew how they were related.

There was nothing sufficiently witty or unpleasant that Alice Roosevelt Longworth, daughter of President Theodore, did not have to say of her cousin President Franklin, who was, I believe, the same relation to President Theodore as the current vice president is to me. Once I teased her when she was going on about Franklin, whom she called 'the Feather Duster' – 'the sort of person you never asked to the dinner but only to come in after.' 'So,' I asked, 'why were you always so down on him?' Alice's gray-yellow eyes blinked as she revealed the huge, snaggled Roosevelt teeth in a thin-lipped smile. 'We were the President Roosevelts, and then along comes these Hyde Park nobodies, and suddenly they were the President Roosevelts, forever and ever. The fact that Eleanor was my first cousin didn't help, either. And, oh, she was so noble! So sickeningly noble. But to tell the truth, I'm afraid that our feelings were nothing more than outraged vanity.' This, in a milder way, was rather my family's view when Albert Sr. went to the Senate in 1952 and became *the* Senator Gore (T.P. had died in 1949).

I seem to have mislaid Gore Day. In honor of me, a dozen hymns were sung, and four Gore preachers spoke the Word, and I was duly drenched – drowned – in the Blood of the Lamb. A few days later, in Jackson, I asked Eudora Welty if this was usual. 'Well,' she said, 'it was a Sunday, and there's not much else to do up there in the country. Of course, I'm from the city. But I did go to school with girls from all over the state, and you could spot where they were from just by the way they looked and talked. We always thought your upstate cousins were a bit on the simple side, while the Delta girls – oh my! – they were *fast*! Even though we all wore uniforms, they *did* things to theirs.'

Significantly, Senator Albert Gore, Jr., due to come, as always, to the reunion of the cousinage, bowed out at the last minute, 'because of a fund-raiser,' he said. But, I was told, this too was in honor of me. I was not only a notorious radical in politics but I had recently written a book about a man still deeply resented in the state, Abraham Lincoln. Even so, the cousinage did not like being stood up for a fund-raiser, that central activity of *fin de siècle* American politics and, perhaps, young Albert's Achilles' heel. I have always avoided him on the ground that one day plausible deniability will be useful to each of us. But I had known Albert Sr. slightly. Once, at a convention, shortly after I'd run for Congress, we were interviewed together on television. When asked the usual questions about how we were related, Albert Sr. said, 'Fourth cousins, I think, but if he'd been elected, it would have been a lot closer than that.'

After Gore Day, I met the last of T.P.'s first cousins, Taffie Gore Griffin. She was in her nineties. In 1951 she was the first woman to be elected to state office. As circuit clerk, she shocked many people by industriously registering blacks to vote. She remembers when T.P. was considered a sure thing as vice president in Woodrow Wilson's second term. Unfortunately, T.P. had opposed our entry into the First World War. When the Chamber of Commerce of Oklahoma City finally ordered him, by telegram, to vote for war, he wired them back: 'How many of your members are of draft age?' Duly defeated in 1920, he returned to the Senate in 1930, where he promptly collided with FDR on monetary policy. Senator Carter Glass told me how he'd been present when T.P., in effect, called the President a liar: 'Franklin turned gray and said nothing. Lucky your grandfather couldn't see his face, because there was this look that said "Kill."' And FDR saw to it that T.P. was defeated in the 1936 primary. Of his overprincipled approach to politics, my grandfather used to say, 'When the Republicans are in, I'm a Democrat, and when the Democrats are in, I'm out of step.'

As you can see, I am uneasily circling a subject that few writers nowadays ever touch upon, and that is character. Ordinarily, I steer clear of such matters, too, out of tact, but as Albert Jr. may be the forty-third president at a crucial time in the republic's life, we had better start finding out where he came from, who he is or if, relevant question, he is anyone at all.

In the matter of race, Albert Arnold Gore, Sr., behaved as well as a senator with a Southern border constituency could. Although he voted against the Civil Rights Act of 1964 (a vote he later said he regretted), he refused to sign Senator Strom Thurmond's 1956 Southern Manifesto, a celebration of the joys and character-building aspects of slavery in the past and of harmonious inequality in the present. But when it comes to the matter of war and peace, Albert Sr. bears a comforting resemblance to T.P. in the previous generation. Alone, I believe, among the usually war-minded Southern legislators, Albert Sr. spoke out against the long idiocy of the Vietnam War. Essentially, populists don't like foreign wars, particularly in lands that they know nothing of and for no demonstrable goals. For exercising good judgment, Albert Sr. was defeated in 1970 by an opponent who used the familiar line that he was 'out of touch with the voters of Tennessee.' If this was true, the voters, supremely misled by three administrations, were seriously out of touch with reality. Exactly fifty years after T. P. Gore departed the Senate because he had been against the First War, his cousin departed because of the Vietnam War. Curiously, the wives of each, though admiring their husbands' integrity, discerned a common tendency to masochism in the name of duty. Albert Sr.'s wife, Pauline, herself a lawyer and a canny politician, has contrasted her son (whom she quietly brought up to be president) with his father: 'Al, by nature, is more of a pragmatist than his father. As am I. I tried to persuade Albert Sr. not to butt at a stone wall just for the sheer joy of butting.' While Nina Kay Gore, wife to T.P., observed, 'The Gores tend to be brilliant, but they've got no sense.' She would sigh whenever confronted with her husband's implacability; as for my own, she used to warn, 'Never stir up more snakes than you can kill with one stick.' Plainly, Albert Jr., his mother's son, need never fear snakebite.

The three Gore senators were never much at money-making, as opposed to fund-raising, where Albert Jr. is willing to be smeared as a pro- or crypto-Buddhist in his Grail-like pursuit of campaign money. Ninety-one years ago, T. P. Gore spent $1,000 on his successful Senate campaign. Although he was later to write the legislation for the oil depletion of resources allowance that made some of his constituents as rich as Saudi Arabs, he was never paid off by them; but then his campaigns were inexpensive. By Albert Sr.'s time, the costs of electioneering were high indeed. In 1938 he was elected to the House of Representatives, on borrowed money. Well, 'family' money, as we shall see.

Albert Jr. was brought up on his father's Carthage, Tennessee, farm as well as in Washington, D.C., where he attended St. Albans, an all-boys school that I had gone to twenty years earlier. The two Alberts had settled down on the eighth floor of our cousin Grady Gore's hotel, the Fairfax (later the Ritz Carlton), where they lived, the Cousins chant, for free. Grady's branch of the family had not gone west like the rest of us and so, staying on in Maryland, they had made a fortune, something the rest of us never quite managed to do. Grady's daughter Louise is a Republican who has inherited that damaged gene that impels some people to public office. Certainly, whenever the moon is full, cousin Louise can be counted on to run for governor of Maryland. Although she has never won, she did persuade Richard Nixon to take as his vice president Maryland's governor, Spiro Agnew, thus earning herself a merry footnote in history. Louise's sister Mary lost her first husband in a crash on Northeast Airlines, a company that my father had founded and owned, showing how our lives crisscross in Faulknerian tragedy as well as in Faulknerian comedy. Later she 'kept company with' Nixon's attorney general John Mitchell, either just before or just after his time in prison. Plainly, we have our devil-may-care side.

I have often thought cousin Grady was the most interesting of the lot. In the 1930s, you could legally give as much as you liked to the candidate of your choice. Cousin Grady had always helped finance Tennessee's senior senator, Kenneth McKellar, until cousin Grady asked McKellar to take on Albert Sr. in his office as an intern, a position of decency in that far-off time. McKellar turned Albert Sr. down. Grady said, 'Why?' 'Don't like him,' said McKellar. Now, there is a saying in the South that 'if a snake bites a Gore, they all puff up.' Grady puffed up. Told Albert Sr., 'I was going to give that old bastard $40,000 for his reelection, but not now. I'm giving it to you. You're running for Congress.' Thus Albert Sr. got to the House.

Later, in 1930, Albert Sr. went into business with one of the century's most gorgeous criminals, Armand Hammer. For those interested in Hammer's life as a Russian-American friend of Lenin's and a financial fixer for Stalin – a bridge, as he might have put it, between Communism and capitalism – I highly recommend Edward Jay Epstein's *Dossier: The Secret History of Armand Hammer*. As chairman of Occidental Petroleum, Hammer befriended (or, as the FBI might say, 'bribed') many American politicians. At one point, he tried to get his hands on 'a huge government-owned refinery in Morgantown, West Virginia,' that the army was willing to lease to the highest bidder. Hammer went after it: 'He had extended . . . largesse to both Republicans and Democrats,' writes Epstein. 'His principal contact among the Democrats in the House was Albert Gore of Tennessee. In 1950, Hammer had made Congressman Gore a partner in a cattle-breeding business, and Gore made a substantial profit.' Hammer failed to get the lease, because of alarm in the government about his close relations with the Soviets. Later, during détente, this connection worked to Hammer's benefit. On January 19, 1961, 'Hammer was Senator Albert Gore's guest at one of the five black-tie inaugural balls.' (JFK had just been inaugurated.) 'He could count on Gore for such invitations. He had made him his partner in the cattle-breeding business – a partnership that had proved profitable – and he had given him each Christmas over the past five years a gift of antique silver.' Gore also helped to get Hammer to Moscow later that winter, where Hammer did business successfully with Anastas Mikoyan and Khrushchev. Rogues have their uses. In 1970, when Albert Sr. was defeated for the Senate, Hammer made him chairman of his Island Creek Coal, the nation's third-largest coal producer.

Hammer had attended five presidential inaugurations as the guest of Albert Sr. He attended Ronald Reagan's 1981 inauguration as the guest of Albert Jr. Hammer not only reveled in reflected glory for its own sake but he had now a specific goal in mind, a presidential pardon. Since 1938 the FBI had six times investigated him for the bribing and blackmailing of public officials. 'Hammer had avoided prosecution,' writes Epstein, 'on a felony charge through a plea bargain.' In 1984 he applied for a pardon for the 'misdemeanors' he had admitted to in order that he might obtain, presumably through a series of aurora borealis bribes, the Nobel Peace Prize (which Hammer actually deserved rather more than some of its recent recipients). But Reagan did not include him in the 1985 round of pardons. 'In 1986, [Hammer] pledged $1 million to the Ronald Reagan Library . . . This made Hammer the largest single pledger of funds for the project.' Again, no pardon. Hammer upped the ante to $1.3 million. Still no pardon. By 1990 he was dead, at ninety-two, vindicated only by a last-chance pardon from George Bush. Happily, the Reagan Library never got a single pledged penny from Hammer's estate. Giants walked the earth in those days.

Albert Jr. The official story of his life makes curiously depressing reading. Certainly by the time he was enrolled at St. Albans, he was running for president, and the other boys knew it, as did several teachers from my era. Since many of the boys came from political families, ambition of a political nature was hardly a surprise if it surfaced in any boy, no matter how young. I, too, was haunted by my grandfather's failure to become vice president – and why not thane of Glamis and Cawdor and king to be? I, too, wanted to complete the family business. But after three years in the army in the Second War, I had become a novelist. I had also been infuriated by American attitudes to same-sexuality, and so, between a political career already mapped out and publishing a book that would, the more effective it was, end all hope of completing the family business, I chose virtue and published *The City and the Pillar*, butting my head against a stone wall that others in the next generation were to dent somewhat. The book was published in January 1948. In March 1948, the Heavenly Campaign Manager of the Gores, aware that I was now a political dud, gave birth to Albert Jr., right on cue. The clan was back on track. There has been a weird symmetry in all this, whose meaning I leave to the witches on the heath.

One of Albert's teachers marveled to me at his no-doubt hard-earned lack of spontaneity: 'He forced himself to be good at sports and win school elections. But he was not a natural at anything except painting, where he was really first-rate.' I asked what sort of paintings he did. 'Miniatures. They were exquisite. The sort of things only someone capable of great concentration and hard work could do.' A Mr. Hank Hillin, in the book *Al Gore Jr., His Life and Career*, thinks the other boys envied Al his hard-won school success and later career, but my impression is they were mocking him for the uncool obviousness of his ambition when they nicknamed him Ozymandias, after Shelley's King of Kings, whose ruined colossal statue lies in the sands with the admonition 'Look on my Works, ye Mighty, and despair!' Al's contemporaries were dealing in irony of a sort not available to Hank or to his subject, Al, who, in order to sound more down-home folksy, changed his name to the bleak, rather unsuitable 'Al Gore,' under the pretense he was just another sharecropper farm boy who had come to pick cotton in Washington's Cathedral Close.

One advantage of being brought up in Washington in a senator's house is that you very quickly get the point to how and why things work. Where someone from outside might come to politics in order to bring justice to the people or, at the very least, Frank Capra, those on the inside know that it is all an intricate game of personalities and what today is called spin. Who you really are is not as important as how you have been made to seem; hence, the universal paranoia about media. Issues that so enthrall the politically minded outside the magic circle of hereditary politicians mean very little to those who start life with a political name that will act as a minimal description of its bearer. A Gore will be – or, let us say, will be thought to be – a mild populist, interested in the welfare of farmers, no open friend to conglomerate America and so on. The classic Gores are against foreign military adventures. It was here that Al Jr. broke with tradition when he was one of only ten Democratic senators to support George Bush's Persian Gulf caper; before that he had approved Reagan's Grenada and Libyan strikes.

At Harvard, Al Jr. met his own eminence grise, Martin Peretz, a sometime schoolteacher who had married a considerable fortune, thus making it possible for him to buy *The New Republic*, a once respectable liberal paper belonging to my brother-in-law Michael Whitney Straight. Yes, our Washington world is astonishingly small, and lives cross and recross for generations. Peretz is a mega-Zionist, and Al Jr. has proved to be a good investment for his lobby – and vice versa, though in Al's 1988 bid for the presidency, the Peretz connection cost him New York's black vote and got him practically none of the Jewish vote, except, possibly, the one cast by Mayor Ed Koch. Peretz has been known to take credit for Al Jr.'s speeches.

In the matter of Vietnam, our hero played it perfectly. He knew that he could not stay out, even though, like his father, he was against the war; and he knew that a visit to Canada's cooler climes would be fatal in the eyes of his patriotic constituency. So he became a journalist for six months with an engineering unit outside Saigon. He never saw action, but he did see to it that, weapon in hand, he was photographed for the Al Gore, Jr., Library. Plainly, the nation had changed after the Second War. I can think of hardly anyone of my generation who dodged the draft, while many of us, especially those with an eye to politics, enlisted and even got killed, something the gung-ho Vietnam generation never did as they found solace in neutral lands or hearkened to a call from God to join His ministry on earth.

Along the way, Al married an appropriate wife and had four appropriate children, all rather better-looking than is usual in the clan, but then they also had a mother as did he. Of Pauline Gore, one of his teachers at St. Albans said, 'She was the driving force, not the father. She was the one who wanted him to be class president and so on.' Where Albert Sr. saw himself as a voice for truth in the world, his wife and his son duly noted that he was not spending as much time at home with the folks as he should, and so number one on the checklist of what the son would *not* do when he began his ascent was neglect the home folks. He would, also, work hard to play down nonfolksy St. Albans and Harvard, as well as Vanderbilt, where he studied, briefly, for the ministry in order 'to atone for the sins' in Vietnam, whatever the sins of a non-combatant might have been; then, once he had exorcised the trauma of man's inhumanity to man, he shifted over to the law school.

A five-year stint at the Nashville *Tennessean* taught him a great deal about how newspapers work, and about publicity. Meanwhile, he took part in his father's various livestock and tobacco dealings. Later he was to share, most publicly at a convention, the guilt he still felt because he had once grown and sold the poisonous leaf that had struck down a beloved sister in her youth. He ceased to traffic with the murderous weed, prayed for forgiveness. He promptly had to face what friends call the 'Gore jinx.' The speech – the work of Marty Peretz? – wetted every eye, including the speaker's. Actually, Al had somehow forced himself to continue in the tobacco business for quite some time after her death. Plainly, the cigarette burned more brightly than the bush on the hard road to Damascus.

The Gore jinx becomes operative whenever Al is inclined, as Sam Goldwyn used to say, to geld the lily. All politicians do this, of course. But Al's air of solemn righteousness sets him up every time for a pratfall, including the astonishing assertion that he and his bride had inspired Erich Segal to write *Love Story* in their common Harvard days. Segal is a brilliant classicist, whose *Roman Laughter*, a study of Plautus, I highly recommend; he sharply denied any connection. Pratfall. Al should have stayed in the family and said that *Myra Breckinridge* had been inspired by the magic couple.

Lily gelding is a harmless activity and, perhaps, a necessity for someone fearful of being thought too young for the presidency in 1988. Al also portrayed himself as a home builder, the developer of a subdivision; actually, others did the work, while he and his father were fairly inactive partners. But Al did make a packet by reselling some of his father's farm after he had first bought it with a Federal Farm Credit System low-interest loan of the sort usually made to finance farmers' crops. Profit to one side, he gelds lilies in order to create an image of himself as farmer, home builder, warrior, relentless crime reporter who sent to jail corrupt officials (they didn't go to jail), and so on. But then, as a member of the House who served with him observed, 'Around here he's what we call a "glory boy." He gets to the House and starts running for the Senate. Gets to the Senate and starts running for the White House. There's no time left to do any of the real work the rest of us have to do.'

Four terms in the House, then to the Senate in 1984. After four years of the Senate, at the age of thirty-nine, Al is ready for the presidency. During the primaries, family lines crossed. Senator

David Boren of Oklahoma told me that the more Al stumped T. P. Gore's state, the closer the family connection became: 'By the end, you'd have thought he was your nephew.' Save for the Peretz connection, a nephew to be proud of, by and large. In politics, credit is taken, if not given, for just about anything admirable or popular at the moment: anything that can't immediately be checked on, that is. The Al Gore résumé is wondrously virtuous, if slightly short on achieved specifics.

T. P. Gore used to say that the most fervent prayer of any politician was 'Would that my opponent had written a book!' In 1992 Al did just that. *Earth in the Balance* was the ominous title of his hostage to fortune. *Ecology and the Human Spirit* was the subtitle, while, under that, '"A powerful summons for the politics of life and hope" – Bill Moyers.' In the introduction, the author says that he has for 'more than twenty-five years . . . [been] in search of a true understanding of the global ecological crisis and how it can be resolved.' All right, so it was not exactly twenty-five years. How about twenty-four? Certainly, the book is solidly researched; the prose as resolutely dull as its author's speeches; the conclusions obvious to nearly everyone who has given the matter thought, except, ironically, the great source of pollution and warming, Corporate America, without whose money and media no one can be elected president. But then, when Al wrote the book, he had taken himself out of the '92 presidential race, never thinking that, within a year, he would be Clinton's vice president and that his 'antibusiness' tract would outrage *The Wall Street Journal*'s fellow polluter-travelers. Since no good deed goes unpunished, one suspects this will convince Al that his unique moment of reasonable altruism is not going to go unpunished and perhaps he'd better go back to endorsing such military-procurement programs as the MX, the Trident D-5, etc. Meanwhile, the Gore jinx again surfaced when the book's greatest fan proved to be the Unabomber.

Dick Morris, the political spin master whose sex life caused him to depart the as yet uncongenial Clinton White House, has written, thus far, the best account of how presidential politics work today. He is particularly intrigued by the Clinton–Gore relationship. 'Gore is the single person in the world whose advice the president most values. He sees Gore as a junior president . . . When he wants a clear-eyed assessment, he turns to Gore, as he does when he wants something really important handled really well.' Yet it was Al who helped bring aboard Leon Panetta as chief of staff: a fatal choice, because when the hard times came, Panetta was one of the first to turn on Clinton. Was this a setup? One almost hopes, out of sheer dramatic imagination, that the deliberately colorless Gore may yet turn out to be Iago, secretly planting handkerchiefs all round the West Wing. Certainly, he has placed a number of his own people in places of power. But he has also, thus far, living up to his own book, done his best to preserve the environmental-protection programs.

About the 1995 battle over the budget, Morris makes an interesting observation: 'A more subtle difference existed between Clinton and Gore. Both wanted a deal [with the congressional Republicans]. But Clinton wanted a compromise, whereas Gore wanted a deal that all but completely protected his priorities: the environment, technology, and so forth. Gore is more interested in specifics than in themes.' This is an important distinction that goes to the heart of American practical politics. By and large, the great presidents have been thematic. FDR never mastered the specifics of anything. But he had a genius for getting across to the electorate his general view of where the country should be going and who should make what deal – New Deal, even – to get us all there. FDR possessed what Bush so memorably disdained as 'the vision thing.' But Al has a graduate student's need to pile up specifics for a good grade. Like Carter, he dotes on facts, figures, blueprints of how to build that tree house. Certainly, it is a sign of seriousness and goodwill that he works on environmental matters not only on TV but behind closed doors; yet it is also a sign of tactical weakness that he has Jimmy Carter's fascination with endless technical detail, more fitting for someone aspiring to a safe berth in Harvard's American Civilization Department than the presidency. FDR was the first to admit that he often stumbled. I may not, he once said, always get a hit each time I come up to bat ... But he had a buoyancy that was contagious. When one thing failed, he'd quickly try another. An over-attention to each tree and not to the forest that contains it could be the fatal flaw in the character of a miniaturist President Gore, whose mind is convergent – only connect things – while the great presidents know that nothing on earth or in politics really connects and that the quick, divergent mentality is the one that best adapts and moves ahead.

In order to be reelected in 1996, the Clinton–Gore administration adopted a series of right-wing Republican, even protofascist, programs, with lots more prisons, death penalties, harassment of the poor, cries of terrorism, and, implicitly, control by government over the citizenry, as the Unabomber duly noted. As one sees these politics evolve in Morris's narrative, one realizes that no one in the White House is thinking about much of anything other than, somehow, finessing the other party, which is slightly more in thrall to the Christian right and somewhat better funded by corporate America than are the Democrats. It is a somber narrative, particularly if one has been studying, as I have, the Bill of Rights lately. But we are now trapped in the rapid erosion of an ever more alien system, currently further skewed by all the atrocious law that Kenneth W. Starr has managed to squeeze from a brain-dead Supreme Court, where only its prince of darkness, Scalia, betrays an inkling of common sense about the harm being done our judicial system as lawyer–client and president–adviser protocols are overthrown in ill-written and worse-conceived judgments.

In 1883 Congress passed a law preventing city and courthouse machines from obliging those on the public payroll to kick back at election time – a sort of tithing to raise money for an election or, perhaps, just riotous living: an evening at Delmonico's with Boss Tweed. Virtue outlawed this practice, officially. Now Janet Reno of Waco ponders a special counsel to investigate Albert Jr., among others, for making calls to raise soft money from a public building, the White House, instead of from a cellular phone in the Lafayette Park convenience parlor. I consulted, in a vision, the Heavenly Campaign Manager of the Gores. He was dismissive. 'If they try making something of that, what about Dole and Gingrich telephoning from Capitol Hill?'

I wondered about the Buddhist fund-raiser for Albert Jr. 'Forget it. Even the Bush family's Heavenly Campaign Manager – dyslexic, by the way – says there's no mileage in it.'

'What about Clinton and Monica? Will that rub off on Albert Jr.?'

'If Clinton goes before 2000 – not much chance, I'd say – Al's in place to run as a sitting president. Anyway, once Bill's gone, end of sex story. You see, Al is sexproof. Designed never to lust in the Oval Office or even in his heart, and – the Beauty Part – no one lusts for him. Oh, we're looking after – really looking after – the family this time.' As the vision started to fade, I was bemused to note that our family's Heavenly Campaign Manager is wearing a saffron robe. A *Buddhist* campaign manager? *Shantih shantih shantih*.

Since there is no earthly reason for Albert Jr. to be president, by the same happy logic there is no unearthly reason for him not to be. But should, by some mishap, the mandate of heaven not come to Albert A. Gore, Jr., the next generation of Gores is bound to succeed, and I am now putting my money on the future president Blake Gore of Houston, Mississippi, who will initiate a golden age not too long after A.D. 2050.

Bad History

Shortly after the publication of David McCullough's prizewinning biography *Truman*, an ad hoc committee of concerned historians was formed to ponder how any historian, no matter how amiably 'in the grain,' could write at such length about so crucial a president and reveal absolutely nothing of his actual politics, whose effects still resonate in the permanent garrison state and economy he bequeathed us. Since this question has many answers, we continue to meet – in secrecy: Tenure is at stake in some cases, while prizes, grants, fellowships, hang in a balance that can go swiftly crashing if any of us dares question openly the image of America the beauteous on its hill, so envied by all that it is subject to attacks by terrorists who cannot bear so much sheer goodness to triumph in a world that belongs to *their* master, the son of morning himself, Satan.

As we discuss in increasing detail the various American history departments, a large portrait of Comer Vann Woodward beams down on us; he is the acknowledged premier conductor of that joyous, glory-bound gravy train. In due course, we plan to give a Vann Woodward Prize to the historian who has shown what biologists term 'absolute maze-brightness,' that is, the ability to get ahead of the pack to the scrumptious cheese at a complex labyrinth's end. Comer's own Pulitzer Prize (bestowed for his having edited the perhaps questionable diary of Mary Chesnut) was the result of a lifetime of successful maze-threading, which ended with a friend, John Blum, awarding him the prime cheddar for what is hardly history writing in our commitee's strict sense. To be fair, Comer did deserve an honorable mention back in 1955 for *The Strange Career of Jim Crow*. Our committee tends to agree that prize-giving is largely a racket in which self-serving schoolteachers look after one another. We shall, in due course, address this interesting if ancillary subject.

Meanwhile, we debate whether or not to create a vulgar splash and give an annual prize to the worst American historian of the year. But the first nominations are coming in so thick and fast that none of us really can, in a single life, read all the evidence – and graduate students are forbidden to do our work for us. So we have tentatively abandoned that notion. Instead, we have been surveying current publications, applying our strict standards to the works of an eclectic group that has only one thing in common (badness aside): the public approbation of like-minded toilers in the field.

Our criteria: First, the book must be badly written. Since this is as true, alas, of some of our best historians, we do not dwell too much on aesthetics. Gibbon and Macaulay and Carlyle knew that history was an important aspect of literature and so made literature; but this secret seems to have got lost by the end of the last century. Even our own wise hero, Edmund Wilson, didn't really write all that good himself. Second, the book in question must be composed in perfect bad faith. This is much easier for us to judge than literary value and very satisfying, particularly when one can figure where the writer is, as they say, coming from. Naturally, our own tastes condition our responses. Most of us are not enthusiasts of the National Security State of 1950 *et seq.* And we suspect that the empire, now spinning out of control, was a bad idea. After all, the federal government must borrow heavily every single day to keep it humming along. But anyone who can make a good case for Truman's invention of the National Security State does not necessarily, on the ground of our own political incorrectness, earn a place in the crowded *galère*. Only if he or she denies that there is such a thing as an American empire (an act of bad faith, since that is the line those who endow universities want taken) will inclusion occur.

In the matter of race, the opportunities for bad faith are beyond mere counting. Even so, our committee has just voted *unanimously* that the worst of the books currently in print is *America in Black and White: One Nation, Indivisible, Race in America,* by Stephan Thernstrom and Abigail Thernstrom. The two nervous subtitles betray unease, just as rapid eye-blinking, behaviorists tell us, signifies a liar in full flood. In presenting the Thernstroms' work as the first of a series of bad histories we do not want to create in them a sense of pride or, indeed, of uniqueness. There are many, many others in their league and, from time to time, they too will be revealed in these pages.

The Thernstroms are a husband-and-wife team: He is a Harvard professor, she a self-proclaimed liberal because, she said to me, she wrote once for *The Economist.* The hearty laughter you now hear from across the Atlantic is that of Evelyn Rothschild, that splendid conservative paper's splendidly conservative proprietor.

The Thernstroms are crude writers, but then if they were not, they would not be so honored here. What they have perfected –

much appreciated by their natural constituency, the anti-blacks – is what we call the Reverse Angle Shot in the matter of race. In the movies a reverse angle is exactly what it sounds like. You shoot a scene one way; then you switch about and shoot it from the exact opposite point of view. In debate, however, the Thernstrom Reverse Angle is supposed to take the place of the master shot: that is, the wide-angle look at the whole scene. Their argument is simple. Affirmative action for minorities is wrong, particularly in the case of African-Americans, because such action takes it for granted that they are by nature inferior to whites and so require more financial aid (and slacker educational standards) than canny whites or those eerily look-alike, overly numerate Asians. This is inspired. Now the Therns can maintain that the true racist is one who believes in affirmative action, because he is anti-black, while the *Economist*-reading Therns believe that blacks can stand on their own two feet alongside the best of whites if only evil liberals, in their condescending racism, would not try to help them out of ghettos of their own feckless making.

To 'prove' this, the Thernstroms have come up with a blizzard of statistics in order to make the case that blacks were really getting their act together from 1945 until the Sixties, when affirmative action, welfare, and other liberal devilries so spoiled them that they took to drugs and murder while, most tragic of all, not living up to 'our' SAT norms.

One of the hallmarks of the truly bad historian is not so much the routine manipulation of the stats as the glee with which it is done, sad and sober though he tries to appear, crocodile tear forever clinging to nose-tip. The Therns' Introduction is high comedy. Quotations routinely turn reality upside down. A state court strikes down a blacks-only scholarship program at the University of Maryland: '"Of all the criteria by which men and women can be judged," the court intoned, "the most pernicious is that of race."' Therefore, special blacks-only scholarships are racist.

But like so many zealots, the Therns cannot control that Strangelovian arm forever going rigid with a life of its own as it rises in salute. A few lines after establishing the overt racism of affirmative action, they up the rhetoric: 'What do we owe those who arrived on our shores in 1619 and remained members of an oppressed caste for more than three centuries?' I like that 'our shores.' After three centuries surely these are African-American shores, too, not to mention the shores of the indigenous Mongol population, which needs quite as much affirmative action these days as do 'our' involuntary African visitors. Certainly the Therns themselves are hardly in the 'our' business; they did not, as idle gossip has it, hit shore with Leif Ericson. Rather, theirs is the disdain, even rage, of recent arrivals against those who preceded them but did less well. Racism, after all, is a complex matter beyond the competence of a pair of publicists for the shrinking white majority and its institutions, among them the Manhattan Institute, where Abigail is 'a senior fellow,' as well as the John M. Olin Foundation and the Bradley, Richardson, Earhart, and Carthage generators of light, fueled by corporate money. Joel Pulliam, one of the Therns' undergraduate helots, 'worked for us part-time throughout his college career.' The Pulliam family are – or were – newspaper proprietors of great malignity. (Our committee is now taking cognizance of these un-American covens and shall, in due course, work to remove their tax exemptions on the ground that they are political activists.)

Now the argument again: Everything was getting better for the blacks until *Brown v. Board of Education*, affirmative action, etc. destroyed their moral fiber. Result: 'Today's typical black twelfth-grader scores no better on a reading test than the average white in

the eighth grade, and is 5.4 years behind the typical white in science.' Our committee is still examining all Thernstrom figures
that 'prove' blacks have never been better off than now, or were
better off before anyone did anything to be of use to them, or
aren't really worth bothering with as they are demonstrably inferior. After all, 'the proportion of blacks in poverty is still triple
that of whites. The unemployment rate for black males is double
the white rate, the rate of death from homicide . . .' and so on.
Then the horror, the horror: 'Blacks from families earning over
$70,000 a year have lower average SAT scores than whites from
families taking in less than $10,000.' So even if they make money
(dealing drugs, entertaining, or playing games), they are still
awfully dumb. Curiously, no Thern has questioned the value of the
SAT score or, indeed, the value of the curriculum that is taught in
'our' high schools or available in universities. 'G.V.' was so bored
at one of the country's best prep schools (prewar) that he made no
effort to do more than pass dull courses. Could it be that African-
American culture might not be satisfied with what passes for
education today? Even – or especially, when one considers the
Therns' polemics – at Harvard?

For the Therns, the political activism of the Sixties is the wrong
road taken. Apparently, 'three of four Southern whites . . . were
ready to concede that racial integration was bound to come,' presumably when the bird of dawning singeth all night long. But
Americans rightly deplored 'brutal tactics' – i.e., demonstrations.
The Therns produce an ancient cold war gloss on the matter of
race: 'Surveys disclosed a pervasive and bizarre skepticism about
whether the civil rights movement reflected the true feelings of
typical African-Americans.' As of a 1963 poll, a quarter of the
white population suspected the Commies of egging on listless
African-Americans. The FBI bugging of Martin Luther King, Jr.,

on the suspicion that he was in with the Commies is justified 'in the context of the deadly struggle between the United States and Soviet totalitarianism.' Thus the Great Red Herring once again makes an obligatory appearance, in a footnote.

'G.V.' must now confess that he met the Therns in 1991. He had come to Harvard to deliver the Massey lectures, which are sponsored by a small, suitably obscure department known, he recalls, as 'American Civilization,' then headed by Professor Thern. 'G.V.' met them at a dinner, which was, he now realizes, a day of apotheosis, particularly for Mrs. Thern, an adorable elfin minx. The Los Angeles Police Department had just beaten Rodney King to a pulp and a video of cops clobbering his fallen figure had been playing on television all day. Abigail was firmly on the side of the police. 'Their work is so dangerous, so unappreciated.' Her panegyric to the LAPD stunned the dinner party. She speculated on Rodney King's as yet unrevealed crimes and shuddered at the thought of his ebondark associates, lying in wait for pink porker cops. Professor Thern gave a secret smile as his helpmeet's aria grew more and more rich and strange.

Now, somewhat sated by numbing stats, the Therns go on attacking blacks in what they appear to think is a sound and sympathetic way. They quote angry citizens like the young black man who says, after King's attackers were let off by a Simi Valley jury, 'Is there a conspiracy to allow and condone the destruction of black people?' Needless to say, there is nothing a Thern likes as much as a conspiracy theory to pooh-pooh. 'That these charges have been repeated so often and so vehemently does not make them true. The issue is complicated.' The Therns conclude that blacks are locked up more often than whites because they commit more crimes, and to try to help them is useless, as the Sixties proved.

As one reads this curiously insistent racist tract, one begins to

sense that there is some sort of demonic spirit on the scene, unac-
knowledged but ever-present, as the Therns make their endless
case. Reading Thern-prose, somewhat more demure than Abby's
table-rant, I was put in uneasy mind of kindly old Dr.
Maimonides. In Book III, Chapter 51 of his *Guide for the
Perplexed* (copyright 1190 C.E.), the revered codifier of the
Talmud lists those who cannot begin to acknowledge, much less
worship, the true God. Among those nonhumans are 'some of the
Turks [he means Mongols] and the nomads in the North and the
Blacks and the nomads in the South, and those who resemble
them in our climates. And their nature is like the nature of mute
animals, and according to my opinion they are not on the level of
human beings, and their level among existing things is below that
of a man and above that of a monkey, because they have the image
and the resemblance of a man more than a monkey does.' When
this celebrated book was translated into English early this century, the translators were embarrassed, as well they should have
been, by the racism. So instead of using the word 'black' or
'Negro,' they went back to the Hebrew word for blacks – Kushim,
which they transliterated as Kushites – a previously unknown and
unidentifiable tribe for Anglophones and so easily despised.

There was an eccentric English duke who, according to legend,
spoke only once a year. His remarks were treasured. At the time of
the abdication of Edward VIII, he suddenly said at a Sunday
dinner, 'If there is any trouble anywhere, look for an archbishop.'
Change 'archbishop' to 'monotheist' and one understands the powerful engine that drives Therns to write bad history. Also, in
fairness, it must be noted that Judaism's two dreary spinoffs,
Christianity and Islam, have given even wider range to the notion
of the true godless folk as 'white man's burden,' 'cursed infidels'
and 'lesser breeds' so much less human than those whipped up in
the true God's bookish image.

Finally, a bad historian is one who dares not say what he means. He must count on his 'evidence' – those stats – to bring us round to his often hidden-in-plain-sight point of view. At the conclusion of their screed, the Therns produce such tautologies as 'the issue of group differences is actually enormously complicated.' This extraordinary insight appears as late as page 541. 'The complexities of the matter become evident when we notice that the socio-economic gap between Jews and Christians today is greater than the gap between blacks and whites. Jewish per capita incomes are nearly double those of non-Jews, a bigger difference than the black-white income gap. Although Jews make up less than 3 per-cent of the population, they constitute more than a quarter of the people on the *Forbes* magazine list of the richest four hundred Americans . . . Asian Americans similarly outrank whites on most measures.' We are also told that Scots are highly educated but don't make all that much money, because they are drawn to 'the ministry and teaching.' Cajuns? Forget it. 'What explains why some of these groups have done so much better than others is very hard to say.' Actually, it is quite easy for a Thern to say, but perhaps a bit dangerous. So at the end of their long book, the matter of race is both a reality and a chimera. In short, *complicated*; yet, to the Therns' credit, we know exactly what they mean.

Perhaps the only literary form perfected by late-twentieth-cen-tury United Statespersons is the blurb for the dust jacket. It is for us what the haiku was for the medieval Japanese. Of all the vari-eties of blurb, the Academic Courtesy is the most exquisite in its balances and reticences and encodements. Now, there was one blurb that the Therns knew that they dare not publish without: that of the chairman of Harvard's Department of Afro-American Studies. Would this elusive, allusive – illusive? – figure misread their text as hoped or, worse for them, would he actually read it for what it is? Great risk either way. One can picture the Therns agonizing over how best to rope him in. He was their White Whale, nay, their Cinqué of Sierra Leone. Night after night, Therns and their ilk flitted about Harvard Yard, suitably hooded against the night air. Meanwhile, the beleaguered chairman, quite aware of their plot, was careful to take the Underground Railroad when crossing the Yard. But in the end, he broke. He gathered loved ones around him. 'I can no longer live like this, in terror of the Therns. I'm going out.' Loved ones keened, 'But not *tonight*. The moon's full. *This is Thern weather.*'

But the chairman said, 'I fear not. My blurb will protect me from all harm.' Blurb? Had he perjured himself? No, he had not, he declared; and so, casting aside fear, he entered the Yard, where a posse of howling Therns promptly held him for ransom in the form of what proved to be the very paradigm of all Harvard blurbs: 'This book is essential reading for anyone wishing to understand the state of race relations at the end of the great American century.' Thus, he tricked his pursuers and freed graduate students as yet unborn from, at the very least, a hoisting by the Thern petard.

The Nation
20 April 1998

Blair

London

In 1964 I watched the election returns in a ballroom at London's Savoy Hotel. The room had been taken by Pamela Berry, whose husband owned *The Daily Telegraph*. As one would expect, considering our hostess's powerful political views, the guests were largely Conservative, though the odd transatlantic visitor could stare at the vast screen which, historically, the first British 'television' election was filling with faces and numbers. Whenever Labour won a seat, there were boos and hisses. When a Tory prevailed, applause. Then the moment of awful truth: Labour had won and the next Prime Minister would be Harold Wilson. Lives and sacred honor, not to mention fortunes, were now at risk as universal darkness buried all.

Gladwyn Jebb, former ambassador to the United Nations, said to me, 'Parish pump politics. Let's go watch the real news.' He led me into a side room where, on a small screen, the fall of Khrushchev was being gloated over. Jebb: 'Now *this* is the real thing.'

A third of a century later I was again in London at the start of the election just concluded. BBC television had hired me to chat about it. Most of the surviving Tories from the Savoy – or their children and grandchildren – were voting for something called New Labour, headed by Tony Blair, while the Conservatives were led by John Major, a Prime Minister who made much of the fact that he was a lower-middle-class Everyman pitted against a posh elitist who had gone to public school. The startling difference between 1964 and 1997 was that where Labour once represented the working classes and poor (today's 'disadvantaged'), it is now a home for prosperous suburbanites on the go as well as disaffected Scots and Welsh. In the end, the Tories did not win a single seat in Scotland or Wales, something that has not happened in a century.

The only real issue was, Should the British, if they ever meet the required standards, join a common European currency? But no politician was about to stick his neck out on that one. Another big issue that the local press was fretting over: Are British elections becoming Americanized? Presidentialized? Devoid of relevant content? The answer is, more or less, yes. The tabloids have created a terrible Clintonian atmosphere. 'Sleaze' is the principal word one sees in every headline. Since Rupert Murdoch, a devotee of honest government, has abandoned the Tories for New Labour, and as this Australian-turned-American is allowed to own Britain's most popular daily paper (*The Sun*) as well as the weekend *News of the World*, Tory politicians are being wildly smeared as sexual degenerates and crooks.

With a BBC crew I made the rounds of the three parties. Each presented its program to the nation. Liberal Democrat Paddy Ashdown received the press in a small crowded ecclesiastical room.

'To make it look like a great crowd,' a journalist whispered in my ear. Pamphlets were distributed. Ashdown is blond, athletic-looking; also quick-witted by American standards, but then any public schoolboy in England speaks more articulately than any American politician except for the great Oval One.

Ashdown played the honesty card, something of a novelty. He wants better education for everyone. He admits that this will cost money. The two other parties swear they will never raise taxes, which, of course, they will . . .

I go to the Royal Albert Hall. Major points out Tony Blair's contradictions and evasions. I suspect a few ancient heads in the audience were at the Savoy that night so many years ago when Harold Wilson won and socialism would level all. (Once in Downing Street, Wilson quickly said that, actually, he had never read Marx.) As the hall filled with the gorgeousness of Elgar, I intoned for the camera: 'Land of hope and glory, of Drake and Nelson, of Clive and Crippen.'

The fascinating kickoff was Mr. Blair's. We were in an early-nineteenth-century building with a dome, dedicated to engineers. Press milled about in the rotunda downstairs, where stood a tall dark man, Peter Mandelson, reputedly Blair's Rasputin. He gave solemn audience to the journalists of the lobby. Words murmured to one, hand held over his mouth. TV cameras, including ours, avoided. He had the insolent manner of one born to the top rung but three. The mood of the Labourites was paranoid, particularly the handsome blonde girls in black suits with curled lips and flashing eyes. Blair's lead was so great in the polls that only a blunder on his part could stop his irresistible rise. So one could not be made. Although the BBC and I had been cleared by the press party office, I suddenly looked like a possible blunder.

We take our seats. Blair enters, followed by what will be much of his Cabinet. He has been told not to smile. The smile has been criticized by the press. Too loopy. Too youthful. He is forty-three, JFK's age in 1960. He is slender with a beaky, mini-Bonaparte sort of nose. The dark hair does not entirely convince. He holds up the party manifesto with his own face, smiling, on the cover. I am close enough to him to realize that he does much of his breathing through his mouth. Lips pressed tight together cause his nostrils to flare as he tries to get enough air in. The speech, his program, was written, we have been told – as if it were from the hand of St. John of Patmos – in his own garden in his own longhand. As it turns out, he has no program. But things will be better, he tells us. Afterward, to every question he says simply, 'Trust me.' He departs.

The press, seeing that I'm all that's left in the room, surround me. The blondes try to shoo them away. Question: 'Are we becoming more Americanized?' Answer: 'Well, you do resemble us in that you now have a single party with two right wings.'

Question: 'Which wing is more to the right?'

Answer (in my gravest and most reverential voice): 'One does not bring a measuring rod to Lilliput.'

Then we were all thrown out. Labour complained to the BBC that I had preempted their affair to 'slag Blair.'

In the next six weeks, Blair makes no errors. He now has a huge majority in the House of Commons. Although he has no plans, I am sure that whatever it was that Mr. Murdoch wanted him to do, he will do. I talked to a Scots MP who knows Blair well. 'He's another Thatcher. Authoritarian. Hands-on control freak.' I go to my splendid ancient friend and former head of the Labour Party, Michael Foot: 'Blair is excellent. Really excellent.' I ask, 'Whatever happened to socialism?' At this Mrs. Foot looked grim. 'Yes,' she asked her husband. 'What did?' He smiles. 'Socialism? Oh, socialism! Yes! Yes! . . . Well, there's time . . .' I move on. 'The young, even in America,' I said, 'are reading Gramsci.' Foot was delighted. 'Good. Good. While you and I are reading Montaigne.'

Question I never got answered by anyone: You are an offshore island. But off whose shore? Europe's or ours?

The Nation
26 May 1997

The Last Empire

It is wonderful indeed, ladies and gentlemen, to have all of you here between covers, as it were – here being the place old John Bunyan called 'Vanity Fair, because the town where 'tis kept, is lighter than vanity.' But these days the town is not so much London or New York as the global village itself, wherein you are this month's movers and shakers, as well as moved and shaken (I feel your pain, Yasser). In a number of ways I find it highly fitting that we meet on the old fairground as twentieth century and Second Christian Millennium are saying goodbye. Personally, I thought they'd never go without taking us with them. There are, of course, 791 days still to go. I also note that the photographers have immortalized a number of smiles. Joy? Or are those anthropologists right who say that the human baring of teeth signals aggression? Let's hope not before 2001 C.E.

Of course, centuries and millennia are just arbitrary markings, like bookkeeping at Paramount Pictures. But, symbolically, they mean a lot to those who are interested in why we are today what we are and doing what we are doing. This goes particularly for those movers and shakers who have spent a lot of this year in meetings, courtesy of the one indisposable – or did President Clinton say indispensable? – nation on earth and last self-styled global power, loaded down with nukes, bases, debts.

Denver and Madrid were two fairgrounds. Nothing much is ever accomplished when the managing world director calls in his regional directors for fun and frolic. But when Clinton chose a cowboy theme at Denver, with boots for all, some regional directors actually dared whine. But they are easily replaced and know it. Later the Seven Leading Economic Powers (plus Russia) decided, at Madrid, to extend the North American Atlantic Organization to include Poland, Czechland, Hungary. Jacques Chirac, the French director of the . . . well, let's be candid: American empire . . . wanted several more Eastern countries to join, while the Russian director wanted *no* Eastern extension of a military alliance that he still thinks, mistakenly, was formed to protect Eastern Europe from the power-mad Soviet Union. Actually, as we shall see, NATO was created so that the United States could dominate *Western* Europe militarily, politically, and economically; any current extension means that more nations and territories will come under American control while giving pleasure to such hyphenate American voters as Poles, Czechs, Hungarians. The French director was heard to use the word *merde* when the American emperor said that only three new countries are to be allowed in this time. The Frenchman was ignored, but then he had lost an election back home. In any case, the North Atlantic confederation of United States–Canada plus Western Europe can now be called the North Atlantic Baltic Danubian Organization, to which the Black Sea will no doubt soon be added.

I see that some of you are stirring impatiently. The United States is *an empire?* The emperor's advisers chuckle at the notion. Are we not a freedom-loving perfect democracy eager to exhibit our state-of-the-art economy to old Europe as a model of what you can do in the way of making money for the few by eliminating labor unions and such decadent frills as public health and education? At Denver a French spearcarrier – always those pesky French – wondered just how reliable our unemployment figures were when one-tenth of the male workforce is not counted, as they are either in prison or on probation or parole. The Canadian Prime Minister, even more tiresome than the French, was heard to say to his Belgian counterpart (over an open mike) that if the leaders of any other country took corporate money as openly as American leaders do, 'we'd be in jail.' Plainly, the natives are restive. But we are still in charge of the Vanity Fair.

I bring up all this not to be unkind. Rather, I should like to point out that those who live too long with unquestioned contradictions are not apt to be able to deal with reality when it eventually befalls them. I have lived through nearly three-quarters of this century. I enlisted in the army of the United States at seventeen; went to the Pacific; did nothing useful – I was just there, as Nixon used to say, WHEN THE BOMBS WERE FALLING. But, actually, the bombs were not really falling on either of us: he was a naval officer making a fortune playing poker, while I was an army first mate writing a novel.

Now, suddenly, it's 1997, and we are 'celebrating' the fiftieth anniversary of the Truman Doctrine and the Marshall Plan. Also, more ominously, July 26 was the fiftieth anniversary of the National Security Act that, without national debate but very quiet bipartisan congressional support, replaced the old American Republic with a National Security State very much in the global-empire business, which explains . . .

But, first, into the Time Machine.

It is the Ides of August 1945. Germany and Japan have

surrendered, and some 13 million Americans are headed home to enjoy – well, being alive was always the bottom line. Home turns out to be a sort of fairground where fireworks go off and the band plays 'Don't Sit Under the Apple Tree,' and an endlessly enticing fun house flings open its doors and we file through. We enjoy halls of mirrors where everyone is comically distorted, ride through all the various tunnels of love, and take scary tours of horror chambers where skeletons and cobwebs and bats brush past us until, suitably chilled and thrilled, we are ready for the exit and everyday life, but, to the consternation of some – and the apparent indifference of the rest – we were never allowed to leave the fun house entirely: it had become a part of our world, as were the goblins sitting under that apple tree.

Officially, the United States was at peace; much of Europe and most of Japan were in ruins, often literally, certainly economically. We alone had all our cities and a sort of booming economy – 'sort of' because it depended on war production, and there was, as far as anyone could tell, no war in the offing. But the arts briefly flourished. *The Glass Menagerie* was staged, Copland's *Appalachian Spring* was played. A film called *The Lost Weekend* – not a bad title for what we had gone through – won an Academy Award, and the as yet unexiled Richard Wright published a much-admired novel, *Black Boy*, while Edmund Wilson's novel *Memoirs of Hecate County* was banned for obscenity in parts of the country. Quaintly, each city had at least three or four daily newspapers in those days, while New York, as befitted *the* world city, had seventeen newspapers. But a novelty, television, had begun to appear in household after household, its cold gray distorting eye relentlessly projecting a fun-house view of the world.

Those who followed the – ugly new-minted word – media began to note that while watching even Milton Berle we kept fading in and out of the Chamber of Horrors. Subliminal skeletons would suddenly flash onto the TV screen; our ally in the recent war, 'Uncle Joe Stalin,' as the accidental President Harry S. Truman had called him, was growing horns and fangs that dripped blood. On earth, we were the only great unruined power with atomic weapons; yet we were now – somehow – at terrible risk. Why? How?

The trouble appeared to be over Germany, which, on February 11, 1945, had been split at the Yalta summit meeting into four zones: American, Soviet, British, French. As the Russians had done the most fighting and suffered the greatest losses, it was agreed that they should have an early crack at reparations from Germany – to the extent of $20 billion. At a later Potsdam meeting the new President Truman, with Stalin and Churchill, reconfirmed Yalta and opted for the unification of Germany under the four victorious powers. But something had happened between the euphoria of Yalta and the edginess of Potsdam. As the meeting progressed, the atom bomb was tried out successfully in a New Mexico desert. We were now able to incinerate Japan – or the Soviet Union, for that matter – and so we no longer needed Russian help to defeat Japan. We started to renege on our agreements with Stalin, particularly reparations from Germany. We also quietly shelved the notion, agreed upon at Yalta, of a united Germany under four-power control. Our aim now was to unite the three Western zones of Germany and integrate them into *our* Western Europe, restoring, in the process, the German economy – hence, fewer reparations. Then, as of May 1946, we began to rearm Germany. Stalin went ape at this betrayal. The cold war was on.

At home, the media were beginning to prepare the attentive few for Disappointment. Suddenly, we were faced with the highest personal income taxes in American history to pay for more and more weapons, among them the world-killer hydrogen bomb – all because *the Russians were coming*. No one knew quite why they were coming or with what. Weren't they still burying 20 million dead? Official explanations for all this made little sense, but then, as Truman's secretary of state, Dean Acheson, merrily observed, 'In the State Department we used to discuss how much time that mythical "average American citizen" put in each day listening, reading, and arguing about the world outside his own country . . . It seemed to us that ten minutes a day would be a high average.' So why bore the people? Secret 'bipartisan' government is best for what, after all, is – or should be – a society of docile workers, enthusiastic consumers, obedient soldiers who will believe just about anything for at least ten minutes. The National Security State, the NATO alliance, the forty-year cold war were all created without the consent, much less advice, of the American people. Of course, there were elections during this crucial time, but Truman-Dewey, Eisenhower-Stevenson, Kennedy-Nixon were of a single mind as to the desirability of inventing, first, a many-tentacled enemy, Communism, the star of the Chamber of Horrors; then, to combat so much evil, installing a permanent wartime state at home with loyalty oaths, a national 'peacetime' draft, and secret police to keep watch over homegrown 'traitors,' as the few enemies of the National Security State were known. Then followed forty years of mindless wars which created a debt of $5 trillion that hugely benefited aerospace and firms like General Electric, whose longtime TV pitchman was Ronald Reagan, eventually retired to the White House.

Why go into all this now? Have we not done marvelously well as the United States of Amnesia? Our economy is the envy of the earth, the President proclaimed at Denver. No inflation. Jobs for all except the 3 percent of the population in prison and the 5 percent who no longer look for work and so are not counted, bringing our actual unemployment close to the glum European average of 11 percent. And all of this accomplished without ever once succumbing to the sick socialism of Europe. We have no health service or proper public education or, indeed, much of anything for the residents of the fun house. But there are lots of ill-paid work-hours for husband and wife with no care for the children while parents are away from home. Fortunately, Congress is now preparing legislation so that adult prisons can take in delinquent fourteen-year-olds. They, at least, will be taken care of, while, economically, it is only a matter of time before the great globe itself is green-spanned.

Certainly European bankers envy us our powerless labor unions (only 14 percent of the lucky funsters are privileged to belong to a labor union) and our industries – lean, mean, downsized, with no particular place for the redundant to go except into the hell of sizzle and fry and burn. Today we give orders to other countries. We tell them with whom to trade and to which of our courts they must show up for indictment should they disobey us. Meanwhile, FBI agents range the world looking for drug fiends and peddlers while the unconstitutional CIA (they don't submit their accounts to Congress as the Constitution requires) chases 'terrorists' now that their onetime colleagues and sometime paymasters in the Russian KGB have gone out of business.

We have arrived at what Tennessee Williams once called A Moon of Pause. When I asked him what on earth the phrase meant, as spoken by an actress in one of his plays, 'It is,' he said loftily, 'the actual Greek translation of menopause.' I said that the word 'moon' did not come from *mensis* (Latin, not Greek, for 'month'). 'Then what,' he asked suspiciously, 'is the Latin for moon?' When I told him it was *luna* and what fun he might have with the word 'lunatic,' he sighed and cut. But at the time of the Madrid conference about the extension of NATO, a moon of pause seemed a nice dotty phrase for the change of life that our empire is now going through, with no enemy and no discernible function.

While we were at our busiest in the fun house, no one ever told us what the North Atlantic Treaty Alliance was really about. March 17, 1948, the Treaty of Brussels called for a military alliance of Britain, France, Benelux to be joined by the U.S. and Canada on March 23. The impetus behind NATO was the United States, whose principal foreign policy, since the administration of George Washington, was to avoid what Alexander Hamilton called 'entangling alliances.' Now, as the Russians were supposed to be coming, we replaced the old republic with the newborn National Security State and set up shop as the major *European* power west of the Elbe. We were now hell-bent on the permanent division of Germany between our western zone (plus the French and British zones) and the Soviet zone to the east. Serenely, we broke every agreement that we had made with our former ally, now horrendous Communist enemy. For those interested in the details, Carolyn Eisenberg's *Drawing the Line (The American Decision to Divide Germany 1944–49)* is a masterful survey of an empire – sometimes blindly, sometimes brilliantly – assembling itself by turning first its allies and then its enemies like Germany, Italy, Japan into client states, permanently subject to our military and economic diktat.

Although the Soviets still wanted to live by our original agreements at Yalta and even Potsdam, we had decided, unilaterally, to restore the German economy in order to enfold a rearmed Germany into Western Europe, thus isolating the Soviet Union, a nation which had not recovered from the Second World War and had no nuclear weapons It was Acheson – again – who elegantly explained all the lies that he was obliged to tell Congress and the ten-minute-attention-spanned average American: 'If we did make our points clearer than truth, we did not differ from most other educators and could hardly do otherwise . . . Qualification must give way to simplicity of statement, nicety and nuance to bluntness, almost brutality, in carrying home a point.' Thus were two generations of Americans treated by their overlords until, in the end, at the word 'Communism,' there is an orgasmic Pavlovian reflex just as the brain goes dead.

In regard to the 'enemy,' Ambassador Walter Bedell Smith – a former general with powerful simple views – wrote to his old boss General Eisenhower from Moscow in December 1947 apropos a conference to regularize European matters: 'The difficulty under which we labor is that in spite of our announced position we really do not want nor intend to accept German unification in any terms the Russians might agree to, even though they seemed to meet most of our requirements.' Hence, Stalin's frustration that led to the famous blockade of the Allied section of Berlin, overcome by General Lucius Clay's successful airlift. As Eisenberg writes, 'With the inception of the Berlin blockade, President Truman articulated a simple story that featured the Russians, trampling the wartime agreements in their ruthless grab for the former German capital. The president did not explain that the United States had abandoned Yalta and Potsdam, that it was pushing the formation of a West German state against the misgivings of many Europeans, and that the Soviets had launched the blockade to prevent partition.' This was fun-house politics at its most tragicomical.

The President, like a distorting mirror, reversed the truth. But then he was never on top of the German situation as opposed to the coming election (November 1948), an election of compelling personal interest to him but, in the great scheme of things, to no one else. He did realize that the few Americans who could identify George Washington might object to our NATO alliance, and so his secretary of state, Acheson, was told to wait until February 1949, *after* the election, to present to Congress our changeover from a Western Hemisphere republic to an imperial European polity, symmetrically balanced by our Asian empire, centered on occupied Japan and, in due course, its tigerish pendant, the ASEAN alliance.

The case for an American world empire was never properly argued, since the debate – what little there was – centered on the alleged desire of the Soviet Union to conquer the whole world, just as Hitler and the Nazis were trying to do until stopped, in 1945, by the Soviet Union with (what Stalin regarded as suspiciously belated) aid from the U.S.

On March 12, 1947, Truman addressed Congress to proclaim what would be known as the Truman Doctrine, in which he targeted our ally of two years earlier as the enemy. The subject at hand was a civil war in Greece, supposedly directed by the Soviets. We could not tolerate this as, suddenly, 'the policy of the United States [is] to support free peoples who are resisting attempted subjugation by armed minorities or by outside pressure.' Thus, Truman made the entire world the specific business of the United States. Although the Greek insurgents were getting some help from Bulgaria and Yugoslavia, the Soviets stayed out. They still hoped that the British, whose business Greece had been, would keep order. But as Britain had neither the resources nor the will, she called on the U.S. to step in. Behind the usual closed doors, Acheson was stirring up Congress with Iago-like intensity: Russian pressure of some sort 'had brought the Balkans to the point where a highly possible Soviet breakthrough might open three continents to Soviet penetration.' Senators gasped; grew pale; wondered how to get more 'defense' contracts into their states.

Of the major politicians, only former vice president Henry

Wallace dared answer Truman's 'clearer than truth' version of history: 'Yesterday, March 12, 1947, marked a turning point in American history, [for] it is not a Greek crisis that we face, it is an American crisis. Yesterday, President Truman . . . proposed, in effect, that America police Russia's every border. There is no regime too reactionary for us provided it stands in Russia's expansionist path. There is no country too remote to serve as the scene of a contest which may widen until it becomes a world war.'

Nine days after Truman declared war on Communism, he installed a federal loyalty-oath program. All government employees must now swear allegiance to the new order. Wallace struck again: 'The President's executive order creates a master index of public servants. From the janitor in the village post office to the Cabinet members, they are to be sifted, and tested and watched and appraised.'

Truman was nervously aware that many regarded Wallace as true heir to Roosevelt's New Deal; Wallace was also likely to enter the presidential race of 1948. Truman now left truth behind in the dust. 'The attempt of Lenin, Trotsky, Stalin, et al. to fool the world and the American Crackpots Association, represented by Jos. Davies, Henry Wallace, Claude Pepper, and the actors and artists in immoral Greenwich Village, is just like Hitler's and Mussolini's so-called socialist states.' Give 'em hell, Harry.

In the wake of Truman's cuckoo-like emergence from the old-fashioned closet of the original American Republic, a new American state was being born in order to save the nation and the great globe itself from Communism. The nature of this militarized state was, from the beginning, beyond rational debate. Characteristically, Truman and Acheson insisted on closed hearings of the Senate Committee on Foreign Relations. These matters were too important to share with the people whose spare ten minutes was now more and more filling up with television. The committee's Republican leader, Arthur H. Vandenberg, the great goose of Grand Rapids, Michigan, was thrilled to be taken into the confidence of the creators of the new empire, but he did suggest that, practically speaking, if hell wasn't scared out of the American people, Congress would have a hard time raising the revenues to pay for a military buildup in what was still thought to be, inside the ever more isolated fun house, peacetime. The media spoke with a single voice. Time Inc. publisher Henry Luce said it loudest: 'God had founded America as a global beacon of freedom.' Dissenters, like Wallace, were labeled Communists and ceased to engage meaningfully in public life or, by 1950, even in debate. Like the voice of a ghost, an ancestral voice, he spoke on May 21, 1947: 'Today in blind fear of communism, we are turning aside from the United Nations. We are approaching a century of fear.' Thus far, he is proved to be half right.

On July 26, 1947, Congress enacted the National Security Act, which created the National Security Council, still going strong, and the Central Intelligence Agency, still apparently going over a cliff as the result of decades of bad intelligence, not to mention all those cheery traitors for whom the country club at Langley, Virginia, was once an impenetrable cover. Years later, a sadder, if not wiser, Truman told his biographer, Merle Miller, that the CIA had become a dangerous mess and ought not to have been set up as it was. But in 1947 the CIA's principal role in Europe was not to counter Soviet activities but to control the politics of NATO members. French and Italian trade unions and publications were subsidized, and a great deal of secret money was poured into Italy to ensure the victory of the Christian Democratic Party in the elections of April 1948.

Acheson, in *Present at the Creation*, a memoir that compensates in elegance what it lacks in candor, alludes delicately to National Security Council document 68 (the 1950 blueprint for our war against Communism). But in 1969, when he was writing, he sadly notes that the memo is still classified. Only in 1975 was it to be declassified. There are seven points. First, never negotiate with the Soviet Union. No wonder the rebuffed Stalin, ever touchy, kept reacting brutally in Mitteleuropa. Second, develop the hydrogen bomb so that when the Russians go atomic we will still be ahead of them. Third, rapidly build up conventional forces. Fourth, to pay for this, levy huge personal income taxes – as high as 90 percent. Fifth, mobilize everyone in the war against internal Communism through propaganda, loyalty oaths, and spy networks like the FBI, whose secret agent Ronald Reagan, president of the Screen Actors Guild, had come into his splendid own, fingering better actors. Sixth, set up a strong alliance system, directed by the United States–NATO. Seventh, make the people of Russia, through propaganda and CIA derring-do, our allies against their government, thus legitimizing, with this highly vague task, our numerous unaccountable secret agents.

So, after five years in the fun house, we partially emerged in January 1950, to find ourselves in a new sort of country. We were also, astonishingly, again at war: this time in Korea. But as Truman-Acheson were nervous about asking Congress for a declaration, the war was called a United Nations police action; and messily lost. Acheson did prepare a memo assuring Truman that, hitherto, eighty-seven presidential military adventures had been undertaken without a congressional declaration of war as required by the old Constitution. Since 1950 the United States has fought perhaps a hundred overt and covert wars. None was declared by the nominal representatives of the American People in Congress Assembled; they had meekly turned over to the executive their principal great power, to wage war. That was the end of that Constitution.

As it will take at least a decade for us to reinvent China as a new evil empire, the moon is in a state of pause over the old fairground. We are entering a phase undreamed of by those 'present at the creation' of the empire. Although many still reflexively object to the word 'empire,' we have military bases in every continent, as well as ten aboard the aircraft carrier called the United Kingdom. For fifty years we have supported too many tyrants, overthrown too many democratic governments, wasted too much of our own money in other people's civil wars to pretend that we're just helping out all those poor little folks all round the world who love freedom and democracy just like we do. When the Russians stabbed us in the back by folding their empire in 1991, we were left with many misconceptions about ourselves and, rather worse, about the rest of the world.

The literature on what we did and why since 1945 is both copious and thin. There are some first-rate biographies of the various players. If one goes digging, there are interesting monographs like Walter LaFeber's 'NATO and the Korean War: A Context.' But the link between universities and imperial Washington has always been a strong one as Kissingers dart back and forth between classroom to high office to even higher, lucrative eminence, as lobbyists for foreign powers, often hostile to our interests. Now, with Carolyn Eisenberg's *Drawing the Line*, there is a step-by-step description of the years 1944–49, when we restored, rearmed, and reintegrated *our* German province into *our* Western Europe. For those who feel that Eisenberg dwells too much on American confusions and mendacities, there is always the elegant Robert H. Ferrell on 'The Formation of the Alliance, 1948–1949.' A court historian, as apologists for empire are known, Ferrell does his best with Harry Truman, reminding us of all the maniacs around him who wanted atomic war at the time of Korea, among them the first secretary of defense, the paranoid James Forrestal, who, while reading Sophocles' *Ajax* in hospital, suddenly defenestrated himself, a form of resignation that has never really caught on as it should.

At one point, Ferrell notes that Truman actually gave thought to the sufferings of women and children should we go nuclear in Korea. As for Truman's original decision to use two atomic bombs on Japan, most now agree that a single demonstration would have been quite enough to cause a Japanese surrender while making an attractive crater lake out of what had been Mount Fujiyama's peak. But Truman was in a bit of a daze at the time, as were the 13 million of us under arms who loudly applauded his abrupt ending of the first out-and-out race war, where the Japanese had taken to castrating Marines, alive as well as dead, while Marines, good brand-name-conscious Americans, would stick Coca-Cola bottles up living Japanese soldiers and then break them off. Welcome to some *pre*-fun-house memories still vivid to ancient survivors. The story that Lieutenant R. M. Nixon tried to persuade the Marines to use Pepsi-Cola bottles has never been verified.

The climate of intimidation that began with the loyalty oath of 1947 remains with us even though two American generations have been born with no particular knowledge of what the weather was like before the great freeze and the dramatic change in our form of government. No thorough history of what actually happened to us and to the world 1945–97 has yet appeared. There are interesting glances at this or that detail. There are also far too many silly hagiographies of gallant little guy Truman and superstatesman George Marshall, who did admit to Acheson that he had no idea what on earth the plan in his name was really about. But aside from all the American and foreign dead from Korea to Vietnam, from Guatemala to the Persian Gulf, the destruction of our old republic's institutions has been the great hurt. Congress has surrendered to the executive not only the first of its great powers, but the second, the power of the purse, looks to be up for grabs as Congress is forcing more money on the Pentagon than even that black hole has asked for, obliging the executive to spend many hot hours in the vast kitchen where the books are forever being cooked in bright-red ink. As for our Ouija-board Supreme Court, it would be nice if they would take time off from holding séances with the long-dead founders, whose original intent so puzzles them, and actually examine what the founders wrought, the Constitution itself and the Bill of Rights.

Did anyone speak out during the half-century that got us $5 trillion into debt while reducing the median household income by 7 percent when . . . No. Sorry. Too boring. Or, as Edward S. Herman writes, 'Paul Krugman admits, in *Age of Diminished Expectations*, that the worsening of the income distribution was "the central fact about economic life in America in the 1980s," but as an issue "it has basically exhausted the patience of the American public"' – the ten-minute attention span, unlike the green-span, has snapped on that one – 'and "no policy change now under discussion seems likely to narrow the gap significantly."'

It was *The New Yorker*'s literary and social critic Edmund Wilson who first sounded the alarm. In 1963 he published *The Cold War and the Income Tax*. Stupidly, he admits, he filed no income-tax returns between 1946 and 1955. As I've noted, one of the great events of our first year in the fun house was the publication in 1946 of Wilson's novel *Memoirs of Hecate County*. Wilson's income – never much – doubled. Then a system of justice, forever alert to sexual indecency, suppressed his book by court order. He was now broke with an expensively tangled marital life. Wilson describes being hounded by agents of the IRS; he also goes into the background of the federal income tax, which dates, as we know it, from 1913. Wilson also notes that, as of the 1960s, we were paying more taxes than we did during the Second World War. Since NSC-68 would remain a secret for another twelve years, he had no way of knowing that punitive income taxes must be borne by the American people in order to build up both nuclear and conventional forces to 'protect' ourselves from a Second World country of, as yet, no danger to anyone except weak neighbors along its borders.

In my review of Wilson's polemic *(Book Week*, November 3, 1963) I wrote: 'In public services, we lag behind all the industrialized nations of the West, preferring that the public money go not to the people but to big business. The result is a unique society in which we have free enterprise for the poor and socialism for the rich.'

It should be noted – but seldom is – that the Depression did not end with the New Deal of 1933–40. In fact, it flared up again, worse than ever, in 1939 and 1940. Then, when FDR spent some $20 billion on defense (1941), the Depression was over and Lord Keynes was a hero. This relatively small injection of public money into the system reduced unemployment to 8 percent and, not unnaturally, impressed the country's postwar managers: if you want to avoid depression, spend money on war. No one told them that the same money spent on the country's infrastructure would have saved us debt, grief, blood.

What now seems to us as Wilson's rather dizzy otherworldly approach to paying taxes is, in the context of his lifetime, reasonable. In 1939, only 4 million tax returns were filed: less than 10 percent of the workforce. According to Richard Polenberg, 'By the summer of 1943, nearly all Americans paid taxes out of their weekly earnings, and most were current in their payments ... [And thus] a foundation for the modern tax structure had been erected.' Then some unsung genius thought up the withholding tax, and all the folks were well and truly locked in. Wilson knew none of this. But he had figured out the causal link between income tax and cold war.

> The truth is that the people of the United States are at the
> present time dominated and driven by two kinds of
> officially propagated fear: fear of the Soviet Union and fear
> of the income tax. These two terrors have been adjusted so
> as to complement one another and thus to keep the citizen
> of our free society under the strain of a double pressure
> from which he finds himself unable to escape – like the
> man in the old Western story, who, chased into a narrow
> ravine by a buffalo, is confronted with a grizzly bear. If we
> fail to accept the tax, the Russian buffalo will butt and
> trample us, and if we try to defy the tax, the federal bear
> will crush us.

At the time the original North American Treaty Organization was created, only the Augustus *manqué* de Gaulle got the point to what we were doing; he took France out of our Cosa Nostra and developed his own atomic bomb. But France was still very much linked to the imperium. Through the CIA and other secret forces, political control was exerted within the empire, not only driving the British Labour Prime Minister Harold Wilson around a bend too far but preventing Italy from ever having a cohesive government by not allowing the 'historic compromise' – a government of Christian Democrats and Communists – to take place. The Soviets, always reactive, promptly cracked down on their client states Czechoslovakia, Hungary, East Germany; and a wall went up in Berlin, to spite their face. From 1950 to 1990, Europe was dangerously divided; and armed to the teeth. But as American producers of weapons were never richer, all was well with their world.

At Yalta, Roosevelt wanted to break up the European colonial empires, particularly that of the French. Of Indochina he said, 'France has milked it for a hundred years.' For the time being, he proposed a UN trusteeship. Then he died. Unlike Roosevelt, Truman was not a philatelist. Had he been a stamp collector, he might have known where the various countries in the world were and who lived in them.

But like every good American, Truman knew he hated Communism. He also hated socialism, which may or may not have been the same thing. No one seemed quite sure. Yet as early as the American election of 1848, socialism – imported by comical German immigrants with noses always in books – was an ominous specter, calculated to derange a raw capitalist society with labor unions, health care, and other Devil's work still being fiercely resisted a century and a half later. In 1946, when Ho Chi Minh asked the United States to take Indochina under its wing, Truman said, No way. You're some kind of Fu Manchu Communist – the worst. In August 1945, Truman told de Gaulle that the French could return to Indochina: we were no longer FDR anti-imperialists. As Ho had his northern republic, the French installed Bao Dai in the south. February 1, 1950, the State Department reported, 'The choice confronting the United States is to support the French in Indochina or face the extension of Communism over the remainder of the continental area of South-east Asia and, possibly, further westward.' Thus, without shepherds or even a napalm star, the domino theory was born in a humble State Department manger. On May 8, 1950, Acheson recommended economic and military aid to the French in Vietnam. By 1955, the U.S. was paying 40 percent of the French cost of war. For a quarter-century, the

United States was to fight in Vietnam because our ignorant leaders and their sharp-eyed financiers never realized that the game, at best, is always chess and never dominoes.

But nothing ever stays the same. During the last days of the waning moon, a haphazard Western European economic union was cobbled together; then, as the Soviet Union abruptly let go its empire, the two Germanys that we had so painstakingly kept apart reunited. Washington was suddenly adrift, and in the sky the moon of empire paused. Neither Reagan nor Bush had much knowledge of history or geography. Nevertheless, orders still kept coming from the White House. But they were less and less heeded because everyone knows that the Oval One has a bank overdraft of $5 trillion and he can no longer give presents to good clients or wage war without first passing the hat to the Germans and Japanese, as he was obliged to do when it came time to sponsor CNN's light show in the Persian Gulf. Gradually, it is now becoming evident to even the most distracted funster that there is no longer any need for NATO, because there is no enemy. One might say there never really was one when NATO was started, but, over the years, we did succeed in creating a pretty dangerous Soviet Union, a fun-house-mirror version of ourselves. Although the United States may yet, in support of Israel, declare war on one billion Muslims, the Europeans will stay out. They recall 1529, when the Turks besieged Vienna not as obliging guest workers but as world conquerors. Never again.

In the wake of the Madrid NATO summit, it is time for the United States to step away from Europe – gracefully. Certainly the Europeans think it is time for us to go, as their disdainful remarks at Denver betrayed, particularly when they were warned not to walk more than a block or two from their hotels for fear of being robbed, maimed, murdered. Yet why do we persist in holding onto empire? *Cherchez la monnaie*, as the clever French say. Ever since 1941, when Roosevelt got us out of the Depression by pumping federal money into rearming, war or the threat of war has been the principal engine to our society. Now the war is over. Or is it? Can we *afford* to give up our – well, cozy unremitting war? Why not – ah, the brilliance, the simplicity! – instead of shrinking, *expand* our phantom empire in Europe by popping everyone into NATO? No reason to have any particular enemy, though, who knows, if sufficiently goaded, Russia might again be persuaded to play Great Satan in our somewhat dusty chamber of horrors.

With an expanded NATO, our armsmakers – if not workers – are in for a bonanza. As it is, our sales of weapons were up 23 percent last year, to $11.3 billion in orders; meanwhile, restrictions on sales to Latin America are now being lifted. Chile, ever menaced by Ecuador, may soon buy as many as twenty-four American-made F-16 jet fighters. But an expanded NATO is the beauty part. Upon joining NATO, the lucky new club member is obliged to buy expensive weapons from the likes of Lockheed Martin, recently merged with Northrop Grumman. Since the new members have precarious economies – and the old ones are not exactly booming – the American taxpayer, a wan goose that lays few eggs, will have to borrow ever more money to foot the bill, which the Congressional Budget Office says should come to $125 billion over fifteen years with the U.S. paying $19 billion. Yeltsin correctly sees this as a hostile move against Russia, not to mention an expensive renewal of the cold war, while our very own Delphic oracle, the ancient Janus-like mandarin George Kennan, has said that such an expansion could 'inflame nationalistic anti-Western and militaristic tendencies in Russian opinion.'

Where once we were told it was better to be dead than Red, now we will be told that it is better to be broke than – what? – slaves of the Knights of Malta? Meanwhile, conservative think tanks (their salaries paid directly or indirectly by interested conglomerates) are issuing miles of boilerplate about the necessity of securing the Free World from enemies; and Lockheed Martin lobbies individual senators, having spent (officially) $2.3 million for congressional and presidential candidates in the 1996 election.

For those interested in just how ruinous NATO membership will be for the new members, there is the special report *NATO Expansion: Time to Reconsider*, by the British American Security Information Council and the Centre for European Security and Disarmament. Jointly published November 25, 1996, the authors regard the remilitarization of the region between Berlin and Moscow as lunacy geopolitically and disastrous economically. Hungary is now aiming at a 22 percent increase in military spending this year. The Czechs and the Poles mean to double their defense spending. The world is again at risk as our 'bipartisan' rulers continue loyally to serve those who actually elect them – Lockheed Martin Northrop Grumman, Boeing, McDonnell Douglas, General Electric, Mickey Mouse, and on and on. Meanwhile, as I write, the U.S. is secretly building a new generation of nuclear weapons like the W-88 Trident missile Cost: $4 billion a year.

There comes a moment when empires cease to exert energy and become symbolic – or existential, as we used to say back in the Forties. The current wrangling over NATO demonstrates what a quandary a symbolic empire is in when it lacks the mind, much less the resources, to impose its hegemony upon former client states. At the end, entropy gets us all. Fun house falls down. Fairground's a parking lot. 'So I awoke, and behold it was a dream.' *Pilgrim's Progress* again. But not quite yet.

It is a truism that generals are always ready to fight the last war. The anachronistic rhetoric at Madrid in July, if ever acted upon, would certainly bring on the next? – last? – big war, if only because, in Francis Bacon's words, 'Upon the breaking and shivering of a great state and empire, you may be sure to have wars.'

Happily, in the absence of money and common will nothing much will probably happen. Meanwhile, there is a new better world ready to be born. The optimum economic unit in the world is now the city-state. Thanks to technology, everyone knows or can know something about everyone else on the planet. The message now pounding over the Internet is the irrelevancy, not to mention sheer danger, of the traditional nation-state, much less empire. Despite currency confusions, Southeast Asia leads the way while the warlords at Peking not only are tolerating vigorous industrial semi-autonomies like Shanghai but also may have an ongoing paradigm in Hong Kong. We do not like the way Singapore is run (hardly our business), but it is, relatively speaking, a greater commercial success than the United States, which might prosper, once the empire's put out of its misery, in smaller units on the Swiss cantonal model: Spanish-speaking Catholic regions, Asian Confucian regions, consensually united mixed regions with, here and there, city-states like New York–Boston or Silicon Valley.

In the next century, barring accident, the common market in Europe will evolve not so much into a union of ancient blood-stained states as a mosaic of homogenous regions and city-states like Milan, say, each loosely linked in trade with a clearinghouse information center at Brussels to orchestrate finance and trade and the policing of cartels. Basques, Bretons, Walloons, Scots who want to be rid of onerous nation-states should be let go in order to pursue and even – why not? – overtake happiness, the goal, or so we Americans have always pretended to believe, of the human enterprise.

On that predictably sententious American note, O movers and

shakers of the month, let us return to 'the wilderness of this world,' recalling the Hippocratic oath, which enjoins doctors: 'Above all do no harm.' Hippocrates also wrote, O moved and shaken, 'Life is short, but the art is long, the opportunity fleeting, the experiment perilous, the judgment difficult.'

Vanity Fair
November 1997

Shredding the Bill of Rights

Most Americans of a certain age can recall exactly where they were and what they were doing on October 20, 1964, when word came that Herbert Hoover was dead. The heart and mind of a nation stopped. But how many recall when and how they first became aware that one or another of the Bill of Rights had expired? For me, it was sometime in 1960 at a party in Beverly Hills that I got the bad news from the constitutionally cheery actor Cary Grant. He had just flown in from New York. He had, he said, picked up his ticket at an airline counter in that magical old-world airport, Idlewild, whose very name reflected our condition. 'There were these lovely girls behind the counter, and they were delighted to help me, or so they said. I signed some autographs. Then I asked one of them for my tickets. Suddenly she was very solemn. "Do you have any identification?" she asked.' (Worldly friends tell me that the 'premise' of this story is now the basis of a series of TV commercials for Visa, unseen by me.) I would be exaggerating if I felt the chill in the air that long-ago Beverly Hills evening.

Actually, we simply laughed. But I did, for just an instant, wonder if the future had tapped a dainty foot on our mass grave.

Curiously enough, it was Grant again who bore, as lightly as ever, the news that privacy itself hangs by a gossamer thread. 'A friend in London rang me this morning,' he said. This was June 4, 1963. 'Usually we have code names, but this time he forgot. So after he asked for me I said into the receiver, "All right. St. Louis, off the line. You, too, Milwaukee," and so on. The operators love listening in. Anyway, after we talked business, he said, "So what's the latest Hollywood gossip?" And I said, "Well, Lana Turner is still having an affair with that black baseball pitcher." One of the operators on the line gave a terrible cry, "Oh, no!"'

Innocent days. Today, as media and Congress thunder their anthem, 'Twinkle, twinkle, little Starr, how we wonder what you are,' the current president is assumed to have no right at all to privacy because, you see, it's really about sex, not truth, a permanent non-starter in political life. Where Grant's name assured him an admiring audience of telephone operators, the rest of us were usually ignored. That was then. Today, in the all-out, never-to-be-won twin wars on Drugs and Terrorism, 2 million telephone conversations a year are intercepted by law-enforcement officials. As for that famous 'workplace' to which so many Americans are assigned by necessity, 'the daily abuse of civil liberties . . . is a national disgrace,' according to the American Civil Liberties Union in a 1996 report.

Among the report's findings, between 1990 and 1996, the number of workers under electronic surveillance increased from 8 million per year to more than 30 million. Simultaneously, employers eavesdrop on an estimated 400 million telephone conversations a year – something like 750 a minute. In 1990, major companies subjected 38 percent of their employees to urine tests for drugs. By 1996, more than 70 percent were thus interfered with. Recourse to law has not been encouraging. In fact, the California Supreme Court has upheld the right of public employers to drug-test not only those employees who have been entrusted with flying jet aircraft or protecting our borders from Panamanian imperialism but also those who simply mop the floors. The court also ruled that governments can screen applicants for drugs and alcohol. This was inspired by the actions of the city-state of Glendale, California, which wanted to test all employees due for promotion. Suit was brought against Glendale on the ground that it was violating the Fourth Amendment's protection against 'unreasonable searches and seizures.' Glendale's policy was upheld by the California Supreme Court, but Justice Stanley Mosk wrote a dissent: 'Drug testing represents a significant additional invasion of those applicants' basic rights to privacy and dignity . . . and the city has not carried its considerable burden of showing that such an invasion is justified in the case of all applicants offered employment.'

In the last year or so I have had two Cary Grant-like revelations, considerably grimmer than what went on in the good old days of relative freedom from the state. A well-known acting couple and their two small children came to see me one summer. Photos were taken of their four-year-old and six-year-old cavorting bare in the sea. When the couple got home to Manhattan, the father dropped the negatives off at a drugstore to be printed. Later, a frantic call from his fortunately friendly druggist: 'If I print these I've got to report you and you could get five years in the slammer for kiddie porn.' The war on kiddie porn is now getting into high gear, though I was once assured by Wardell Pomeroy, Alfred Kinsey's colleague in sex research, that pedophilia was barely a blip on the statistical screen, somewhere down there with farm lads and their animal friends.

It has always been a mark of American freedom that unlike

countries under constant Napoleonic surveillance, we are not obliged to carry identification to show to curious officials and pushy police. But now, due to Terrorism, every one of us is stopped at airports and obliged to show an ID which must include a mug shot (something, as Allah knows, no terrorist would ever dare fake). In Chicago after an interview with Studs Terkel, I complained that since I don't have a driver's license, I must carry a passport in my own country as if I were a citizen of the old Soviet Union. Terkel has had the same trouble. 'I was asked for my ID – with photo – at this Southern airport, and I said I didn't have anything except the local newspaper with a big picture of me on the front page, which I showed them, but they said that that was not an ID. Finally, they got tired of me and let me on the plane.'

Lately, I have been going through statistics about terrorism (usually direct responses to crimes our government has committed against foreigners – although, recently, federal crimes against our own people are increasing). Only twice in twelve years has an American commercial plane been destroyed in flight by terrorists; neither originated in the United States. To prevent, however, a repetition of these two crimes, hundreds of millions of travelers must now be subjected to searches, seizures, delays.

The state of the art of citizen-harassment is still in its infancy. Nevertheless, new devices, at ever greater expense, are coming onto the market – and, soon, to an airport near you – including the dream machine of every horny schoolboy. The 'Body Search' Contraband Detection System, created by American Science and Engineering, can 'X-ray' through clothing to reveal the naked body, whose enlarged image can then be cast onto a screen for prurient analysis. The proud manufacturer boasts that the picture is so clear that even navels, unless packed with cocaine and taped over, can be seen winking at the voyeurs. The system also has what is called, according to an ACLU report, 'a joystick-driven Zoom Option' that allows the operator to enlarge interesting portions of the image. During all this, the victim remains, as AS&E proudly notes, fully clothed. Orders for this machine should be addressed to the Reverend Pat Robertson and will be filled on a first-come, first-served basis, while the proud new owner of 'Body Search' will be automatically included in the FBI's database of Sexual Degenerates – Class B. Meanwhile, in February 1997, the 'Al' Gore Commission called for the acquisition of fifty-four high-tech bomb-detection machines known as the CTX 5000, a baggage scanner that is a bargain at a million dollars and will cost only $100,000 a year to service. Unfortunately, the CTX 5000 scans baggage at the rate of 250 per hour, which would mean perhaps a thousand are needed to 'protect' passengers at major airports from those two putative terrorists who might – or might not – strike again in the next twelve years, as they twice did in the last twelve years. Since the present scanning system seems fairly effective, why subject passengers to hours of delay, not to mention more than $54 million worth of equipment?

Presently, somewhat confused guidelines exist so that airline personnel can recognize at a glance someone who fits the 'profile' of a potential terrorist. Obviously, anyone of mildly dusky hue who is wearing a fez gets busted on the spot. For those terrorists who do not seem to fit the 'profile,' relevant government agencies have come up with the following behavioral tips that should quickly reveal the evil-doer. A devious drug smuggler is apt to be the very first person off the plane unless, of course, he is truly devious and chooses to be the last one off. Debonair master criminals often opt for a middle position. Single blonde young women are often used, unwittingly, to carry bombs or drugs given them by Omar Sharif look-alikes in sinister Casbahs. Upon arrival in freedom's land, great drug-sniffing dogs will be turned loose on them; unfortunately, these canine detectives often mistakenly target as drug carriers women that are undergoing their menstrual period: the sort of icebreaker that often leads to merry laughter all around the customs area. Apparently one absolutely sure behavioral giveaway is undue nervousness on the part of a passenger though, again, the master criminal will sometimes appear to be too much at ease. In any case, whatever mad rule of thumb is applied, a customs official has every right to treat anyone as a criminal on no evidence at all; to seize and to search without, of course, due process of law.

Drugs. If they did not exist our governors would have invented them in order to prohibit them and so make much of the population vulnerable to arrest, imprisonment, seizure of property, and so on. In 1970, I wrote in *The New York Times*, of all uncongenial places,

> It is possible to stop most drug addiction in the United States within a very short time. Simply make all drugs available and sell them at cost. Label each drug with a precise description of what effect – good or bad – the drug will have on the taker. This will require heroic honesty. Don't say that marijuana is addictive or dangerous when it is neither, as millions of people know – unlike 'speed,' which kills most unpleasantly, or heroin, which can be addictive and difficult to kick. Along with exhortation and warning, it might be good for our citizens to recall (or learn for the first time) that the United States was the creation of men who believed that each person has the right to do what he wants with his own life as long as he does not interfere with his neighbors' pursuit of happiness

(that his neighbor's idea of happiness is persecuting others does confuse matters a bit).

I suspect that what I wrote twenty-eight years ago is every bit as unacceptable now as it was then, with the added problem of irritable ladies who object to my sexism in putting the case solely in masculine terms, as did the sexist founders.

I also noted the failure of the prohibition of alcohol from 1919 to 1933. And the crime wave that Prohibition set in motion so like the one today since 'both the Bureau of Narcotics and the Mafia want strong laws against the sale and use of drugs because if drugs are sold at cost there would be no money in them for anyone.' Will anything sensible be done? I wondered. 'The American people are as devoted to the idea of sin and its punishment as they are to making money – and fighting drugs is nearly as big a business as pushing them. Since the combination of sin and money is irresistible (particularly to the professional politician), the situation will only grow worse.' I suppose, if nothing else, I was a pretty good prophet.

The media constantly deplore the drug culture and, variously, blame foreign countries like Colombia for obeying that iron law of supply and demand to which we have, as a notion and as a nation, sworn eternal allegiance. We also revel in military metaphors. Czars lead our armies into wars against drug dealers and drug takers. So great is this permanent emergency that we can no longer afford such frills as habeas corpus and due process of law. In 1989 the former drug czar and TV talk-show fool, William Bennett, suggested de jure as well as de facto abolition of habeas corpus in 'drug' cases as well as (I am not inventing this) public beheadings of drug dealers. A year later, Ayatollah Bennett declared, 'I find no merit in the [drug] legalizers' case. The simple fact is that drug use is wrong. And the moral argument, in the end, is the most compelling argument.' Of course, what this dangerous comedian thinks is moral James Madison and the Virginia statesman and Rights-man George Mason would have thought dangerous nonsense, particularly when his 'morality' abolishes their gift to all of us, the Bill of Rights. But Bennett is not alone in his madness. A special assistant to the President on drug abuse declared, in 1984, 'You cannot let one drug come in and say, "Well, this drug is all right." We've drawn the line. There's no such thing as a soft drug.' There goes Tylenol-3, containing codeine. Who would have thought that age-old palliatives could, so easily, replace the only national religion that the United States has ever truly had, anti-Communism?

On June 10, 1998, a few brave heretical voices were raised in *The New York Times*, on an inner page. Under the heading BIG NAMES SIGN LETTER CRITICIZING WAR ON DRUGS. A billionaire named 'George Soros has amassed signatures of hundreds of prominent people around the world on a letter asserting that the global war on drugs is causing more harm than drug abuse itself.' Apparently, the Lindesmith Center in New York, funded by Soros, had taken out an ad in the *Times*, thereby, expensively, catching an editor's eye. The signatories included a former secretary of state and a couple of ex-senators, but though the ad was intended to coincide with a United Nations special session on Satanic Substances, it carried no weight with one General Barry McCaffrey, President Clinton's war director, who called the letter 'a 1950s perception,' whatever that may mean. After all, drug use in the Fifties was less than it is now after four decades of relentless warfare. Curiously, the *New York Times* story made the signatories seem to be few and eccentric while the Manchester *Guardian* in England reported that among the 'international signatories are the former prime minister of the Netherlands . . . the former presidents of Bolivia and

Colombia . . . three [U.S.] federal judges . . . senior clerics, former drugs squad officers . . .' But the *Times* always knows what's fit to print.

It is ironic – to use the limpest adjective – that a government as spontaneously tyrannous and callous as ours should, over the years, have come to care so much about our health as it endlessly tests and retests commercial drugs available in other lands while arresting those who take 'hard' drugs on the parental ground that they are bad for the user's health. One is touched by their concern – touched and dubious. After all, these same compassionate guardians of our well-being have sternly, year in and year out, refused to allow us to have what every other First World country simply takes for granted, a national health service.

When Mr. and Mrs. Clinton came up to Washington, green as grass from the Arkansas hills and all pink and aglow from swift-running whitewater creeks, they tried to give the American people such a health system, a small token in exchange for all that tax money which had gone for 'defense' against an enemy that had wickedly folded when our back was turned. At the first suggestion that it was time for us to join the civilized world, there began a vast conspiracy to stop any form of national health care. It was hardly just the 'right wing,' as Mrs. Clinton suggested. Rather, the insurance and pharmaceutical companies combined with elements of the American Medical Association to destroy forever any notion that we be a country that provides anything for its citizens in the way of health care.

One of the problems of a society as tightly controlled as ours is that we get so little information about what those of our fellow citizens whom we will never know or see are actually thinking and feeling. This seems a paradox when most politics today involves minute-by-minute polltaking on what looks to be every conceivable subject, but, as politicians and pollsters know, it's how the question is asked that determines the response. Also, there are vast areas, like rural America, that are an unmapped ultima Thule to those who own the corporations that own the media that spend billions of dollars to take polls in order to elect their lawyers to high office.

Ruby Ridge. Waco. Oklahoma City. Three warning bells from a heartland that most of us who are urban dwellers know little or nothing about. Cause of rural dwellers' rage? In 1996 there were 1,471 mergers of American corporations in the interest of 'consolidation.' This was the largest number of mergers in American history, and the peak of a trend that had been growing in the world of agriculture since the late 1970s. One thing shared by the victims at Ruby Ridge and Waco, and Timothy McVeigh, who may have committed mass murder in their name at Oklahoma City, was the conviction that the government of the United States is their implacable enemy and that they can only save themselves by hiding out in the wilderness, or by joining a commune centered on a messianic figure, or, as revenge for the cold-blooded federal murder of two members of the Weaver family at Ruby Ridge, blow up the building that contained the bureau responsible for the murders.

To give the media their due, they have been uncommonly generous with us on the subject of the religious and political beliefs of rural dissidents. There is a neo-Nazi 'Aryan Nations.' There are Christian fundamentalists called 'Christian Identity,' also known as 'British Israelism.' All of this biblically inspired nonsense has taken deepest root in those dispossessed of their farmland in the last generation. Needless to say, Christian demagogues fan the flames of race and sectarian hatred on television and, illegally, pour church money into political campaigns.

Conspiracy theories now blossom in the wilderness like night-blooming dementia praecox, and those in thrall to them are mocked invariably by the . . . by the actual conspirators. Joel Dyer, in *Harvest of Rage: Why Oklahoma City Is Only the Beginning*, has discovered some very real conspiracies out there, but the conspirators are old hands at deflecting attention from themselves. Into drugs? Well, didn't you know Queen Elizabeth II is overall director of the world drug trade (if only poor Lilibet had had the foresight in these republican times!). They tell us that the Trilateral Commission is a world-Communist conspiracy headed by the Rockefellers. Actually, the commission is excellent shorthand to show how the Rockefellers draw together politicians and academics-on-the-make to serve their business interests in government and out. Whoever it was who got somebody like Lyndon LaRouche to say that this Rockefeller Cosa Nostra is really a Communist front was truly inspired.

But Dyer has unearthed a genuine ongoing conspiracy that affects everyone in the United States. Currently, a handful of agro-conglomerates are working to drive America's remaining small farmers off their land by systematically paying them less for their produce than it costs to grow, thus forcing them to get loans from the conglomerates' banks, assume mortgages, undergo foreclosures and the sale of land to corporate-controlled agribusiness. But is this really a conspiracy or just the Darwinian workings of an efficient marketplace? There is, for once, a smoking gun in the form of a blueprint describing how best to rid the nation of small farmers. Dyer writes: 'In 1962, the Committee for Economic Development comprised approximately seventy-five of the nation's most powerful corporate executives. They represented not only the food industry but also oil and gas, insurance, investment and retail industries. Almost all groups that stood to gain from consolidation were represented on that committee. Their report [*An Adaptive*

Program for Agriculture] outlined a plan to eliminate farmers and farms. It was detailed and well thought out.' Simultaneously, 'as early as 1964, Congressmen were being told by industry giants like Pillsbury, Swift, General Foods, and Campbell Soup that the biggest problem in agriculture was too many farmers.' Good psychologists, the CEOs had noted that farm children, if sent to college, seldom return to the family farm. Or as one famous economist said to a famous senator who was complaining about jet lag on a night flight from New York to London, 'Well, it sure beats farming.' The committee got the government to send farm children to college. Predictably, most did not come back. Government then offered to help farmers relocate in other lines of work, allowing their land to be consolidated in ever vaster combines owned by fewer and fewer corporations.

So a conspiracy had been set in motion to replace the Jeffersonian ideal of a nation whose backbone was the independent farm family with a series of agribusiness monopolies where, Dyer writes, 'only five to eight multinational companies have, for all intents and purposes, been the sole purchasers and transporters not only of the American grain supply but that of the entire world.' By 1982 'these companies controlled 96 percent of U.S. wheat exports, 95 percent of U.S. corn exports,' and so on through the busy aisles of chic Gristedes, homely Ralph's, sympathetic Piggly Wigglys.

Has consolidation been good for the customers? By and large, no. Monopolies allow for no bargains, nor do they have to fuss too much about quality because we have no alternative to what they offer. Needless to say, they are hostile to labor unions and indifferent to working conditions for the once independent farmers, now ill-paid employees. For those of us who grew up in the prewar United States there was the genuine ham sandwich. Since consolidation, ham has been so rubberized that it tastes of nothing at all while its texture is like rosy plastic. Why? In the great hogariums a hog remains in one place, on its feet, for life. Since it does not root about – or even move – it builds up no natural resistance to disease. This means a great deal of drugs are pumped into the prisoner's body until its death and transfiguration as inedible ham.

By and large, the Sherman antitrust laws are long since gone. Today three companies control 80 percent of the total beef-packing market. How does this happen? Why do dispossessed farmers have no congressional representatives to turn to? Why do consumers get stuck with mysterious pricings of products that in themselves are inferior to those of an earlier time? Dyer's answer is simple but compelling. Through their lobbyists, the corporate executives who drew up the 'adaptive program' for agriculture now own or rent or simply intimidate Congresses and presidents while the courts are presided over by their former lobbyists, an endless supply of white-collar servants since two-thirds of all the lawyers on our small planet are Americans. Finally, the people at large are not represented in government while corporations are, lavishly.

What is to be done? Only one thing will work, in Dyer's view: electoral finance reform. But those who benefit from the present system will never legislate themselves out of power. So towns and villages continue to decay between the Canadian and the Mexican borders, and the dispossessed rural population despairs or rages. Hence, the apocalyptic tone of a number of recent nonreligious works of journalism and analysis that currently record, with fascinated horror, the alienation of group after group within the United States.

Since the *Encyclopaedia Britannica* is Britannica and not America, it is not surprising that its entry for 'Bill of Rights, United States' is a mere column in length, the same as its neighbor on the page 'Bill of Sale,' obviously a more poignant document to the island compilers. Even so, they do tell us that the roots of our rights are in Magna Carta and that the genesis of the Bill of Rights that was added as ten amendments to our Constitution in 1791 was largely the handiwork of James Madison, who, in turn, echoed Virginia's 1776 Declaration of Rights. At first, these ten amendments were applicable to American citizens only as citizens of the entire United States and not as Virginians or as New Yorkers, where state laws could take precedence according to 'states' rights,' as acknowledged in the tenth and last of the original amendments. It was not until 1868 that the Fourteenth Amendment forbade the states to make laws counter to the original bill. Thus every United States person, in his home state, was guaranteed freedom of 'speech and press, and the right to assembly and to petition as well as freedom from a national religion.' Apparently, it was Charlton Heston who brought the Second Amendment, along with handguns and child-friendly Uzis, down from Mount DeMille. Originally, the right for citizen militias to bear arms was meant to discourage a standing federal or state army and all the mischief that an armed state might cause people who wanted to live not under the shadow of a gun but peaceably on their own atop some sylvan Ruby Ridge.

Currently, the Fourth Amendment is in the process of disintegration, out of 'military necessity' – the constitutional language used by Lincoln to wage civil war, suspend habeas corpus, shut down newspapers, and free Southern slaves. The Fourth Amendment guarantees 'the right of the people to be secure in their persons, houses, papers, and effects, against unreasonable searches and seizures, shall not be violated, and no Warrants shall issue, but upon probable cause, supported by Oath or affirmation, and particularly describing the place to be searched, and the persons or things to be seized.' The Fourth is the people's principal defense against totalitarian government; it is a defense that is now daily breached both by deed and law.

In James Bovard's 1994 book, *Lost Rights*, the author has assembled a great deal of material on just what our law enforcers are up to in the never-to-be-won wars against Drugs and Terrorism, as they do daily battle with the American people in their homes and cars, on buses and planes, indeed, wherever they can get at them, by hook or by crook or by sting. Military necessity is a bit too highbrow a concept for today's federal and local officials to justify their midnight smashing in of doors, usually without warning or warrant, in order to terrorize the unlucky residents. These unlawful attacks and seizures are often justified by the possible existence of a flush toilet on the fingered premises. (If the warriors against drugs don't take drug fiends absolutely by surprise, the fiends will flush away the evidence.) This is intolerable for those eager to keep us sin-free and obedient. So in the great sign of Sir Thomas Crapper's homely invention, they suspend the Fourth, and conquer.

Nineteen ninety-two. Bridgeport, Connecticut. *The Hartford Courant* reported that the local Tactical Narcotics Team routinely devastated homes and businesses they 'searched.' Plainclothes policemen burst in on a Jamaican grocer and restaurant owner with the cheery cry 'Stick up, niggers. Don't move.' Shelves were swept clear. Merchandise ruined. 'They never identified themselves as police,' the *Courant* noted. Although they found nothing but a registered gun, the owner was arrested and charged with 'interfering with an arrest' and so booked. A judge later dismissed the case. Bovard reports, 'In 1991, in Garland, Texas, police dressed in black and wearing black ski-masks burst into a trailer, waved guns in the air and kicked down the bedroom door where Kenneth Baulch had been sleeping next to his seventeen-month-old son. A policeman claimed that Baulch posed a deadly threat because he held an ashtray in his left hand, which explained why he shot Baulch in the back and killed him. (A police internal investigation found no wrongdoing by the officer.) In March 1992, a police SWAT team killed Robin Pratt, an Everett, Washington, mother, in a no-knock raid carrying out an arrest warrant for her husband. (Her husband was later released after the allegations upon which the arrest warrant were based turned out to be false.)' Incidentally, this KGB tactic – hold someone for a crime, but let him off if he then names someone else for a bigger crime, also known as Starr justice – often leads to false, even random allegations which ought not to be acted upon so murderously without a bit of homework first. *The Seattle Times* describes Robin Pratt's last moments. She was with her six-year-old daughter and five-year-old niece when the police broke in. As the bravest storm trooper, named Aston, approached her, gun drawn, the other police shouted, '"Get down," and she started to crouch onto her knees. She looked up at Aston and said, "Please don't hurt my children . . ." Aston had his gun pointed at her and fired, shooting her in the neck. According to [the Pratt family attorney John] Muenster, she was alive another one to two minutes but could not speak because her throat had been destroyed by the bullet. She was handcuffed, lying face down.' Doubtless Aston was fearful of a divine resurrection; and vengeance. It is no secret that American police rarely observe the laws of the land when out wilding with each other, and as any candid criminal judge will tell you, perjury is often their native tongue in court.

The IRS has been under some scrutiny lately for violations not only of the Fourth but of the Fifth Amendment. The Fifth requires a grand-jury indictment in prosecutions for major crimes. It also provides that no person shall be compelled to testify against himself, forbids the taking of life, liberty, or property without due process of law, or the taking of private property for public use without compensation.

Over the years, however, the ever secretive IRS has been seizing property right and left without so much as a postcard to the nearest grand jury, while due process of law is not even a concept in their single-minded pursuit of loot. Bovard notes:

> Since 1980, the number of levies – IRS seizures of bank accounts and pay checks – has increased fourfold, reaching 3,253,000 in 1992. The General Accounting Office (GAO) estimated in 1990 that the IRS imposes over 50,000 incorrect or unjustified levies on citizens and businesses per year. The GAO estimated that almost 6 percent of IRS levies on business were incorrect . . . The IRS also imposes almost one and a half million liens each year, an increase of over 200 percent since 1980. *Money* magazine conducted a survey in 1990 of 156 taxpayers who had IRS liens imposed on their property and found that 35 percent of the taxpayers had never received a thirty-day warning notice from the IRS of an intent to impose a lien and that some first learned of the liens when the magazine contacted them.

The current Supreme Court has shown little interest in curbing so powerful and clandestine a federal agency as it routinely disobeys the Fourth, Fifth, and Fourteenth Amendments. Of course, this particular court is essentially authoritarian and revels in the state's exercise of power while its livelier members show great wit when it comes to consulting Ouija boards in order to discern exactly what the founders originally had in mind, ignoring just how clearly Mason, Madison, and company spelled out such absolutes as you can't grab someone's property without first going to a grand jury and finding him guilty of a crime as law requires. In these matters, sacred original intent is so clear that the Court prefers to look elsewhere for its amusement. Lonely voices in Congress are sometimes heard on the subject. In 1993, Senator David Pryor thought it would be nice if the IRS were to notify credit agencies once proof was established that the agency wrongfully attached a lien on a taxpayer's property, destroying his future credit. The IRS got whiny. Such an onerous requirement would be too much work for its exhausted employees.

Since the U.S. statutes that deal with tax regulations comprise some 9,000 pages, even tax experts tend to foul up, and it is possible for any Inspector Javert at the IRS to find flawed just about any conclusion as to what Family X owes. But, in the end, it is not so much a rogue bureau that is at fault as it is the system of taxation as imposed by key members of Congress in order to exempt their friends and financial donors from taxation. Certainly, the IRS itself has legitimate cause for complaint against its nominal masters in Congress. The IRS's director of taxpayer services, Robert LeBaube, spoke out in 1989: 'Since 1976 there have been 138 public laws modifying the Internal Revenue Code. Since the Tax Reform Act of 1986 there have been thirteen public laws changing the code, and in 1988 alone there were seven public laws affecting the code.' As Bovard notes but does not explain, 'Tax law is simply the latest creative interpretation by government officials of the mire of tax legislation Congress has enacted. IRS officials can take five, seven, or more years to write the regulations to implement a new tax law – yet Congress routinely changes the law before new regulations are promulgated. Almost all tax law is provisional – either waiting to be revised according to the last tax bill passed, or already proposed for change in the next tax bill.'

What is this great busyness and confusion all about? Well, corporations send their lawyers to Congress to make special laws that will exempt their corporate profits from unseemly taxation: this is done by ever more complex – even impenetrable – tax laws which must always be provisional as there is always bound to be a new corporation requiring a special exemption in the form of a private bill tacked onto the Arbor Day Tribute. Senators who save corporations millions in tax money will not need to spend too much time on the telephone begging for contributions when it is time for him – or, yes, her – to run again. Unless – the impossible dream – the cost of elections is reduced by 90 percent, with no election lasting longer than eight weeks. Until national TV is provided free for national candidates and local TV for local candidates (the way civilized countries do it), there will never be tax reform. Meanwhile, the moles at the IRS, quite aware of the great untouchable corruption of their congressional masters, pursue helpless citizens and so demoralize the state.

It is nicely apt that the word 'terrorist' (according to the *OED*) should have been coined during the French Revolution to describe 'an adherent or supporter of the Jacobins, who advocated and practised methods of partisan repression and bloodshed in the propagation of the principles of democracy and equality.' Although our rulers have revived the word to describe violent enemies of the United States, most of today's actual terrorists can be found within our own governments, federal, state, municipal. The Bureau of Alcohol, Tobacco, and Firearms (known as ATF), the Drug Enforcement Agency, FBI, IRS, etc., are so many Jacobins at war against the lives, freedom, and property of our citizens. The FBI slaughter of the innocents at Waco was a model Jacobin enterprise. A mildly crazed religious leader called David Koresh had started a commune with several hundred followers – men, women, and children. Koresh preached world's end. Variously, ATF and FBI found him an ideal enemy to persecute. He was accused of numerous unsubstantiated crimes, including this decade's favorite, pedophilia, and was never given the benefit of due process to determine his guilt or innocence. David Kopel and Paul H. Blackman have now written the best and most detailed account of the American government's current war on its unhappy citizenry in *No More Wacos: What's Wrong with Federal Law Enforcement and How to Fix It*.

They describe, first, the harassment of Koresh and his religious group, the Branch Davidians, minding the Lord's business in their commune; second, the demonizing of him in the media; third, the February 28, 1993, attack on the commune: seventy-six agents stormed the communal buildings that contained 127 men, women, and children. Four ATF agents and six Branch Davidians died. Koresh had been accused of possessing illegal firearms even though he had previously invited law-enforcement agents into the commune to look at his weapons and their registrations. Under the Freedom of Information Act, Kopel and Blackman have now discovered that, from the beginning of what would become a siege and then a 'dynamic entry' (military parlance for all-out firepower and slaughter), ATF had gone secretly to the U.S. Army for advanced training in terrorist attacks even though the Posse Comitatus Law of 1878 forbids the use of federal troops for civilian law enforcement. Like so many of our laws, in the interest of the war on Drugs, this law can be suspended if the army is requested by the Drug Law Enforcement Agency to fight sin. Koresh was secretly accused by ATF of producing methamphetamine that he was importing from nearby Mexico, 300 miles to the south. Mayday! The army must help out. They did, though the charges against drug-hating Koresh were untrue. The destruction of the Branch Davidians had now ceased to be a civil affair where the Constitution supposedly rules. Rather, it became a matter of grave military necessity: hence a CS-gas attack (a gas which the U.S. had just signed a treaty swearing never to use in war) on April 19, 1993, followed by tanks smashing holes in the buildings where twenty-seven children were at risk; and then a splendid fire that destroyed the commune and, in the process, the as yet uncharged, untried David Koresh. Attorney general Janet Reno took credit and 'blame,' comparing herself and the president to a pair of World War II generals who could not exercise constant oversight . . . the sort of statement World War II veterans recognize as covering your ass.

Anyway, Ms. Reno presided over the largest massacre of Americans by American Feds since 1890 and the fireworks at Wounded Knee. Eighty-two Branch Davidians died at Waco, including thirty women and twenty-five children. Will our Jacobins ever be defeated as the French ones were? Ah . . . The deliberate erasure of elements of the Bill of Rights (in law as opposed to in fact when the police choose to go on the rampage, breaking laws and heads) can be found in loony decisions by lower courts that the Supreme Court prefers not to conform with the Bill of Rights. It is well known that the Drug Enforcement Agency and the IRS are inveterate thieves of private property without due process of law or redress or reimbursement later for the person who has been robbed by the state but committed no crime. Currently, according to Kopel and Blackman, U.S. and some state laws go like this: whenever a police officer is permitted, with or without judicial approval, to investigate a potential crime, the officer may seize and keep as much property associated with the alleged criminal as the police officer considers appropriate. Although forfeiture is predicated

on the property's being used in a crime, there shall be no requirement that the owner be convicted of a crime. It shall be irrelevant
that the person was acquitted of the crime on which the seizure
was based, or was never charged with any offense. Plainly, Judge
Kafka was presiding in 1987 (*United States v. Sandini*) when
this deranged formula for theft by police was made law: 'The
innocence of the owner is irrelevant,' declared the court. 'It is
enough that the property was involved in a violation to which
forfeiture attaches.' Does this mean that someone who has committed no crime, but may yet someday, will be unable to get his
property back because *U.S. v. Sandini* also states firmly, 'The
burden of proof rests on the party alleging ownership'?

This sort of situation is particularly exciting for the woof-woof
brigade of police since, according to onetime attorney general
Richard Thornburgh, over 90 percent of all American paper currency contains drug residue; this means that anyone carrying, let us
say, a thousand dollars in cash will be found with 'drug money,'
which must be seized and taken away to be analyzed and, somehow, never returned to its owner if the clever policeman knows his
Sandini.

All across the country high-school athletes are singled out for
drug testing while random searches are carried out in the classroom. On March 8, 1991, according to Bovard, at the Sandburg
High School in Chicago, two teachers (their gender is not given so
mental pornographers can fill in their own details) spotted a six-
teen-year-old boy wearing sweatpants. Their four eyes glitteringly
alert, they cased his crotch, which they thought 'appeared to be
"too well endowed."' He was taken to a locker room and stripped
bare. No drugs were found, only a nonstandard scrotal sac. He was
let go as there is as yet no law penalizing a teenager for being
better hung than his teachers. The lad and his family sued. The
judge was unsympathetic. The teachers, he ruled, 'did all they

could to ensure that the plaintiff's privacy was not eroded.' Judge Kafka never sleeps.

Although drugs are immoral and must be kept from the young, thousands of schools pressure parents to give the drug Ritalin to any lively child who may, sensibly, show signs of boredom in his classroom. Ritalin renders the child docile if not comatose. Side effects? 'Stunted growth, facial tics, agitation and aggression, insomnia, appetite loss, headaches, stomach pains and seizures.' Marijuana would be far less harmful.

The bombing of the Alfred P. Murrah Federal Building in Oklahoma City was not unlike Pearl Harbor, a great shock to an entire nation and, one hopes, a sort of wake-up call to the American people that all is not well with us. As usual, the media responded in the only way they know how. Overnight, one Timothy McVeigh became the personification of evil. Of motiveless malice. There was the usual speculation about confederates. Grassy knollsters. But only one other maniac was named, Terry Nichols; he was found guilty of 'conspiring' with McVeigh, but he was not in on the slaughter itself.

A journalist, Richard A. Serrano, has just published *One of Ours: Timothy McVeigh and the Oklahoma City Bombing*. Like everyone else, I fear, I was sick of the subject. Nothing could justify the murder of those 168 men, women, and children, none of whom had, as far as we know, anything at all to do with the federal slaughter at Waco, the ostensible reason for McVeigh's fury. So why write such a book? Serrano hardly finds McVeigh sympathetic, but he does manage to make him credible in an ominously fascinating book.

Born in 1968, McVeigh came from a rural family that had been, more or less, dispossessed a generation earlier. Father Bill had been in the U.S. Army. Mother worked. They lived in a western New

York blue-collar town called Pendleton. Bill grows vegetables; works at a local GM plant; belongs to the Roman Catholic Church. Of the area, he says, 'When I grew up, it was all farms. When Tim grew up, it was half and half.'

Tim turns out to be an uncommonly intelligent and curious boy. He does well in high school. He is, as his defense attorney points out, 'a political animal.' He reads history, the Constitution. He also has a lifelong passion for guns: motivation for joining the army. In Bush's Gulf War he was much decorated as an infantryman, a born soldier. But the war itself was an eye-opener, as wars tend to be for those who must fight them. Later, he wrote a journalist how 'we were falsely hyped up.' The ritual media demonizing of Saddam, Arabs, Iraqis had been so exaggerated that when McVeigh got to Iraq he was startled to 'find out they are normal like me and you. They hype you to take these people out. They told us we were to defend Kuwait where the people had been raped and slaughtered. War woke me up.'

As usual, there were stern laws against American troops fraternizing with the enemy. McVeigh writes a friend, 'We've got these starving kids and sometimes adults coming up to us begging for food . . . It's really "trying" emotionally. It's like the puppy dog at the table; but much worse. The sooner we leave here the better. I can see how the guys in Vietnam were getting killed by children.' Serrano notes, 'At the close of the war, a very popular war, McVeigh had learned that he did not like the taste of killing innocent people. He spat into the sand at the thought of being forced to hurt others who did not hate him any more than he them.'

The army and McVeigh parted once the war was done. He took odd jobs. He got interested in the far right's paranoid theories and in what Joel Dyer calls 'The Religion of Conspiracy.' An army buddy, Terry Nichols, acted as his guide. Together they obtained a book called *Privacy*, on how to vanish from the government's view, go underground, make weapons. Others had done the same, including the Weaver family, who had moved to remote Ruby Ridge in Idaho. Randy Weaver was a cranky white separatist with Christian Identity beliefs. He wanted to live with his family apart from the rest of America. This was a challenge to the FBI. When Weaver did not show up in court to settle a minor firearms charge, they staked him out August 21, 1992. When the Weaver dog barked, they shot him; when the Weavers' fourteen-year-old son fired in their direction, they shot him in the back and killed him. When Mrs. Weaver, holding a baby, came to the door, FBI sniper Lon Horiuchi shot her head off. The next year the Feds took out the Branch Davidians.

For Timothy McVeigh, the ATF became the symbol of oppression and murder. Since he was now suffering from an exaggerated sense of justice, not a common American trait, he went to war pretty much on his own and ended up slaughtering more innocents than the Feds had at Waco. Did he know what he was doing when he blew up the Alfred P. Murrah Federal Building in Oklahoma City because it contained the hated bureau? McVeigh remained silent throughout his trial. Finally, as he was about to be sentenced, the court asked him if he would like to speak. He did. He rose and said. 'I wish to use the words of Justice Brandeis dissenting in *Olmstead* to speak for me. He wrote, "Our government is the potent, the omnipresent teacher. For good or ill, it teaches the whole people by its example."' Then McVeigh was sentenced to death by the government.

Those present were deeply confused by McVeigh's quotation. How could the Devil quote so saintly a justice? I suspect that he did it in the same spirit that Iago answered Othello when asked why he had done what he had done: 'Demand me nothing: what you know, you know: from this time forth I never will speak word.' Now we know, too: or as my grandfather used to say back in Oklahoma, 'Every pancake has two sides.'

Vanity Fair
November 1998

The New Theocrats

June 18, 1997, proved to be yet another day that will live in infamy in the history of *The Wall Street Journal*, or t.w.m.i.p., 'the world's most important publication,' as it bills itself – blissfully unaware of just how unknown this cheery neofascist paper is to the majority of Americans, not to mention those many billions who dwell in darkness where the sulfurous flashes of Wall Street's little paper are no more than marsh gas from the distant marches of the loony empire. June 18 was the day that t.w.m.i.p. took an ad in *The New York Times*, the paper that prints only the news that will fit its not-dissimilar mindset. The ad reprinted a t.w.m.i.p. editorial titled 'Modern Morality,' a subject I should have thought alien to the core passions of either paper. But then for Americans morality has nothing at all to do with ethics or right action or who is stealing what money – and liberties – from whom. Morality is SEX. SEX. SEX.

The edit's lead is piping hot. 'In the same week that an Army general with 147 Vietnam combat missions' (remember the *Really*

Good War, for lots of Dow Jones listings?) 'ended his career over an adulterous affair 13 years ago' (t.w.m.i.p. is on strong ground here; neither the general nor the lady nor any other warrior should be punished for adulteries not conducted while on watch during enemy attack) 'the news broke' – I love that phrase in a journal of powerful opinion and so little numberless news – 'that a New Jersey girl gave birth to a baby in the bathroom at her high school prom, put it in the trash and went out to ask the deejay to play a song by Metallica – for her boyfriend. The baby is dead.'

Misled by the word 'girl,' I visualized a panicky pubescent tot. But days later, when one Melissa Drexler was indicted for murder, she was correctly identified by the *Times* as a 'woman, 18.' In a recently published photograph of her alongside her paramour at the prom, the couple look to be in their early thirties. But it suited t.w.m.i.p. to misrepresent Ms. Drexler as yet another innocent child corrupted by laissez-faire American liberal 'values,' so unlike laissez-faire capitalism, the great good.

All this is 'moral chaos,' keens the writer. I should say that all this is just plain old-fashioned American stupidity where a religion-besotted majority is cynically egged on by a ruling establishment whose most rabid voice is *The Wall Street Journal.*

'We have no good advice on how the country might extricate itself anytime soon from a swamp of sexual confusion . . .' You can say that again and, of course, you will. So, rather than give bad advice, cease and desist from taking out ads to blame something called The Liberals. In a country evenly divided between political reactionaries and religious maniacs, I see hardly a liberal like a tree – or even a burning bush – walking. But the writer does make it clear that the proscribed general was treated unfairly while the 'girl' with baby is a statistic to be exploited by right-wing journalists, themselves often not too far removed from the odious Metallica-listening orders who drop babies in johns, a bad situation that might have been prevented by the use, let us say, of a rubber when 'girl' and 'boy' had sex.

But, no. We are assured that the moral chaos is the result of sexual education and 'littering,' as the ad puts it, 'the swamp' with 'condoms that for about the past five years have been dispensed by adults running our high schools . . . or by machines located in, by coincidence, the bathroom.' Presumably, the confessional would be a better venue, if allowed. So, on the one hand, it is bad, as we all agree, for a woman to give birth and then abandon a baby; but then too, it's wrong, for some metaphysical reason, to help prevent such a birth from taking place. There is no sense of cause/effect when these geese start honking. Of course, t.w.m.i.p. has its own agendum: Outside marriage, no sex of any kind for the lower classes and a policing of everyone, including generals and truly valuable people, thanks to the same liberals who now 'forbid nothing and punish anything.' This is spaceship-back-of-the-comet reasoning.

The sensible code observed by all the world (except for certain fundamentalist monotheistic Jews, Christians, and Muslims) is that 'consensual' relations in sexual matters are no concern of the state. The United States has always been backward in these matters, partly because of its Puritan origins and partly because of the social arrangements arrived at during several millennia of family-intensive agrarian life, rudely challenged a mere century ago by the Industrial Revolution and the rise of the cities and, lately, by the postindustrial work-world of services in which 'safe' prostitution should have been, by now, a bright jewel.

Although the 'screed' (a favorite right-wing word) in the *Times* ad is mostly rant and not to be taken seriously, the spirit behind all this blather is interestingly hypocritical. T.w.m.i.p. is not interested in morality. In fact, any company that can increase quarterly profits through the poisoning of a river is to be treasured. But the piece does reflect a certain unease that the people at large, most visibly through sex, may be trying to free themselves from their masters, who grow ever more insolent and exigent in their pro-hibitions – one strike and you're out is their dirty little secret. In mid-screed, the paper almost comes to the point: 'Very simply [*sic*], what we're suggesting here is that the code of sexual behavior formerly set down by established religion in the U.S. more or less kept society healthy, unlike the current manifest catastrophe.' There it is. Where is Norman Lear, creator of *Mary Hartman, Mary Hartman*, now that we need him? Visualize on the screen gray clapboard, slate-colored sky, om*ni*-ous (as Darryl Zanuck used to say) music. Then a woman's plaintive voice calling, 'Hester Prynne, Hester Prynne!' as the screen fills with a pulsing scarlet 'A.'

So arrière-garde that it is often avant-garde, t.w.m.i.p. is actually on to something. Although I shouldn't think anyone on its pre-mises has heard of the eighteenth-century Neapolitan scholar Vico, our readers will recall that Vico, working from Plato, established various organic phases in human society. First, Chaos. Then Theocracy. Then Aristocracy. Then Democracy – but as republics tend to become imperial and tyrannous, they collapse and we're back to Chaos and to its child Theocracy, and a new cycle. Currently, the United States is a mildly chaotic imperial republic headed for the exit, no bad thing unless there is a serious outbreak of Chaos, in which case a new age of religion will be upon us. Anyone who ever cared for our old Republic, no matter how flawed it always was with religious exuberance, cannot *not* prefer Chaos to the harsh rule of Theocrats. Today, one sees them at their savage worst in Israel and in certain Islamic countries, like Afghanistan, etc. Fortunately, thus far their social regimentation is still no match for the universal lust for consumer goods, that brave new world at the edge of democracy. As for Americans, we can still hold the fort against our very own praying mantises – for the most part, fundamentalist Christians abetted by a fierce, decadent capitalism in thrall to totalitarianism as proclaimed so saucily in *The New York Times* of June 18, 1997.

The battle line is now being drawn. Even as the unfortunate 'girl' in New Jersey was instructing the deejay, the Christian right was organizing itself to go after permissiveness in entertainment. On June 18 the Southern Baptists at their annual convention denounced the Disney company and its TV network, ABC, for showing a lesbian as a human being, reveling in *Pulp Fiction* violence, flouting Christian family values. I have not seen the entire bill of particulars (a list of more than 100 'properties' to be boycotted was handed out), but it all sounds like a pretrial deposition from Salem's glory days. Although I have criticized in these pages the Disney cartel for its media domination, I must now side with the challenged octopus.

This is the moment for Disney to throw the full weight of its wealth at the Baptists, who need a lesson in constitutional law they will not soon forget. They should be brought to court on the usual chilling-of-First-Amendment grounds as well as for restraint of trade. Further, and now let us for once get to the root of the matter. The tax exemptions for the revenues of all the churches from the Baptists to the equally absurd – and equally mischievous – Scientologists must be removed.

The original gentlemen's agreement between Church and State was that *We the People* (the State) will in no way help or hinder any religion while, absently, observing that as religion is 'a good thing,' the little church on Elm Street won't have to pay a property tax. No one envisaged that the most valuable real estate at the heart of most of our old cities would be tax-exempt, as churches and temples and orgone boxes increased their holdings and portfolios. The *quo* for this huge *quid* was that religion would stay out of politics and not impose its superstitions on *Us the People*. The agreement broke down years ago. The scandalous career of the Reverend Presidential Candidate Pat Robertson is a paradigm.

As Congress will never act, this must be a grass-roots movement to amend the Constitution, even though nothing in the original First Amendment says a word about tax exemptions or any other special rights to churches, temples, orgone boxes. This is a useful war for Disney to fight, though I realize that the only thing more cowardly than a movie studio or TV network is a conglomerate forced to act in the open. But if you don't, Lord Mouse, it will be your rodentian ass 15.7 million Baptists will get, not to mention the asses of all the rest of us.

The Nation
21 July 1997

Coup de Starr

Like so many observers of the mysterious Starr Ship that President Clinton seemed to sink so gracefully on television, I was mystified by the marauding pirates' inability to go for any loot other than details of his indecorous sex life, a matter of no great interest to anyone but partisans of the far right and a press gone mad with bogus righteousness. But along with mystification over the pirates' obsession with whether or not a blow job is sex (neatly finessed by Clinton because the wise judge in the Paula Jones case had forgotten to include lips in her court's menu of blue-plate delights), I had a sense that I had, somehow, been through something like this once before. Where had I stumbled over the notion that a presidential election could be overthrown because of sexual behavior that is not a crime, at least beyond the city limits of Atlanta, Georgia? Sex as politics. Politics as sex. *Sex Is Politics*. Then I remembered. In January 1979 I had written a piece in *Playboy* with that title, because something new was happening in American politics back then.

The ERA and gay rights were, at that time, under fire . . . At that time! Clinton's support for women and gays, at the beginning of his first term, was more than enough to launch the Starr Ship. But twenty years ago, the right had already vowed that so-called valence issues would be its principal choice of weapon. Or, as a member of the Conservative Caucus put it then, with engaging candor, 'We're going after people on the basis of their hot buttons.' In other words, sex, sex, sex. Save the Family and Save Our Children were the slogans of that moment, and one Richard Viguerie was the chief money raiser for the powers of darkness. 'Viguerie is not just a hustler,' I wrote in *Playboy*. 'He is also an ideologue.' He was thinking of creating a new political party. 'I have raised millions of dollars for the conservative movement over the years,' he said, 'and I am not happy with the result. I decided to become more concerned with how the money is spent.' Viguerie was working with a group called Gun Owners of America.

> Another of Viguerie's clients is Utah's Senator Orrin Hatch, a proud and ignorant man who is often mentioned as a possible candidate for President if the far right should start a new political party . . . 'I want,' says Viguerie, 'a massive assault on Congress in 1978. I don't want any token efforts. We now have the talent and the resources to move in a bold, massive way. I think we can move against Congress in 1978 in a way that's never been conceived of.'

I duly noted that this sounded like revolution.

As it was, the bold, massive move against Congress did not take place until 1994, thanks to the twelve-year Reagan/Bush snooze, capped by Clinton's political ineptitude. But now that the Man from Hope has gained a personal, if temporary, victory against our would-be revolutionaries, I suggest that before the obligatory Capitol Reichstag fire, a charge of treason be brought against Kenneth Starr. Since all sovereignty rests with We the People, Starr's attempt to overthrow the presidential elections of 1992 and 1996 constitutes a bold, massive blow at the American people themselves: a unique attempt in our history and one that must be swiftly addressed in order to discover just who his co-conspirators are and how best to undo their plots. Yes, Hillary, there was – and there is – a right-wing plot with deep roots. Meanwhile, Senator Orrin Hatch, do you solemnly swear to tell the truth, the whole truth, and nothing but the truth, so help you Moroni?

The Nation
26 October 1998

Starr Conspiracy

On August 17 the forty-second president of the United States, William Jefferson Clinton, will commit what could be a fatal political error by allowing himself to be questioned under oath by a special prosecutor, Kenneth W. Starr, who has taken over four years and spent 40 million taxpayer dollars in trying to prove that Mr. Clinton must be guilty of something or other and so should be impeached by the House of Representatives and tried and convicted by the Senate (as the Constitution requires) for what the peculiar Mr. Starr will argue is a high crime or misdemeanor, like treason or taking bribes or insufficient racial bigotry.

Foreigners are mystified by the whole business while thoughtful Americans – there are several of us – are equally mystified that the ruling establishment of the country has proved to be so mindlessly vindictive that it is willing, to be blunt, to overthrow the lawful government of the United States – that is, a president elected in 1992 and reelected in 1996 by *We the People*, that sole source of all political legitimacy, which takes precedence over the Constitution and the common law and God himself. This last was a concept highly uncongenial to the enlightened eighteenth-century founders but not, we are told, to a onetime judge of meager intellectual capacity but deep faith in all the superstitions that ruling classes encourage the lower orders to believe so that they will not question authority.

First, what is the President guilty of? Attempts to prove that he did something criminal fifteen years ago in Arkansas in a real estate deal came to nothing. Undeterred, Mr. Starr kept on searching for 'high crime and misdemeanors' as the Constitution puts it. Had one of Clinton's associates in the White House been murdered, possibly by Mrs. Clinton, said to be his mistress? This 'murder' was found to be a suicide, the result of depression brought on by savage attacks from a fascist newspaper called *The Wall Street Journal*. The restless Starr moved on to other areas. Meanwhile, in 1994, Congress became Republican and political partisans are now reveling in the political paralysis of the Democratic White House. According to Starr, the fate of the Republic now depends upon whether or not Clinton lied under oath when he denied having had sexual relations with a White House intern, Monica Lewinsky, assuming anyone can define, satisfactorily, a sexual relation. Does a blow job performed on a passive president, idly daydreaming of the budget, count as intercourse? Finally, semanticists are stuck with the English word 'intercourse.' *Inter* means between at least two people. *Intra* would be what we call a gang bang, not practical in the Oval Offfice unless sturdy Secret Service lads join in. Did they? As I write, the nation awaits the laboratory analysis of what is, according to Monica, a presidential semen stain on her elegant blue dress, carefully preserved so that, when her time comes, she can take her place in history alongside if not Joan of Arc, Charlotte Corday.

A few years ago two pollsters did an elaborate study of a wide spectrum of the American population. Many questions were asked on many subjects. The results were published in a book called *The Day America Told the Truth*, not a confidence-inspiring title when over 90 percent of those polled confessed to being 'habitual liars.' That the president of such an electorate should lie about sex makes him more sympathetic than not. Certainly, if so irrelevant a question was asked of George Washington, he would have run Mr. Starr through with his sword while Abraham Lincoln would have thrown him out the window. But irrelevance is now the American condition, both as a global empire and incoherent domestic polity. Two-thirds of all the world's lawyers are American and they have made a highly profitable, for them, mess of our legal system. They could not prove, in the Fifties, that Alger Hiss had been a spy for the Soviets so they sent him to prison on an unconvincing perjury charge. Al Capone was never convicted of murder or extortion: he was put in jail for income tax evasion. This is law in its decadence.

After four years, Starr has found no crime that Clinton has committed except denying a sexual relationship with Monica which she has already said, under oath, never took place but now says, under oath and with a wink from Starr for her previous perjury, did take place. The President cannot be indicted by a civil grand jury. He need not speak to Starr, who is, ironically, his employee. The President's attorney general, Janet Reno, with the connivance of two right-wing senators (one is Jesse Helms, tobacco's best friend) and a panel of three right-wing judges, came up with Starr as special prosecutor to investigate, originally, Whitewater and then anything else that might undo the results of two presidential elections.

What is behind this vendetta against Clinton, a popular president? First, the most powerful emotion in American political life is the undying hatred of certain whites for all blacks. For American blacks, Clinton is white knight. Arkansas is also a Southern state where the Ku Klux Klan is still a force. When the schools were desegregated in the Fifties, a battle line was drawn. A former judge and a member of the White Citizens Council known as 'Justice' Jim Johnson waged a war against blacks in general and Clinton in particular. 'Justice Jim' is also associated with someone *The Observer* (U.K.) calls 'a convicted fraudster,' David Hale, in charge of the 'Arkansas Project,' funded by a conservative billionaire named Richard Mellon Scaife. This brings us to the Clintons' other nemesis: the wealthy conservative ruling class. In order to avoid taxation, they have through their lawyers, both in and out of government, placed their capital in tax-free foundations for 'charitable' purposes. But to have such a foundation one must never use it to meddle in politics. But Mr. Scaife does meddle. He gives money to such disreputable papers as *The American Spectator*, which has published numerous wild stories about the Clintons. A year or so ago, Mr. Scaife rewarded Starr with a professorship at Pepperdine University, which Starr accepted and then, as the publicity was bad, he hastily returned to his war on Clinton. Presumably, he will be paid off by Scaife once his holy work is done. Every society gets the Titus Oates it deserves.

Mrs. Clinton is correct when she says that there is a right-wing conspiracy against them. Unfortunately for her, Americans have been trained by the media to go into Pavlovian giggles at the mention of the word 'conspiracy' because for an American to believe in a conspiracy he must also believe in flying saucers or, craziest of all, that more than one person was involved in the JFK murder. Mrs. Clinton, perhaps, emphasizes too heavily the 'right-wing' aspect of her enemies. It is corporate America, quite wingless in political as opposed to money matters, that declared war on the Clintons in 1993 when the innocent couple tried to give the American people a national health service, something every civilized country has but we must never enjoy because the insurance companies now get one-third of the money spent on health care and the insurance companies are the piggy banks – the cash cows – of corporate America.

In order to destroy the health service plan, insurance and pharmaceutical companies, in tandem with lively elements of the American Medical Association, conspired to raise a half-billion dollars to create and then air a barrage of TV advertisements to convince the electorate that such a service was Communist, not to mention an affront to the Darwinian principle that every American has the right to die unhelped by the state, which collects half his income in life with which to buy, thus far, $5.5 trillion's worth of military hardware at stupendous – to this day – cost. Then, not content with the political destruction of the Clintons' health plan, corporate America decided to destroy their reputations. Nothing personal in this, by the way. But how else can the ownership of the country send a warning to other feckless politicians that the country and its people exist only to make money for corporations now so internationalized that they cannot be made to pay tax on much – if any – of their profits. Starr is now the most visible agent of corporate America wielding a new weapon under the sun: endless legal harassment of a twice-elected President so that he cannot exercise his office as first magistrate.

All sovereignty in the United States rests, most vividly, on the concept of 'We the People of the United States' (with the sometime addition of 'in Congress Assembled'). The Constitution, the common law, and even the wealth of corporate America or the rage of lumpen white Americans against the blacks must bow to this great engine which could, through a constitutional convention, sweep into limbo all our current arrangements. President John Adams wanted a republic not of men but of laws. He could not have foreseen the madness of our present condition with everyone at law and expensive prisons filling up while a partisan lawyer, through legal harassment, is busy undoing the presidential elections of 1992 and 1996 because his paymasters did not like the results.

Happily when the collapse begins, there may yet be time for that most feared (Pavlov again) rendezvous with destiny – a constitutional convention. Meanwhile, I should not in the least be surprised if yet another 'conspiracy,' in the name of We the People, is set in motion against Kenneth W. Starr, who, no matter how meticulously he has observed the rules of the statute creating his monstrous office, did, in effect, attempt to overthrow two lawful elections reflective of the People's will and he is put on trial for – why not? – treason against the United States. If nothing else, such an exercise might reveal all sorts of highly interesting co-conspirators.

International Herald Tribune
11 August 1998

Birds and Bees and Clinton

How time flies! Seven fairly long years have now passed since I explained the Birds and the Bees to *Nation* readers, thus putting the finis to the cold war and, may I boast, more than one case of nervous tic douloureux, which ticked no more ['A Few Words About Sex: The Birds and the Bees,' October 28, 1991]. But since that long-ago October day when I explained the mysteries of sex and scales fell from readers' eyes, new hordes have grown up in darkness, among them Kenneth Starr, as well as his numerous investigators and co-conspirators on the House Judiciary Committee, as well as in Pittsburgh's Mellon Patch and Marietta, Georgia, where the nation's Renaissance Man awaits rebirth as commander of the armies of a sinless America, troops whose powder is kept dry as, nervously, they closely shave hairy palms while their minds slowly rattle into madness from abuse of self and others.

It was not until Mr. Starr published his dirty book at public expense that I realized how far off-track I have allowed these sad dummies to get. Simple truths about the birds and the bees have been so distorted by partisanship that blow jobs and hand jobs are now confused with The Real Thing, which can only be classic in-and-out as Anthony Burgess so snappily put it in *A Clockwork Orange*. I take full responsibility for not providing a booster shot of Sex Ed. So, as the old impeachment train leaves the station, let me demonstrate how the President did not commit perjury when he said he did not have sexual intercourse with . . . surely not Abigail Thernstrom . . . I seem to have mislaid my notes. Anyway, you know who I mean.

First, let us quickly – or 'briefly' as every question on CNN now begins – review the bidding from our last symposium. 'Men and women are *not* alike.' That was the first shocker I had for you in 1991. 'They have different sexual roles to perform.' At this point Andrea Dworkin, with a secret smile, began to load her bazooka. 'Despite the best efforts of theologians and philosophers to disguise our condition, there is no point to us, or to any species, except proliferation and survival. This is hardly glamorous, and so to give Meaning to Life, we have invented some of the most bizarre religions that . . . alas, we have nothing to compare ourselves to. We are biped mammals filled with red seawater (reminder of our oceanic origin), and we exist to reproduce until we are eventually done in by the planet's changing weather or a stray meteor.' Thus, I wrapped up the Big Picture.

Next: Lubricious Details. 'The male's function is to shoot semen as often as possible into as many women (or attractive surrogates) as possible, while the female's function is to be shot briefly' by Wolf Blitzer . . . no, no, by a male, any male, 'in order to fertilize an egg, which she will lay nine months later.'

Seven years ago, apropos same-sex versus other-sex, or homosexuality versus heterosexuality, two really dumb American sports invented by the spiritual heirs of Gen. Abner Doubleday, who gave us baseball, I wrote, 'In the prewar Southern town of Washington, D.C., it was common for boys to have sex with one another. It was called "messing around" and it was no big deal.' I went into no more detail because I assumed most readers would get the point.

Recently, the sexologist George Plimpton, a James Moran Institute professor emeritus, explained in *The New Yorker* how boys in his youth would go through mating stages with girls, using, significantly, baseball terminology like 'getting to first base,' which meant . . . and so on. 'Going all the way,' however, was used instead of 'home run' for full intercourse, the old in-and-out or mature penis-vagina intercourse.

Arguably, Southerners are somewhat different from other residents of that shining city on a hill that has brought so much light and joy to all the world in the past two centuries. In balmy climes, human beings mature early. They also have a lot of chiggery outdoors to play baseball and other games in.

When I was a boy, Fairfax County, Virginia, where I lived, was Li'l Abner country. No glamorous houses. No CIA lords hidden away in Georgian mansions on the Potomac Heights. There was just a Baptist church. A Methodist church. And a lot of Sunday. Also, a whole hierarchy of do's and don'ts when it came to boy–girl sex. What is now harshly called groping was the universal sentimental approach (put down that bazooka, Andrea). All players understood touching. Even without a thong. Endless kissing. First, second, third bases to be got to. Then a boy shootist was allowed, more soon than late, to shoot. Otherwise he might *die*, of dreaded blueballs. Girls tended to be understanding. Even so, all-the-way intercourse was not on offer unless he was 'serious.' Now add to these age-old rituals of mating cold war Pentagon-CIA terminology, the concept of 'plausible deniability,' and one starts to understand the truth of the President's denial under oath that he had sexual relations with Miss Monica. From the Testimony: 'The President maintained that there can be no sexual relationship without sexual intercourse, regardless of what other sexual activities may transpire. He stated that "most ordinary Americans" would embrace this distinction.' Certainly most lads and lassies in Arkansas or the Fairfax County of sixty years ago would agree.

It is true that in the age of Freud, now drawing to a close, it used to be argued by those who preached the good news in his name that *everything* was sexual. Two men shaking hands. The embrace between baseball players on the diamond. Two women friends weeping in each other's arms, and so on. One can argue that, yes, there is a sexual element to everything if one wants to go digging but even the most avid Freudian detective would have to admit that what might be construed as sexuality by other means falls literally short of plain old in-and-out, which is the name of the game that takes precedence even over General Doubleday's contribution to the boredom of nations.

In reference to Miss Monica's first sworn denial of sexual relations with the President, which Clinton had originally confirmed, he later said, 'I believe at the time she filled out this affidavit, if she believed that the definition of sexual relationship was two people having intercourse, then this is accurate.' To support Clinton's reading of the matter, one has only to overhear Miss Monica and her false friend/fiend Linda Tripp bemoaning the fact that the President will not perform the absolute, complete, all-the-way act of becoming as one with her in mature heterosexual land forever glimmering somewhere over the rainbow. Without sexual intercourse there can be no sexual relationship. If this sounds like quibbling, it is. But that is the way we have been speaking in lawyerland for quite some time. The honor system at West Point regarded quibbling as worse than lying. So the officer corps became adept at quibbling, even in the ruins of the city of Ben Tre, which 'we destroyed in order to save it.'

A nation not of men but of laws, intoned John Adams as he, among other lawyers, launched what has easily become the most demented society ever consciously devised by intelligent men. We are now enslaved by laws. We are governed by lawyers. We create little but litigate much. Our monuments are the ever-expanding prisons, where millions languish for having committed victimless crimes or for simply not playing the game of plausible deniability (a.k.a. lying) with a sufficiently good legal team. What began as a sort of Restoration comedy, *The Impeachment of the President*, on a frivolous, irrelevant matter, is suddenly turning very black indeed, and all our political arrangements are at risk as superstitious Christian fundamentalists and their corporate manipulators seem intent on overthrowing two presidential elections in a Senate trial. This is no longer comedy. This is usurpation.

With that warning, I invite the Senate to contemplate Vice President Aaron Burr's farewell to the body over which he himself had so ably presided: 'This house is a sanctuary, a citadel of law, of order, and of liberty; and it is here in this exalted refuge; here, if anywhere, will resistance be made to the storm of political frenzy and the silent arts of corruption; and if the Constitution be destined ever to perish by the sacrilegious hands of the demagogue or the usurper, which God avert, its expiring agonies will be witnessed on this floor.' Do no harm to this state, Conscript Fathers.

The Nation
28 December 1998

A Letter to be Delivered

I am writing this note a dozen days before the inauguration of the loser of the year 2000 presidential election. Lost republic as well as last empire. We are now faced with a Japanese seventeenth-century-style arrangement: a powerless Mikado ruled by a shogun vice president and his Pentagon warrior counselors. Do they dream, as did the shoguns of yore, of the conquest of China? We shall know more soon, I should think, than late. Sayonara.

January 11, 2001

*Congratulations, Mr. President-Elect. Like everyone else, I'm eagerly looking forward to your inaugural address. As you must know by now, we could never get enough of your speeches during

* This was written for *Vanity Fair* before the November 7, 2000, presidential election.

the recent election in which the best man won, as he always does in what Spiro Agnew so famously called 'the greatest nation in the country.'

Apropos your first speech to us as president. I hope you don't mind if I make a few suggestions, much as I used to do in the Sixties when I gave my regular States of the Union roundups on David Susskind's TV show of blessed memory. Right off, it strikes me that this new beginning may be a good place to admit that for the last fifty years we have been waging what the historian Charles A. Beard so neatly termed 'perpetual war for perpetual peace.'

It is my impression, Mr. President-Elect, that most Americans want our economy converted from war to peace. Naturally, we still want to stand tall. We also don't want any of our tax money wasted on health care because that would be Communism, which we all abhor. But we would like some of our tax dollars spent on education. Remember what you said in your terminal debate with your opponent, now so much charred and crumbling toast? 'Education is the key to the new millennium.' (Actually, looking at my notes, all four of you said that.)

In any case, it is time we abandon our generally unappreciated role as world policeman, currently wasting Colombia, source of satanic drugs, while keeping Cuba, Iraq, and, until recently, Serbia 'in correction,' as policepersons call house arrest. This compulsive interference in the affairs of other states is expensive and pointless. Better we repair our own country with 'internal improvements,' as Henry Clay used to say. But in order to do this your first big job will be to curb the Pentagon warlords and their fellow conspirators in Congress and the boardrooms of corporate America. Ever since the Soviet Union so unsportingly disbanded in order to pursue proto-capitalism and double-entry bookkeeping, our warlords have been anxiously searching for new enemies in order to justify an ever increasing military budget. Obviously, there is Terrorism to be fought. There is also the war on Drugs, to be fought but never won. Even so, in the failed attempt, the coming destruction of Colombia, a once liberal democratic nation, promises to be great fun for warlords and media, if not the residents of a once happy nation. Lately, a new clear and present danger has been unveiled: Rogue States, or 'states of concern.' Currently, North Korea, Iraq, and Iran have been so fingered, while the world's one billion Muslims have been demonized as crazed fanatics, dedicated to destroying all that is good on earth, which is us.

Since we have literally targeted our enemies, the Pentagon assumes that, sooner or later, Rogues will take out our cities, presumably from spaceships. So to protect ourselves, the Ronald Reagan Memorial Nuclear Space Shield must be set in place at an initial cost of $60 billion even though, as of July, tests of the system, no matter how faked by the Pentagon, continued to fail. The fact that, according to polls, a majority of your constituents believe that we already have such a shield makes it possible for you to say you're updating it and then do nothing. After all, from 1949 to 1999 the U.S. spent $7.1 trillion on 'national defense.' As a result, the national debt is $5.6 trillion, of which $3.6 trillion is owed to the public, and $2 trillion to the Social Security–Medicare Trust Funds, all due to military spending and to the servicing of the debt thus incurred.

Mr. President-Elect, since Treasury figures are traditionally juggled, it would be nice if you were to see to it that the actual income and outgo of federal money are honestly reported. Last year the government told us, falsely, that its income was just over $1.8 trillion while it spent just under $1.8 trillion; hence, the famous, phantom surplus when there was, of course, our usual homely deficit of around $90 billion. Year after year, the government's official income is inflated by counting as revenue the income of the people's Social Security and Medicare Trust Funds. These funds are not federal revenue. This year Social Security has a healthy surplus of $150 billion. No wonder corporate America and its employees in Congress are eager to privatize this healthy fund, thus far endangered only by them.

Although actual military spending was indeed lower last year than usual, half the budget still went to pay for wars to come as well as to blowing up the odd aspirin factory in the Sudan. Cash outlays for the military were $344 billion while interest on the military-caused national debt was $282 billion: sorry to bore you with these statistics, but they are at the heart of our – what was Jimmy Carter's unfortunate word? – malaise (that's French for broke). The Clinton administration's airy promise of a $1.8 trillion budget surplus over the next decade was, of course, a bold if comforting fiction, based on surreal estimates of future federal income – not to mention expenditures which, if anything like last September's congressional spending spree, will drown us in red ink.

Sir, if you are going to be of any use at all to the nation and to the globe that it holds hostage, you will have to tame the American military. Discipline the out-of-control service chiefs. Last September, the Chairman of the Joint Chiefs of Staff, General H. H. Shelton, declared that more, not less, dollars were needed. Specifically, the Marines want an extra $1.5 billion per year, the army wants over $30 billion, the navy $20 billion, the air force $30 billion, all in the absence of an enemy (we spend twenty-two times more than our seven potential enemies – Cuba, Iran, Iraq, Libya, North Korea, Sudan, and Syria – combined). You must not grant these ruinous increases.

In August 1961, I visited President Kennedy at Hyannis Port. The Berlin Wall was going up, and he was about to begin a huge military buildup – reluctantly, or so he said, as he puffed on a cigar liberated by a friend from Castro's Cuba. It should be noted that

Jack hated liberals more than he did conservatives. 'No one can ever be liberal enough for *The New York Post*,' he said. 'Well, the *Post* should be happy now. Berlin's going to cost us at least three and a half billion dollars. So, with this military buildup, we're going to have a seven-billion-dollar deficit for the year. That's a lot of pump priming.' He scowled. 'God, I hate the way they throw money around over there at the Pentagon.'

'It's not they,' I said. 'It's you. It's your administration.' Briskly, he told me the facts of life, and I repeat them now as advice from the thirty-fifth to the – what are you, Mr. President? Forty-third president? 'The only way for a president to control the Pentagon would be if he spent the entire four years of his first term doing nothing else but investigating that mess, which means he really could do nothing else . . .'

'Like getting reelected?'

He grinned. 'Something like that.'

So I now propose, Mr. President-Elect, while there is still time, that you zero in on the links between corporate America and the military and rationalize as best you can the various procurement policies, particularly the Ronald Reagan Memorial Nuclear Shield. You should also leak to the American people certain Pentagon secrets. In 1995, we still had our missiles trained on 2,500 foreign targets. Today, to celebrate peace in the world, our missiles are trained on 3,000 targets – of which 2,260 are in Russia; the rest are directed at China and the Rogue States. Although President Clinton had spoken eloquently of the need for a reduction in such dangerous nuclear targeting, the Pentagon does as it pleases, making the world unsafe for everyone. But then *USA Today* recently reported that the military enjoys the highest popularity rating (64 percent) of any group in the country – the Congress and Big Business are among the lowest. Of course, the services do spend $265 million annually on advertising.

Jack Kennedy very much enjoyed Fletcher Knebel's thriller *Seven Days in May*, later a film. The story: a jingo based on the real-life Admiral Arthur Radford plans a military coup to take over the White House. Jack found the book riveting. 'Only,' he chuckled, rather grimly, 'it's a lot more likely that this president will one day raise his own army and occupy their damned building.' No, I don't agree with Oliver Stone that the generals killed him. But there is, somewhere out there, a watchdog that seems never to bark in the night. Yet the dog that doesn't bark is the one that should be guarding the house from burglars, in this case the military-industrial complex that Eisenhower so generously warned us against. Although there are many media stories about costly overruns in the defense industries as well as the slow beginning of what may yet turn into an actual debate over the nuclear shield that Reagan envisaged for us after seeing Alfred Hitchcock's *Torn Curtain*, a movie nowhere near as good as *Seven Days in May*, there is, as yet, no debate over the role of the military in the nation's life and its ongoing threat to us all, thanks to the hubris of senior officers grown accustomed to dispensing vast amounts of the people's money for missiles that can't hit targets and bombers that can't fly in the rain. Congress, which should ride herd, does not because too many of its members are financed by those same companies that absorb our tax money, nor is it particularly helpful that senior officers, after placing orders with the defense industries, so often go to work as salesmen for the very same companies they once bought from.

Of all recent presidents, Clinton was expected to behave the most sensibly in economic matters. He understood how the economy works. But because he had used various dodges to stay out of the Vietnam War, he came to office ill at ease with the military. When Clinton tried to live up to his pledge to gay voters that the private life of any military person was no one's business but his own, the warlords howled that morale would be destroyed. Clinton backed down. When Clinton went aboard the aircraft carrier U.S.S. *Theodore Roosevelt* to take the salute, sailors pranced around with mop ends on their heads, doing fag imitations while hooting at the President, who just stood there. These successful insults to civilian authority have made the military ever more truculent and insolent. And now they must be brought to heel.

This summer, the warlords of the Pentagon presented the secretary of defense with their Program Objective memorandum. Usually, this is a polite wish list of things that they would like to see under the Christmas tree. By September, the wish list sounded like a harsh ultimatum. As one dissenting officer put it, 'Instead of a budget based on a top-line budget number, the chiefs are demanding a budget based on military strategy.' Although their joint military strategies, as tested in war over the last fifty years, are usually disastrous, military strategy in this context means simply extorting from the government $30 billion a year over and above the 51 percent of the budget that now already goes for war. Mr. President-Elect, I would advise you to move your office from the West Wing of the White House to the Pentagon, across the river. Even though every day you spend there could prove to be your Ides of March, you will at least have the satisfaction of knowing that you tried to do something for us, the hitherto unrepresented people.

Fifty years ago, Harry Truman replaced the old republic with a National Security State whose sole purpose is to wage perpetual wars, hot, cold, and tepid. Exact date of replacement? February 27, 1947. Place: White House Cabinet Room. Cast: Truman, Undersecretary of State Dean Acheson, a handful of congressional leaders. Republican senator Arthur Vandenberg told Truman that he could have his militarized economy only *if* he first 'scared the hell out of the American people' that the Russians were coming. Truman obliged. The perpetual war began. Representative government of, by, and for the people is now a faded memory. Only corporate America enjoys representation by the Congresses and presidents that it pays for in an arrangement where no one is entirely accountable because those who have bought the government also own the media. Now, with the revolt of the Praetorian Guard at the Pentagon, we are entering a new and dangerous phase. Although we regularly stigmatize other societies as rogue states, we ourselves have become the largest rogue state of all. We honor no treaties. We spurn international courts. We strike unilaterally wherever we choose. We give orders to the United Nations but do not pay our dues. We complain of terrorism, yet our empire is now the greatest terrorist of all. We bomb, invade, subvert other states. Although We the People of the United States are the sole source of legitimate authority in this land, we are no longer represented in Congress Assembled. Our Congress has been hijacked by corporate America and its enforcer, the imperial military machine. We the unrepresented People of the United States are as much victims of this militarized government as the Panamanians, Iraqis, or Somalians. We have allowed our institutions to be taken over in the name of a globalized American empire that is totally alien in concept to anything our founders had in mind. I suspect that it is far too late in the day for us to restore the republic that we lost a half-century ago.

Even so, Mr. President-Elect, there is an off chance that you might actually make some difference if you start now to rein in the warlords. Reduce military spending, which will make you popular because you can then legitimately reduce our taxes instead of doing what you have been financed to do, freeing corporate America of its small tax burden. The 1950 taxes on corporate profits accounted for 25 percent of federal revenue; in 1999 only 10.1

percent. Finally, as sure as you were not elected by We the People by the vast sums of unaccountable corporate money, the day of judgment is approaching. Use your first term to break the Pentagon. Forget about a second term. After all, if you succeed on the other side of the Potomac, you will be a hero to We the People. Should you fail or, worse, do nothing, you may be the last president, by which time history will have ceased to notice the United States and all our proud rhetoric will have been reduced to an ever diminishing echo. Also, brood upon an odd remark made by your canny, if ill-fated, predecessor Clinton. When Gingrich and his Contract on (rather than with) America took control of Congress, Clinton said, 'The president is not irrelevant.' This was a startling admission that he could become so. Well, sir, be relevant. Preserve, protect, and defend what is left of our ancient liberties, not to mention our heavily mortgaged fortune.*

Vanity Fair
December 2000

---

* Repeated with the following message to the troops: And so Mr. President, elected by the Supreme Court (5–4), has now, in addition to a vice-preident who was a former secretary of defense, appointed another former defense secretary to his old post as well as a general to be secretary of state; thus the pass was sold.

Democratic Vistas

The vice president to Richard Nixon and bribe-taker to many, Spiro Agnew, was once inspired to say, 'The United States, for all its faults, is still the greatest nation in the country.' Today, even in the wake of the Supreme Court's purloining of the election for the forty-third President, Spiro must be standing tall among his fellow shades. Have we not come through, yet again? As we did in 1888 when Grover Cleveland's plurality of the popular vote was canceled by the intricacies of the Electoral College, and as we even more famously did in 1876 when the Democrat Samuel Tilden got 264,000 more votes than the Republican Rutherford B. Hayes, whose party then challenged the votes in Oregon, South Carolina, Louisiana and – yes, that slattern Florida. An electoral commission chosen by Congress gave the election to the loser, Hayes, by a single vote, the result of chicanery involving a bent Supreme Court Justice appointed by the sainted Lincoln. Revolution was mooted but Tilden retired to private life and to the pleasures of what old-time New Yorkers used to recall, wistfully, as one of the greatest collections of pornography in the Gramercy Park area of Manhattan.

Until December 12, we enjoyed a number of quietly corrupt elections, decently kept from public view. But the current Supreme Court, in devil-may-care mood, let all sorts of cats out of its bag – such as a total commitment to what the far right euphemistically calls family values. Justice Antonin Scalia – both name and visage reminiscent of a Puccini villain – affirmed family values by not recusing himself from the Bush–Gore case even though his son works for the same law firm that represented Bush before the Court. Meanwhile, Justice Clarence Thomas's wife works for a far-right think tank, the Heritage Foundation, and even as her husband attended gravely to arguments, she was vetting candidates for office in the Bush administration.

Elsewhere, George W. Bush, son of a failed Republican president, was entrusting his endangered Florida vote to the state's governor, his brother Jeb.

On the other side of family values, the Gore clan has, at times, controlled as many as a half-dozen Southern legislatures. They are also known for their forensic skill, wit, learning – family characteristics the vice president modestly kept under wraps for fear of frightening the folks at large.

American politics is essentially a family affair, as are most oligarchies. When the father of the Constitution, James Madison, was asked how on earth any business could get done in Congress when the country contained a hundred million people whose representatives would number half a thousand, Madison took the line that oligarchy's iron law always obtains: A few people invariably run the show; and keep it, if they can, in the family.

Finally, those founders, to whom we like to advert, had such a fear and loathing of democracy that they invented the Electoral College so that the popular voice of the people could be throttled, much as the Supreme Court throttled the Floridians on December 12. We were to be neither a democracy, subject to majoritarian tyranny, nor a dictatorship, subject to Caesarean folly.

Another cat let out of the bag is the Supreme Court's dedication to the 1 percent that own the country. Justice Sandra Day O'Connor couldn't for the life of her see why anyone would find the Palm Beach butterfly ballot puzzling. The subtext here was, as it is so often with us, race. More votes were invalidated by aged Votomatic machines in black districts than in white. This made crucial the uncounted 10,000 Miami-Dade ballots that recorded no presidential vote. Hence the speed with which the Bush campaign, loyally aided and abetted by a 5-to-4 majority of the Supreme Court, invented a series of delays to keep those votes from ever being counted because, if they were, Gore would have won the election. Indeed he did win the election until the Court, through ever more brazen stays and remands, with an eye on that clock ever ticking, delayed matters until, practically speaking, in the eyes of the five, if not all of the four, there was no longer time to count, the object of an exercise that had sent trucks filled with a million ballots from one dusty Florida city to the next, to be kept uncounted.

During this slow-paced comedy, there was one riveting moment of truth that will remain with us long after G.W. Bush has joined the lengthening line of twilight presidents in limbo. On the Wednesday before the Thursday when we gave thanks for being the nation once hailed as the greatest by Agnew, the canvassing board in Dade County was, on the orders of the Florida Supreme Court, again counting ballots when an organized crowd stormed into the county building, intimidating the counters and refusing to give their names to officials. *The Miami Herald,* a respectable paper, after examining various voting trends, etc., concluded that Gore had actually carried Florida by 23,000 votes. The *Herald* plans to examine those much-traveled ballots under Florida's 'sunshine' law. I suspect that the ballots and their chads will be found missing.

Thanksgiving came and went. The ballots toured up and down the Florida freeways. Gore was accused of trying to steal an election that he had won. The black population was now aware that, yet again, it had not been taken into account. There had been riots. Under Florida law, anyone with a criminal record – having been convicted of a felony – loses all civil rights. Thousands of blacks were so accused and denied the vote; yet most so listed were not felons or were guilty only of misdemeanors. In any case, the calculated delays persuaded two of the four dissenting judges that there was no time left to count.

Justice John Paul Stevens, a conservative whose principal interest seems to be conserving our constitutional liberties rather than the privileges of corporate America, noted in his dissent: 'One thing, however, is certain. Although we may never know with complete certainty the identity of the winner of this year's presidential election, the identity of the loser is perfectly clear. It is the nation's confidence in the judge as an impartial guardian of the rule of law.'

What will the next four years bring? With luck, total gridlock. The two houses of Congress are evenly split. Presidential adventurism will be at a minimum. With bad luck (and adventures), Chancellor Cheney will rule. A former secretary of defense, he has said that too little money now goes to the Pentagon even though last year it received 51 percent of the discretionary budget. Expect a small war or two in order to keep military appropriations flowing. There will also be tax relief for the very rich. But bad scenario or good scenario, we shall see very little of the charmingly simian George W. Bush. The military – Cheney, Powell, et al. – will be calling the tune, and the whole nation will be on constant alert, for, James Baker has already warned us, Terrorism is everywhere on the march. We cannot be too vigilant. Welcome to Asunción. Yes! We have no bananas.

The Nation
8/15 January 2001

Three Lies to Rule By

In the end, the American presidential campaign of 2000 ostensibly (pre-fraud) came down to a matter of Character. Specifically, to the characters of two male citizens of hitherto no particular interest to the polity. But then personality is about all that our media can cope with, since the American political system, despite ever more expensive elections, sees to it that nothing of an overtly political nature may be discussed. It is true that one candidate, daringly, if briefly, suggested that since 1 percent of the population owns most of the country, as well as quite a bit of the globe elsewhere, perhaps that 1 percent ought not to pay even less tax than it currently does. This tore it. For a moment, the red flag snapped in CNN's early light, but by twilight's last gleaming, that banner was struck, and no real issue was touched on again.

What then is a real issue? Currently, the United States spends twenty-two times as much as our potential enemies (the seven designated rogue states of concern) spend combined. It used to be that true politics involved an accounting of where the people's tax money goes and why. Since the American military currently gets over half of each year's federal revenue, that should have been the most important subject to chat about. But not this year, and so, dutifully, each candidate pledged himself to ever greater spending for the Great War Machine, as it idly trawls about the globe in search of enemies, leaving us with nothing to chatter about except Character. With *moral* character. Or, as Dr. Elaine May once put it so well: 'I like a moral problem so much better than a real problem.'

Although one candidate was immediately perceived to be something of a dope – and dyslexic to boot (defense: it's not *his* fault, so why are you picking on him?) – there are, we were sternly told, worse things in a president. Like what? *Like lying.* When this bunch of garlic was hoisted high, a shudder went through us peasants in our Transylvanian villages as we heard, across haunted moors, the sound of great leathern wings. The undead were aloft.

One candidate was deemed a liar because he exaggerated. He never actually said that he alone had invented the Internet, but he implied that he might have had more to do with its early inception than he had. Worse, he said that his mother-in-law's medicine cost more than his dog's identical medicine, when he had – I've already forgotten which – either no mother-in-law or no dog. By now the Republic was reeling. The vileness of it all! Could we entrust so false a figure to hold in his hand war's arrows, peace's laurel? All in all, the two to three billion dollars that the election cost the generous 1 percent through its corporate paymasters was, by all reckoning, the most profoundly irrelevant in a political history which seems determined to make a monkey of Darwin while exalting the creationist point of view, Manichaean version.

Today's sermon is from Montaigne: 'Lying is an accursed vice. It is only our words which bind us together and make us human. If we realized the horror and weight of lying, we would see that it is more worthy of the stake than other crimes . . . Once let the tongue acquire the habit of lying and it is astonishing how impossible it is to make it give it up.'

But our subject is not the people, those quadrennial spear-carriers, but the two paladins, one of whom will presently be entrusted with the terrible swift nuclear sword, thus becoming the greatest goodest nation that ever was robustly incarnate.

'We are a nation based on Truth,' the Republican managers of the impeachment of sex-fibber President Clinton constantly reminded us, unaware that his constituents were, perversely, rallying round him. Pleased, no doubt, by the metaphysics of his 'What is *is*?' After all, what is truth, as a Roman bureaucrat once rather absently put it. Yet . . .

'Yet' is the nicest of words in English when logically, non-pregnantly used. The American global empire rests on a number of breathtaking presidential lies that our court historians seldom dare question. It would seem that the Hitler team got it about right when it comes to human credulity: the greater the lie, the more apt it is to be believed. The price of the perhaps nonexistent dog's medicine is not going to go unchallenged, but President Franklin Delano Roosevelt's deliberate provocation of the Japanese, in order to force them into attacking us and thus bring us into the Second World War, is simply not admissible. Contemporary journalism's first law, 'What ought not to be true is not true,' is swiftly backed up by those who write the 'history' stories to be used in schools. Happily, I have lived long enough to indulge in the four most beautiful words in the English language: 'I told you so.'

In *Burr* (1973), I relit, as it were, the image of that demonized figure, Aaron Burr. In passing, I duly noted that his chief de-monizer, the admirable-in-most-things, save a tendency toward hypocrisy, Thomas Jefferson, had lived connubially with a slave girl, Sally Hemings, by whom he had a number of children, kept on as slaves. Dumas Malone, the leading Jefferson biographer of the day, denounced my portrait of Jefferson as 'subversive,' because, as he put it, no gentleman could have had sexual relations with a slave and, since Mr. Jefferson was the greatest gentleman of that era, he could not have . . . On such false syllogisms are national myths set. Recent testing shows that many of Hemings's descendants contain the golden DNA of Jefferson himself. Loyalists say that it was an idiot nephew who fathered Sally's children. How? Since Jefferson and Sally lived pretty much as man and wife at Monticello, the idea of the nephew, banjo in hand, making his way up the hill to the house, time and again, to get laid by Jefferson's companion boggles the mind. So much for a great lie that court historians and other propagandists insist that Americans believe. Why is it so grimly important? Since the relationship between black and white is still the most delicate of subjects for Americans, Jefferson must be marble-pure and so outside his own great formulation and invitation to the peoples of all the world: the pursuit of happiness.

That was yesterday. Today, any scrutiny of the three powerful myths which Americans and their helpers in other lands are obliged to accept will set off fire alarms. In *The Golden Age* (largely covering the years 1940–50 as viewed from Washington, D.C., by our rulers), I make three cases involving presidential whoppers. One, Franklin Delano Roosevelt (whose domestic policies – the New Deal – I admire) deliberately provoked the Japanese into attacking us at Pearl Harbor. Why? As of 1940, he wanted us in the war against Hitler, but 80 percent of the American people wanted no European war of any kind after the disappointments of 1917. He could do nothing to budge an isolationist electorate. Luckily for him (and perhaps the world), Japan had a military agreement with Germany and Italy. For several years, Japan had been engaged in an imperial mission to conquer China. Secretly, FDR began a series of provocations to goad the Japanese into what turned out to be an attack on our fleet at Pearl Harbor, thus making inevitable our prompt, wholehearted entry into the Second World War. There is a vast literature on this subject, beginning as early as 1941 with Charles A. Beard's *President Roosevelt and the Coming of War* and continuing to the current *Day of Deceit* by Robert B. Stinnett, now being argued about in the U.S. Stinnett gives the most detailed account of the steps toward war initiated by FDR, including the November 26, 1941, ultimatum to Japan, ordering them out of China while insisting they renounce their pact with the Axis powers; this left Japan with no alternative but war, the object of the exercise.

The second great myth was that Harry Truman, FDR's successor, dropped his two atom bombs on Hiroshima and Nagasaki because he feared that a million American lives would be lost in an invasion (that was the lie he told at the time). Admiral Nimitz, on the spot in the Pacific, and General Eisenhower, brooding elsewhere, disagreed: the Japanese had already lost the war, they said. No nuclear bombs, no invasion was needed; besides, the Japanese had been trying to surrender since the May 1945 devastation of Tokyo by U.S. B-29 bombers.

The third great myth was that the Soviets began the cold war because, driven by the power-mad would-be world conqueror, Stalin, they divided Germany, forcing us to create the West German republic, and then, when Stalin viciously denied us access to our section of Berlin (still under four-power rule as determined at Yalta), we defied him with an airlift. He backed down, foiled in his invasion of France, his crossing of the Atlantic, and so on.

These are three very great myths which most historians of the period knew to be myths but which court historians, particularly those with salaries that are paid by universities with federal grants for research and development, either play down or flatly deny.

David Hume tells us that the Many are kept in order by the Few through Opinion. *The New York Times* in the U.S. is the Opinion-maker of the Few for some of the Many; so when the paper draws the line, as it were, other papers in other lands take heed and toe it. In *The Golden Age*, I revealed, tactfully I thought, life in Washington during the decade from the fall of France to Pearl Harbor to the Cold War and Korea. No one needs to know any history at all to follow the story. Even so, one American reviewer was upset that I did not know how 'dumbed-down' (his phrase) Americans were, and how dare I mention people that they had never heard of, such as Harry Hopkins?

But I am a fairly experienced narrator, and each character is, painlessly I hope, explained in context. Unfortunately, the new pop wisdom is that you must only write about what the readers already know about, which, in this case at least, would be an untrue story.

The New York Times hired a British journalist, once associated with *The New Republic,* a far-right paper unfavorable to me (it is a propagandist for Israel's Likudite faction, much as *The Washington Times* supports the line of its proprietor, Korea's Dr. Sun Moon). The hired journalist knew nothing of the period I was writing about. He quotes an aria from Herbert Hoover which he thinks I made up, when, as always with the historical figures that I quote, I only record what they are said to have said.

Hoover regarded, rightly or wrongly, FDR as in the same totalitarian mold as he saw Hitler, Mussolini, and Stalin: 'You cannot extend the mastery of the government over the daily working life of a people without at the same time making it the master of the people's souls and thoughts.' Our best modern historian, William Appleman Williams, in *Some Presidents: Wilson to Nixon* (1972), noted that it was Hoover's intuition that, in the first third of the twentieth century, the virus of totalitarian government was abroad in the world, and that Hitler in his demonic way and Stalin in his deadly bureaucratic way and FDR in his relatively melioristic way were each responding to a common Zeitgeist.

For a right-wing hired hand this should have been a profound analysis, but the reviewer fails to grasp it. He also ignores Hoover's astonishing aside: 'What this country needs is a great poem.' Most damaging to the integrity of my narrative (and the historians I relied on), the reviewer declares, without evidence, that . . . But let me quote from a letter by the historian Kai Bird which, to my amazement, *The New York Times* published (usually they suppress anything too critical of themselves or their Opinion-makers):

> Twice the reviewer dismisses as 'silly' Vidal's assertion that Harry Truman's use of the atomic bomb on Hiroshima was unnecessary because Japan had been trying for some months to surrender.
>
> Such assertions are neither silly nor . . . a product of Vidal's 'cranky politics.' Rather Vidal has cleverly drawn on a rich and scholarly literature published in the last decade to remind his readers that much of what orthodox court historians have written about the Cold War was simply wrong. With regard to Hiroshima, perhaps Vidal had in mind Truman's July 18, 1945, handwritten diary reference to a 'telegram from Jap emperor asking for peace.'

Or this August 3, 1945, item from the diary of Walter Brown:

> Brown notes a meeting with Secretary of State James F. Byrnes, Admiral W. D. Leahy, and Truman at which all

three agreed, 'Japs looking for peace' . . . But Truman wanted to drop the bomb; and did. Why? To frighten Stalin, a suitable enemy for the U.S. as it was about to metamorphose from an untidy republic into a national security state at 'perpetual war,' in Charles A. Beard's phrase, 'for perpetual peace.'

I fear that the *TLS* review of *The Golden Age* battened on the inaccuracies of *The New York Times* review; your reviewer is plainly an American neoconservative who enjoys crude reversals of categories. The American hard right has no known interest in the people at large, and a reverence for the 1 percent that pays for their journals and think tanks. He refers to my 'universally contemptuous Leftism' which involves 'sneering in its disregard for "the lower orders . . . the rather shadowy American people."' This is the oldest trick in bad book-reviewing. A novelist writes: '"I hate America," shrieked the Communist spy.' This will become, for the dishonest book reviewer, 'At one point, the author even confesses that he hates America.' But I know of no 'Leftist' (define) who sneers at the people, while no populist could. Rather I concentrate on what has been done to the people by the 1 percent through its mastery of the national wealth and made-in-the-house, as it were, Opinion. Your reviewer even misunderstands my own sharp conclusion that an era ended, happily in my view, when the traditional American servant class ceased to exist, thanks to the 13 million of us in the armed services and the full employment of women in the Second World War. That some of my sillier grandees mourn this state of affairs is a part of the social comedy of the narrative, admittedly not of quite so high an order as the inadvertent comedy of rightists affecting unrequited passion for Demos.

The final myth is that Stalin started the cold war by dividing

Germany into two sections, while trying to drive us out of our sector of Berlin. I'll quote the best authority, thus far, on what Truman was up to after Potsdam when he met Stalin, who, after Yalta, had expected to live in some sort of reasonable balance with the U.S. Here is Carolyn Eisenberg in *Drawing the Line: The American Decision to Divide Germany, 1944–1949* (1996):

> With the inception of the Berlin blockade, President
> Truman articulated a simple story that featured the
> Russians trampling the wartime agreements in their
> ruthless grab for the former German capital. The President
> did not explain that the United States had [unilaterally –
> my adverb] abandoned Yalta and Potsdam, that it was
> pushing the formation of a Western German state against
> the misgivings of many Europeans and that the Soviets had
> launched the blockade to prevent partition.

This great lie remains with us today. Please no letters about the horrors of the Gulag, Stalin's mistreatment of the buffer states, and so on. Our subject is the serious distortions of the truth on our side and why, unless they are straightened out, we are forever doomed to thrash about in a permanent uncomprehending fog. Good morning, Vietnam!

The attitude toward truth on the part of Truman's administration was best expressed by his secretary of state, Dean Acheson, in the memoir *Present at the Creation: My Years in the State Department* (1969). It was Acheson who launched the global empire on February 27, 1947. Place: Cabinet Room of the White House. Present: Truman, Secretary of State Marshall, Under Secretary Acheson, a half-dozen congressional leaders. The British had, yet again, run out of money. They could not honor their agreements to keep Greece tethered to freedom.

Could we take over? Although Stalin had warned the Greek Communists that their country was in the U.S. sphere and they should therefore expect no aid from him, Truman wanted a military buildup. We had to stand tall. But Marshall failed to convince the congressional leaders. Acheson, a superb corporate lawyer and a most witty man, leaped into the breach. He was impassioned. The free world stood at the brink. Yes, at Armageddon. Should the Russians occupy Greece and then Turkey, three continents would be at risk. He used the evergreen homely metaphor of how one rotten apple in a barrel could . . . Finally, were we not the heirs of the Roman Empire? Was not the Soviet Union our Carthage? Had not our Punic Wars begun? We dared not lose. 'America has no choice. We must act now to protect our security . . . to protect freedom itself.' It was then agreed that if Truman addressed the country in these terms and scared the hell out of the American people, Congress would finance what has turned out to be a half-century of cold war, costing, thus far, some $7.1 trillion.

In retrospect, Acheson wrote, cheerfully, 'If we did make our points clearer than truth, we did not differ from most other educators and could hardly do otherwise.' After all, as he noted, it was the State Department's view that the average American spent no more than ten minutes a day brooding on foreign policy; he spends less now that television advertising can make anything clearer than truth.

Today, we are not so much at the brink as fallen over it. Happily, as of this election, we were not at our old stamping ground, Armageddon. Rather, we were simply fretting about fibs involving drunken driving and the true cost of that mother-in-law's medicine as opposed to the pampered dog's, when, had the candidate been true to his roots, he could have found, in a back alley of Carthage, Tennessee, two pinches of cheap sulphur that would have dewormed both mother-in-law and dog in a jiffy.*

The Times Literary Supplement
10 November 2000

---

* It should be remembered that J. Q. Adams complained of Thomas Jefferson's 'large stories.' Example? Jefferson claimed to have learned Spanish in nineteen days aboard a transatlantic ship.

Japanese Intentions in the Second World War

Sir, – I am in Clive James's debt for the succinct way that he has assembled what must be at least 90 percent of all the Received Opinion having to do with the start and finish of the American–Japanese war of 1941–45 (Letters, November 24). Were it not for occasional Jacobean resonances, one might suspect that Dr. Barry Humphries had been working overtime in his bat-hung lab, assembling yet another Australian monster: a retired Lt. Col. with a powerful world-view fueled by the tabloid press of Oz.

James begins briskly: Vidal has an 'admonitory vision' to the effect that the 'leadership class' of the American empire thinks 'that Washington is the center of the world. Unfortunately, Vidal seems to think the same.'

Indeed they do. Indeed I do. Indeed, Washington has been the uncontested global center for most of the twentieth century, which I tend to deplore – Washington's primacy, that is. In a recent book, *The Golden Age*, I concentrate on the decade 1940–50 when the New World gave birth to the global arrangement.

I start with the convergence on Washington of more than 3,000 British agents, propagandists, spies. Yes, I was there. At the heart of an isolationist family that 'entertained,' as they used to say, everyone, I personally observed the brilliant John Foster in action. Foster was attached to Lord Lothian's British Embassy. He enchanted the Washingtonians while secretly working with Ben Cohen, a White House lawyer, to draft the Lend-Lease agreement which proved to be the first blow that President Roosevelt was able to strike for England. Residents of that other center, Canberra, no doubt have a different tale to tell.

I make the hardly original case that Franklin Roosevelt provoked the Japanese into attacking us for reasons that I shall come to presently.

James, armed to the teeth with Received Opinion (henceforth RO), tells us that Japan was provoked into war by the Japanese Army, 'which had been in a position to blackmail the Cabinet since 1922 and never ceased to do so until surrender in 1945,' brought on, as RO has it, by gallant Harry Truman's decision to drop a pair of atomic bombs. None of this conforms to what we have known for some time about the internal workings of Japan's intricate system of governance, not to mention our own. There was indeed a gung-ho Japanese military war party that was busy trying to conquer as much of China as possible en route to Southeast Asia where the oil was. There was also a peace party, headed by Prince Konoye, who was eager, as of August 1941, to meet with FDR, who kept postponing a face-to-face discussion to sort out differences. Had FDR been interested in peace in the Pacific, he could have met with Konoye, much as he was secretly meeting with Churchill on a soon-to-be-related matter.

James correctly notes that we had broken Japan's diplomatic code, Purple, but he seems unaware that, by early October 1940, we had also broken many of the Japanese military codes, specifically parts of the Kaigun Ango: the twenty-nine separate naval codes which gave us a good idea of what their fleet was up to during the entire year before Pearl Harbor. RO assures James that, if FDR wanted war, he would not have sent the Emperor, on December 6, a cable whose only message seemed to be a wistful hope that the Japanese would not try to replace the defeated French in Indo-China. James seems ignorant of the context of that message.

Here it is. On Saturday, November 15, 1941, General Marshall, the U.S. Army Chief of Staff, called in various Washington newspaper bureau chiefs. After swearing them to secrecy, he told them that we had broken Japan's naval codes, and that war with Japan would start sometime during the first ten days of December. On November 26, Cordell Hull, FDR's secretary of state, presented Japan's two special envoys to Washington with a ten-point proposal, intended, as Hull told Secretary of War Stimson, 'to kick the whole thing over.' Of FDR's ultimatum, Hull later remarked, 'We [had] no serious thought Japan would accept . . .' What was the proposal? Complete Japanese withdrawal from China and Indo-China, Japan to support China's Nationalist government and to abandon the tripartite agreement with the Axis. FDR had dropped a shoe. Now he waited for the Japanese to drop the other. They did. RO has it that we were taken by surprise. Certainly, FDR was not. But apparently the unwarned military commanders at Pearl Harbor were, and 3,000 men were killed in a single strike.

RO always had a difficult time with motive. Since FDR could never, ever, have set us up, why would the Japanese want to attack a wealthy continental nation 4,000 miles away? Fortunately, RO can always fall back on the demonic view of history. As a race, the Japanese were prone to suicide. Hardly human, they were a bestial people whose eyes were so configured that they could never handle modern aircraft or bombsights. As a young soldier in the Pacific, I was, along with everyone else, marinated in this racist nonsense. But should this demonic reading of the Japanese character not be true, one must wonder why the Japanese military, with a difficult war of conquest in China that was using up their wealth and energy in every sense, would want to provoke a war with the United States so far away? RO has had sixty years to come up with an answer; and failed to do so.

Today, no one seriously contests that FDR wanted the U.S. in the war against Hitler. But 60 to 80 percent of the American people were solidly against any European war. In November 1940, FDR had been elected to a third term with the pledge that none of America's sons would ever fight in a foreign war 'unless attacked.' Privately, more than once, he had said to others that the Japs must strike the first blow or, as he put it to Admiral James O. Richardson (October 8, 1940), 'as the war continued and the area of operations expanded, sooner or later they would make a mistake and we would enter the war'; hence, FDR's series of provocations culminating not in a Japanese 'mistake' but in the ultimatum of November 26 that left the Japanese with no alternative but war, preferably with a 'sneak' knockout attack of the sort that had succeeded so well against Russia in 1904, at Port Arthur. Did FDR know that the Japanese would attack Pearl Harbor, where much of our Pacific fleet was at anchor? Or did he think they would strike at some lesser venue like Manila? This matter is, yet again, under scrutiny.

James's RO is correct when he notes that the German-Italian-Japanese tripartite agreement was of a defensive nature. They were not obliged to join in each other's offensive wars. Why Hitler declared war upon the U.S. is still a 'puzzle,' according to no less a historian than Dr. Henry Kissinger, not a bad historian when not obliged to gaze into a mirror (cf. his *Diplomacy*).

At war at least in the Pacific, how could FDR be so sure that he would get his war in Europe? Well, FDR is easily the most intricate statesman of our time: as Nixon once said admiringly of Eisenhower, 'He was a far more sly and devious man than most people suspected, and I mean those words in their very best sense.'

Once the U.S. was wholeheartedly at war on December 8, 1941, our artful dodger could, under wartime powers, aid Britain and the Soviets, as he was already doing with Lend-Lease and other virtuous if quasi-legal measures. Also, FDR's problem with his election pledge ceased to exist when the Japanese responded so fiercely to his provocations and ultimatums. As usual, he got what he wanted.

Received Opinion: without Truman's pair of atom bombs, the famous Japanese war party that had seized control of the government would have ordered a million Japanese to jump off cliffs onto the invading Americans had not the Emperor, distressed by the bombs, etc. . . . Let us turn from comfortable RO to Authority, to Ambassador Joseph C. Grew's memoir, *Turbulent Era: A Diplomatic Record of Forty Years, 1904–1945*. As U.S. ambassador to Japan, Grew was dedicated to bringing together FDR and Prince Konoye, little suspecting that, where Konoye was apparently sincere in wanting peace, FDR was not. By autumn 1941, Grew was exasperated by Washington's unrelenting line that the Japanese government was completely dominated by the military war party:

> We in Tokyo were closer to the scene than was the
> Administration in Washington and we believed, on the
> basis of the highest possible intelligence, and so reported,

that the Japanese government at the time was in a position to control the armed forces of the country. We explained in several of our telegrams to our Government that Germany's attack on Soviet Russia had given those elements in Japan which controlled national policies further and convincing evidence that confidence could not be placed in Germany's promises . . . No one, I think, would contest the view that the Japanese government was in a far better position to control its forces in the summer of 1941 than it was in December 1938 . . .

The problem with RO, even when served up by so sensitive a writer as Clive James, is that contrary evidence must not be admitted. RO still clings to the myth that Japan would have fought to the end if Truman had not dropped his A-bombs. But Japanese envoys had been making overtures for a year in, variously, Sweden, Switzerland, Portugal, the Vatican, etc. Message: the war is over if the Emperor is retained.

Finally, the most important Japanese player, as I noted in my piece (November 10), the Emperor himself, on July 18, 1945, wrote Truman a letter 'looking for peace' (Truman's words). On August 3, 1945, an official's diary notes that Truman, Byrnes, and Leahy were discussing a telegram 'from the Emperor asking for peace.' Truman, inspired, some believe, by Secretary of State Byrnes, wanted to intimidate the Soviets with our super-weapon. So he had his two big bangs, contrary to the advice of his chief military commanders. Here is Eisenhower: 'I had been conscious of a feeling of depression and so I voiced to [Secretary of War Henry L. Stimson] my grave misgivings . . . I thought that our country should avoid shocking world opinion by the use of a weapon whose employment was, I thought, no longer mandatory as a measure to save American lives.'

FDR, like so many Americans of his generation, found irresistible the phrase 'unconditional surrender' – General U. S. Grant's adamantine message to the Confederacy. FDR applied it to the Axis powers. Truman inherited this policy. Then, once he had dropped his bombs, he promptly abandoned unconditional surrender and kept the Emperor. For Clive of Canberra, I recommend the latest, if not last, word on the subject, *The Decision To Use the Bomb and the Architecture of an American Myth* by Gar Alperovitz. For the why and what of Pearl Harbor, there is now R. B. Stinnett's *Day of Deceit*, soon to be a subject of strenous debate in another journal.

Again, how could FDR have known Hitler would declare war on us after Pearl Harbor? James's RO provides him with no sensible motive. So he falls back on the demonic – 'megalomania' which drove Hitler to ensure that he would be at war on every side. But this won't do. Hitler was certainly subject to fits of inspiration, but he was usually very cautious in his dealings with the 'mongrel' Americans. In his December 11 declaration of war to the Reichstag, he gave a seemingly rational if odd reason. On December 4, at the President's request, General Marshall had presented FDR with a war plan in which he proposed that, as Hitler was the principal enemy of the U.S. and the world, the United States should raise an expeditionary force of 5 million men and send it to invade Germany by July 1, 1943. The plan – one hopes of no more than a contingency nature – was leaked onto the front page of *The Chicago Tribune*, the great trumpet of isolationism. The headline, 'F.D.R.'S WAR PLANS!' Three days later, Pearl Harbor erased the story, but Hitler had seen it and mentioned it as 'proof' of FDR's predatory designs on the Axis, noting (more in sorrow than in anger?), 'Without any attempt at an official denial on the part of the American Government, President Roosevelt's plan has been published under which Germany and Italy are to be attacked with military force in Europe by 1943 at the latest.' (This is from *A World to Gain* by Thomas Toughill, an intriguing amateur sleuth.)

Finally, for an analysis of the persisting myth about the dropping of the A-bombs, Mr. Alperovitz is hearteningly shrewd.

The Times Literary Supplement
1 December 2000

Sir, – When Kenneth Tynan came to New York to practice his trade as drama critic, he had only recently become a Marxist. Brecht had had something to do with it, and I think he may have read some of Marx. Certainly he often quoted him, usually at midpoint during one of our late evenings at the Mayfair workers' canteen, Mirabelle. 'Money should not breed money,' Ken would stammer. Upon arrival in New York, he began to evangelize. I watched him with an ancient *Partisan Review* editor, a former Stalinist, Trotskyite, Reichian. Fiercely, Ken told him what it was that money must never do. When Ken had run out of breath, the weary old class warrior said, 'Mr. Tynan, your arguments are so old that I have forgotten all the answers to them.'

The estimable Clive James (Letters, December 8) is in a time warp similar to Ken's. Thirty years of incremental information about the American–Japanese war have passed him by. He thinks 'the real [Japanese] fleet sent no radio messages' en route to Pearl Harbor: that 'was long ago invalidated.' No. What has been invalidated is the myth that the Japanese kept complete radio silence. In 1993 and 1995 (under the Freedom of Information Act), all sorts of transcripts came to light, as well as Communication Intelligence Summaries such as this one for December 6, 1941, where an American code-breaker reported: 'The Commander in Chief Combined (Japanese) Fleet originated several messages to

Carriers, Fourth Fleet and the Major Commanders.' Each headed toward Hawaii and interacting. Although there is some evidence that James has kept up with the latest Hirohito books (Chrysanthemum Porn, as we call it in the trade), he has no interest in political revelations. I do. But then I spent five years researching *The Golden Age*, trying to figure out what actually happened at Pearl Harbor, and why the A-bombs were dropped after Japan was ready to surrender, and why . . . I shall not repeat myself, but I must note, in passing, the purity of a certain midtwentieth-century journalistic style that continues to reverberate like the beat beat beat of the tom-tom in Clive of Canberra's burnished prose. Ingredients? High Moral Indignation, no matter how hoked up, linked to *ad hominem* zingers from right field. I referred to the leader of the peace party at the Japanese court, Prince Konoye. I was interested in his proposals. Our period journalist is interested in Konoye as an anti-Semite who faked his own suicide note. Is it possible that I have misjudged Konoye's dedication to peace? Was he also, like so many Japanese princes, an adulterer? If so, was that the reason FDR refused to meet him at Juneau, an Alaskan beauty spot that is, in summer, a breeding ground for the largest mosquitoes in North America? FDR's sense of fun seldom abandoned him In any case, for whatever reason, after suggesting a comical venue, FDR backed down. Peace in the Pacific was not his dream.

Next, Charles Lindbergh, my 'other questionable hero,' is dragged in, so that we can be told, with righteous anger, how 'his isolationism was *de facto* an instrument of Axis policy.' Surely James the Latinist means *ad hoc* in a sentence admittedly quite as meaningless as that tom-tom pounding you you you. He does admit that 'Lindbergh did loyal service [in the war] and even shot down a Japanese plane but [one] can't help wondering about the American planes he shot down with his mouth'; moral outrage is now in high gear – pass me the sick bag, Alice, or whatever that splendid gel was called. In real life, Lindbergh was sent by FDR to take a look at the German Air Force and plane production. Lindbergh was sufficiently alarmed by what he saw to urge increased American production of aircraft for war, particularly the B-17. He was, of course, an isolationist, and so was reflective of a majority of the American people before Pearl Harbor.

Then, alas, we hear that 'Ambassador Joseph Grew, alas, won't do for a hero either.' Plainly my world contained no heroes. Although Grew was much admired for his brilliance and probity by those of us who had relations with him, the great Canberra moralist tells us that he was worse than an anti-Semite, he was a snob. Could it be that this terrible flaw in his character encouraged the war party in Tokyo to attack the United States? But Mr. James – again alas – never connects his enticing dots. Actually, Grew's problem as a diplomat was that he tried to maintain the peace between Japan and the U.S., when his president had other plans which involved maneuvering the Japanese into striking the first blow so that we could go to war. But then James always dodges the great unanswered question: unless provoked by us, *why did the Japanese attack?* He waffles a bit about their desire for 'unopposed expansion.' To where? Chicago?

Finally, a rhetorical question to me. If I had been told in 1945 that we had a weapon 'so devastating that it could end that . . . war in a week,' what would I have said? Well, none of us was consulted. But we were, most of us, highly in favor of using the Bomb. On the other hand, had we been told that the war could have been concluded as of May 1945, I would have gone to work for the impeachment of a president who had wasted so many lives and destroyed so many cities in his power game with the Soviet Union which led, inexorably, to a half-century of unnecessary cold war. I am also bemused that a witness so all-knowing, if not knowledge-able, as Clive James, still doesn't understand what happened to him, to all of us, for most of our lives.

The Times Literary Supplement
15 December 2000

The Meaning of
Timothy McVeigh

Toward the end of the last century but one, Richard Wagner made a visit to the southern Italian town of Ravello, where he was shown the gardens of the thousand-year-old Villa Rufolo. 'Maestro,' asked the head gardener, 'do not these fantastic gardens 'neath yonder azure sky that blends in such perfect harmony with yonder azure sea closely resemble those fabled gardens of Klingsor where you have set so much of your latest interminable opera, *Parsifal*? Is not this vision of loveliness your inspiration for Klingsor?' Wagner muttered something in German. 'He say,' said a nearby translator, '"How about that?"'

How about that indeed, I thought, as I made my way toward a corner of those fabled gardens, where ABC-TV's *Good Morning America* and CBS's *Early Show* had set up their cameras so that I could appear 'live' to viewers back home in God's country.

This was last May. In a week's time 'the Oklahoma City Bomber,' a decorated hero of the Gulf War, one of Nature's Eagle Scouts, Timothy McVeigh, was due to be executed by lethal injection in Terre Haute, Indiana, for being, as he himself insisted, the sole maker and detonator of a bomb that blew up a federal building in which died 168 men, women, and children. This was the greatest massacre of Americans by an American since two years earlier, when the federal government decided to take out the compound of a Seventh-Day Adventist cult near Waco, Texas. The Branch Davidians, as the cultists called themselves, were a peaceful group of men, women, and children living and praying together in anticipation of the end of the world, which started to come their way on February 28, 1993. The Federal Bureau of Alcohol, Tobacco and Firearms, exercising its mandate to 'regulate' firearms, refused all invitations from cult leader David Koresh to inspect his licensed firearms. The ATF instead opted for fun. More than 100 ATF agents, without proper warrants, attacked the church's compound while, overhead, at least one ATF helicopter fired at the roof of the main building. Six Branch Davidians were killed that day. Four ATF agents were shot dead, by friendly fire, it was thought.

There was a standoff. Followed by a fifty-one-day siege in which loud music was played twenty-four hours a day outside the compound. Then electricity was turned off. Food was denied the children. Meanwhile, the media were briefed regularly on the evils of David Koresh. Apparently, he was making and selling crystal meth; he was also – what else in these sick times? – not a Man of God but a Pedophile. The new attorney general, Janet Reno, then got tough. On April 19 she ordered the FBI to finish up what the ATF had begun. In defiance of the Posse Comitatus Act (a basic bulwark of our fragile liberties that forbids the use of the military against civilians), tanks of the Texas National Guard and the army's Joint Task Force Six attacked the compound with a gas deadly to children and not too healthy for adults while ramming holes in the building. Some Davidians escaped. Others were shot by FBI snipers. In an investigation six years later, the FBI denied ever shooting off anything much more than a pyrotechnic tear-gas canister. Finally, during a six-hour assault, the building was set fire to and then bulldozed by Bradley armored vehicles. God saw to it that no FBI man was hurt while more than eighty cult members were killed, of whom twenty-seven were children. It was a great victory for Uncle Sam, as intended by the FBI, whose code name for the assault was Show Time.

It wasn't until May 14, 1995 that Janet Reno, on *60 Minutes*, confessed to second thoughts. 'I saw what happened, and knowing what happened, I would not do it again.' Plainly, a learning experience for the Florida daughter of a champion lady alligator rassler.

The April 19, 1993, show at Waco proved to be the largest massacre of Americans by their own government since 1890, when a number of Native Americans were slaughtered at Wounded Knee, South Dakota. Thus the ante keeps upping.

Although McVeigh was soon to indicate that he had acted in retaliation for what had happened at Waco (he had even picked the second anniversary of the slaughter, April 19, for his act of retribution), our government's secret police, together with its allies in the media, put, as it were, a heavy fist upon the scales. There was to be only one story: one man of incredible innate evil wanted to destroy innocent lives for no reason other than a spontaneous joy in evildoing. From the beginning, it was ordained that McVeigh was to have no coherent motive for what he had done other than a Shakespearean motiveless malignity. Iago is now back in town, with a bomb, not a handkerchief. More to the point, he and the prosecution agreed that he had no serious accomplices.

I sat on an uncomfortable chair, facing a camera. Generators hummed amid the delphiniums. *Good Morning America* was first. I had been told that Diane Sawyer would be questioning me from

New York, but ABC has a McVeigh 'expert,' one Charles Gibson, and he would do the honors. Our interview would be something like four minutes. Yes, I was to be interviewed In Depth. This means that only every other question starts with 'Now, tell us, briefly . . .' Dutifully, I told, briefly, how it was that McVeigh, whom I had never met, happened to invite me to be one of the five chosen witnesses to his execution.

Briefly, it all began in the November 1998 issue of *Vanity Fair*. I had written a piece about 'the shredding of our Bill of Rights.' I cited examples of IRS seizures of property without due process of law, warrantless raids and murders committed against innocent people by various drug-enforcement groups, government collusion with agribusiness's successful attempts to drive small farmers out of business, and so on. Then, as a coda, I discussed the illegal but unpunished murders at Ruby Ridge, Idaho (a mother and child and dog had been killed in cold blood by the FBI); then, the next year, Waco. The media expressed little outrage in either case. Apparently, the trigger words had not been spoken. Trigger words? Remember *The Manchurian Candidate*? George Axelrod's splendid 1962 film, where the brainwashed (by North Koreans) protagonist can only be set in murderous motion when the gracious garden-club lady, played by Angela Lansbury, says, 'Why don't you pass the time by playing a little solitaire?'

Since we had been told for weeks that the Branch Davidian leader, David Koresh, was not only a drug dealer but the sexual abuser of the twenty-seven children in his compound, the maternal Ms. Reno in essence decreed: Better that they all be dead than defiled. Hence, the attack. Later, eleven members of the Branch Davidian Church were put on trial for the 'conspiracy to commit murder' of the federal agents who had attacked them. The jury found all eleven innocent on that charge. But after stating that the defendants were guilty of attempted murder – the very charge of which they had just been acquitted – the judge sentenced eight innocent church members up to forty years on lesser charges. One disgusted juror said, 'The wrong people were on trial.' Show Time!

Personally, I was sufficiently outraged to describe in detail what had actually happened. Meanwhile, the card players of 1998 were busy shuffling and dealing. Since McVeigh had been revealed as evil itself, no one was interested in why he had done what he had done. But then 'why' is a question the media are trained to shy away from. Too dangerous. One might actually learn why something had happened and become thoughtful. I wrote in these pages:

For Timothy McVeigh, [Waco and Ruby Ridge] became the symbol of [federal] oppression and murder. Since he was now suffering from an exaggerated sense of justice, not a common American trait, he went to war pretty much on his own and ended up slaughtering more innocents than the Feds had at Waco. Did he know what he was doing when he blew up the Alfred P. Murrah Federal Building in Oklahoma City because it contained the hated [Feds]? McVeigh remained silent throughout his trial. Finally, as he was about to be sentenced, the court asked him if he would like to speak. He did. He rose and said, 'I wish to use the words of Justice Brandeis dissenting in *Olmstead* to speak for me. He wrote, "Our government is the potent, the omnipresent teacher. For good or ill, it teaches the whole people by its example."' Then McVeigh was sentenced to death by the government.

Those present were deeply confused by McVeigh's quotation. How could the Devil quote so saintly a justice? I suspect that he did it in the same spirit that Iago answered Othello when asked why he had done what he had done: 'Demand me nothing, what you know you know, from this time forth I never will speak word.' Now we know, too: or as my grandfather used to say back in Oklahoma, 'Every pancake has two sides.'

When McVeigh, on appeal in a Colorado prison, read what I had written he wrote me a letter and . . .

But I've left you behind in the Ravello garden of Klingsor, where, live on television, I mentioned the unmentionable word 'why,' followed by the atomic trigger word 'Waco.' Charles Gibson, 3,500 miles away, began to hyperventilate. 'Now, wait a minute . . .' he interrupted. But I talked through him. Suddenly I heard him say, 'We're having trouble with the audio.' Then he pulled the plug that linked ABC and me. The soundman beside me shook his head. 'Audio was working perfectly. He just cut you off.' So, in addition to the governmental shredding of Amendments Four, Five, Six, Eight, and Fourteen, Mr. Gibson switched off the journalists' sacred First.

Why? Like so many of his interchangeable TV colleagues, he is in place to tell the viewers that former senator John Danforth had just concluded a fourteen-month investigation of the FBI that cleared the bureau of any wrongdoing at Waco. Danforth did admit that 'it was like pulling teeth to get all this paper from the FBI.'

In March 1993, McVeigh drove from Arizona to Waco, Texas, in order to observe firsthand the federal siege. Along with other protesters, he was duly photographed by the F.B.I. During the siege the cultists were entertained with twenty-four-hour ear-shattering tapes (Nancy Sinatra: 'These boots are made for walkin' / And that's just what they'll do, / One of these days these boots are gonna walk all over you') as well as the recorded shrieks of dying rabbits, reminiscent of the first George Bush's undeclared war on Panama, which after several similar concerts outside the Vatican Embassy yielded up the master drug criminal (and former CIA agent) Noriega, who had taken refuge inside. Like the TV networks, once our government has a hit it will be repeated over and over again. Oswald? Conspiracy? Studio laughter.

TV-watchers have no doubt noted so often that they are no longer aware of how often the interchangeable TV hosts handle anyone who tries to explain why something happened. 'Are you suggesting that there was a conspiracy?' A twinkle starts in a pair of bright contact lenses. No matter what the answer, there is a wriggling of the body, followed by a tiny snort and a significant glance into the camera to show that the guest has just been delivered to the studio by flying saucer. This is one way for the public never to understand what actual conspirators – whether in the FBI or on the Supreme Court or toiling for Big Tobacco – are up to. It is also a sure way of keeping information from the public. The function, alas, of Corporate Media.

In fact, at one point, former senator Danforth threatened the recalcitrant FBI director Louis Freeh with a search warrant. It is a pity that he did not get one. He might, in the process, have discovered a bit more about Freeh's membership in Opus Dei (meaning 'God's work'), a secretive international Roman Catholic order dedicated to getting its membership into high political, corporate, and religious offices (and perhaps even heaven too) in various lands to various ends. Lately, reluctant medialight was cast on the order when it was discovered that Robert Hanssen, an FBI agent, had been a Russian spy for 22 years but also that he and his director, Louis Freeh, in the words of their fellow traveler William Rusher (*The Washington Times*, March 15, 2001), 'not only [were] both members of the same Roman Catholic Church in suburban Virginia but . . . also belonged to the local chapter of Opus Dei.'

Mr. Rusher, once of the devil-may-care *National Review*, found this 'piquant.' Opus Dei was founded in 1928 by José-Maria Escrivá. Its lay godfather, in early years, was the Spanish dictator Francisco Franco. One of its latest paladins was the corrupt Peruvian president Alberto Fujimoro, still *in absentia*. Although Opus Dei tends to fascism, the current Pope has beatified Escrivá, disregarding the caveat of the Spanish theologian Juan Martin Velasco: 'We cannot portray as a model of Christian living some-one who has served the power of the state [the fascist Franco] and who used that power to launch his Opus, which he ran with obscure criteria – like a Mafia shrouded in white – not accepting papal magisterium when it failed to coincide with his way of thinking.'

Once, when the mysterious Mr. Freeh was asked whether or not he was a member of Opus Dei, he declined to respond, obliging an FBI special agent to reply in his stead. Special Agent John E. Collingwood said, 'While I cannot answer your specific questions, I note that you have been "informed" incorrectly.'

It is most disturbing that in the secular United States, a nation whose Constitution is based upon the perpetual separation of church and state, an absolutist religious order not only has placed one of its members at the head of our secret (and largely unac-countable) police but also can now count on the good offices of at least two members of the Supreme Court.

From *Newsweek*, March 9, 2001:

[Justice Antonin] Scalia is regarded as the embodiment of
the Catholic conservatives . . . While he is not a member of
Opus Dei, his wife Maureen has attended Opus Dei's
spiritual functions . . . [while their son], Father Paul Scalia,
helped convert Clarence Thomas to Catholicism four years
ago. Last month, Thomas gave a fiery speech at the

American Enterprise Institute, a conservative think-tank,
to an audience full of Bush Administration officials. In the
speech Thomas praised Pope John Paul II for taking
unpopular stands.

And to think that Thomas Jefferson and John Adams opposed
the presence of the relatively benign Jesuit order in our land of laws
if not of God. President Bush has said that Scalia and Thomas are
the models for the sort of justices that he would like to appoint in
his term of office. Lately, in atonement for his wooing during the
election of the fundamentalist Protestants at Bob Jones University,
Bush has been 'reaching out' to the Roman Catholic far right. He
is already solid with fundamentalist Protestants. In fact, his attorney general, J. D. Ashcroft, is a Pentecostal Christian who starts
each day at eight with a prayer meeting attended by Justice
Department employees eager to be drenched in the blood of the
lamb. In 1999, Ashcroft told Bob Jones University graduates that
America was founded on religious principles (news to Jefferson et
al.) and 'we have no king but Jesus.'

I have already noted a number of conspiracies that are beginning to register as McVeigh's highly manipulated story moves
toward that ghastly word 'closure,' which, in this case, will simply
mark a new beginning. The Opus Dei conspiracy is – was? – central to the Justice Department. Then the FBI conspired to withhold
documents from the McVeigh defense as well as from the department's alleged master: *We the People* in Congress Assembled as
embodied by former senator Danforth. Finally, the ongoing spontaneous media conspiracy to demonize McVeigh, who acted alone,
despite contrary evidence.

But let's return to the FBI conspiracy to cover up its crimes at
Waco. Senator Danforth is an honorable man, but then, so was

Chief Justice Earl Warren, and the findings of his eponymous commission on the events at Dallas did not, it is said, ever entirely convince even him. On June 1, Danforth told *The Washington Post*, 'I bet that Timothy McVeigh, at some point in time, I don't know when, will be executed and after the execution there will be some box found, somewhere.' You are not, Senator, just beating your gums. Also, on June 1, *The New York Times* ran an A.P. story in which lawyers for the Branch Davidians claim that when the FBI agents fired upon the cultists they used a type of short assault rifle that was later not tested. Our friend FBI spokesman John Collingwood said that a check of the bureau's records showed that 'the shorter-barreled rifle was among the weapons tested.' Danforth's response was pretty much, Well, if you say so. He did note, again, that he had got 'something less than total cooperation' from the FBI As H. L. Mencken put it, '[The Department of Justice] has been engaged in sharp practices since the earliest days and remains a fecund source of oppression and corruption today. It is hard to recall an administration in which it was not the center of grave scandal.'

Freeh himself seems addicted to dull sharp practices. In 1996 he was the relentless Javert who came down so hard on an Atlanta security guard, Richard Jewell, over the Olympic Games bombing. Jewell was innocent. Even as he sent out for a new hair shirt (Opus Dei members mortify the flesh) and gave the order to build a new guillotine, the FBI lab was found to have routinely bungled investigations (read *Tainting Evidence*, by J. F. Kelly and P. K. Wearne). Later, Freeh led the battle to prove Wen Ho Lee a Communist spy. Freeh's deranged charges against the blameless Los Alamos scientist were thrown out of court by an enraged federal judge who felt that the FBI had 'embarrassed the whole nation.' Well, it's always risky, God's work.

Even so, the more one learns about the FBI, the more one

realizes that it is a very dangerous place indeed. Kelly and Wearne, in their investigation of its lab work, literally a life-and-death matter for those under investigation, quote two English forensic experts on the subject of the Oklahoma City bombing. Professor Brian Caddy, after a study of the lab's findings: 'If these reports are the ones to be presented to the courts as evidence then I am appalled by their structure and information content. The structure of the reports seems designed to confuse the reader rather than help him.' Dr. John Lloyd noted, 'The reports are purely conclusory in nature. It is impossible to determine from them the chain of custody, on precisely what work has been done on each item.' Plainly, the time has come to replace this vast inept and largely unaccountable secret police with a more modest and more efficient bureau to be called 'the United States Bureau of Investigation.'

It is now June 11, a hot, hazy morning here in Ravello. We've just watched Son of Show Time in Terre Haute, Indiana. CNN duly reported that I had not been able to be a witness, as McVeigh had requested: the attorney general had given me too short a time to get from here to there. I felt somewhat better when I was told that, lying on the gurney in the execution chamber, he would not have been able to see any of us through the tinted glass windows all around him. But then members of the press who were present said that he had deliberately made 'eye contact' with his witnesses and with them. He did see his witnesses, according to Cate McCauley, who was one. 'You could tell he was gone after the first shot,' she said. She had worked on his legal case for a year as one of his defense investigators.

I asked about his last hours. He had been searching for a movie on television and all he could find was *Fargo*, for which he was in no mood. Certainly he died in character; that is, in control. The first shot, of sodium pentothal, knocks you out. But he kept his eyes open. The second shot, of pancuronium bromide, collapsed his lungs. Always the survivalist, he seemed to ration his remaining breaths. When, after four minutes, he was officially dead, his eyes were still open, staring into the ceiling camera that was recording him 'live' for his Oklahoma City audience.

McVeigh made no final statement, but he had copied out, it appeared from memory, 'Invictus,' a poem by W. E. Henley (1849–1903). Among Henley's numerous writings was a popular anthology called *Lyra Heroica* (1892), about those who had done selfless heroic deeds. I doubt if McVeigh ever came across it, but he would, no doubt, have identified with a group of young writers, among them Kipling, who were known as 'Henley's young men,' forever standing on burning decks, each a master of his fate, captain of his soul.

Characteristically, no talking head mentioned Henley's name, because no one knew who he was. Many thought this famous poem was McVeigh's work. One irritable woman described Henley as 'a nineteenth-century cripple.' I fiercely E-mailed her network: the one-legged Henley was 'extremities challenged.'

The stoic serenity of McVeigh's last days certainly qualified him as a Henley-style hero. He did not complain about his fate; took responsibility for what he was thought to have done; did not beg for mercy as our always sadistic media require. Meanwhile, conflicting details about him accumulate – a bewildering mosaic, in fact – and he seems more and more to have stumbled into the wrong American era. Plainly, he needed a self-consuming cause to define him. The abolition of slavery or the preservation of the Union would have been more worthy of his life than anger at the excesses of our corrupt secret police. But he was stuck where he was and so he declared war on a government that he felt had declared war on its own people.

One poetic moment in what was largely an orchestrated hymn of hatred. Outside the prison, a group of anti-death-penalty people prayed together in the dawn's early light. Suddenly, a bird appeared and settled on the left forearm of a woman, who continued her prayers. When, at last, she rose to her feet the bird remained on her arm – consolation? *Ora pro nobis.*

CNN gave us bits and pieces of McVeigh's last morning. Asked why he had not at least said that he was sorry for the murder of innocents, he said that he could say it but he would not have meant it. He was a soldier in a war, not of his making. This was Henleyesque. One biographer described him as honest to a fault. McVeigh had also noted that Harry Truman had never said that he was sorry about dropping two atomic bombs on an already defeated Japan, killing around 200,000 people, mostly collateral women and children. Media howled that that was wartime. But McVeigh considered himself, rightly or wrongly, at war, too. Incidentally, the inexorable beatification of Harry Truman is now an important aspect of our evolving imperial system. It is widely believed that the bombs were dropped to save American lives. This is not true. The bombs were dropped to frighten our new enemy, Stalin. To a man, our leading World War II commanders, including Eisenhower, C. W. Nimitz, and even Curtis LeMay (played so well by George C. Scott in *Dr Strangelove*), were opposed to Truman's use of the bombs against a defeated enemy trying to surrender. A friend from live television, the late Robert Alan Aurthur, made a documentary about Truman. I asked him what he thought of him. 'He just gives you all these canned answers. The only time I got a rise out of him was when I suggested that he tell us about his decision to drop the atomic bombs in the actual ruins of Hiroshima. Truman looked at me for the first time. "O.K.," he said, "but I won't kiss their asses."' Plainly another Henley hero, with far more collateral damage to his credit than McVeigh. Was it Chaplin's M. Verdoux who said that when it comes to calibrating liability for murder it is all, finally, a matter of scale?

After my adventures in the Ravello gardens (CBS's Bryant Gumbel was his usual low-key, courteous self and did not pull the cord), I headed for Terre Haute by way of Manhattan. I did several programs where I was cut off at the word 'Waco.' Only CNN's Greta Van Susteren got the point. 'Two wrongs,' she said, sensibly, 'don't make a right.' I quite agreed with her. But then, since I am against the death penalty, I noted that three wrongs are hardly an improvement.

Then came the stay of execution. I went back to Ravello. The media were now gazing at me. Time and again I would hear or read that I had written McVeigh first, congratulating him, presumably, on his killings. I kept explaining, patiently, how, after he had read me in *Vanity Fair*, it was he who wrote me, starting an off-and-on three-year correspondence. As it turned out, I could not go so I was not able to see with my own eyes the bird of dawning alight upon the woman's arm.

The first letter to me was appreciative of what I had written. I wrote him back. To show what an eager commercialite I am – hardly school of Capote – I kept no copies of my letters to him until the last one in May.

The second letter from his Colorado prison is dated '28 Feb 99.' 'Mr. Vidal, thank you for your letter. I received your book United States last week and have since finished most of Part 2 – your political musings.' I should say that spelling and grammar are perfect throughout, while the handwriting is oddly even and slants to the left, as if one were looking at it in a mirror. 'I think you'd be surprised at how much of that material I agree with . . .

As to your letter, I fully recognize that 'the general rebellion against what our gov't has become is the most interesting (and I think important) story in our history this century.' This is why I have been mostly disappointed at previous stories attributing the OKC bombing to a simple act of 'revenge' for Waco – and why I was most pleased to read your Nov. article in Vanity Fair. In the 4 years since the bombing, your work is the first to really explore the underlying motivations for such a strike against the U.S. Government – and for that, I thank you. I believe that such in-depth reflections are vital if one truly wishes to understand the events of April 1995.

Although I have many observations that I'd like to throw at you, I must keep this letter to a practical length – so I will mention just one: if federal agents are like 'so many Jacobins at war' with the citizens of this country, and if federal agencies 'daily wage war' against those citizens, then should not the OKC bombing be considered a 'counter-attack' rather than a self-declared war? Would it not be more akin to Hiroshima than Pearl Harbor? (I'm sure the Japanese were just as shocked and surprised at Hiroshima – in fact, was that anticipated effect not part and parcel of the overall strategy of that bombing?)

Back to your letter, I had never considered your age as an impediment [here he riots in tact!] until I received that letter – and noted that it was typed on a *manual typewriter?* Not to worry, recent medical studies tell us that Italy's taste for canola oil, olive oil and wine helps extend the average lifespan and helps prevent heart disease in Italians – so you picked the right place to retire to.

Again, thank you for dropping me a line – and as far as

any concern over what or how to write someone 'in my situation,' I think you'd find that many of us are still just 'regular Joes' – regardless of public perception – so there need be no special consideration(s) given to whatever you wish to write. Until next time, then . . .

Under this line he has put in quotes ' "Every normal man must be tempted at times to spit on his hands, hoist the black flag, and begin slitting throats." – H. L. Mencken. Take good care.'

He signed off with scribbled initials. Needless to say, this letter did not conform to any notion that I had had of him from reading the rabid U.S. press led, as always, by *The New York Times*, with their clumsy attempts at Freudian analysis (e.g., he was a broken blossom because his mother left his father in his sixteenth year – actually he seemed relieved). Later, there was a year or so when I did not hear from him. Two reporters from a Buffalo newspaper (he was born and raised near Buffalo) were at work interviewing him for their book, *American Terrorist*. I do think I wrote him that Mencken often resorted to Swiftian hyperbole and was not to be taken too literally. Could the same be said of McVeigh? There is always the interesting possibility – prepare for the grandest conspiracy of all – that he neither made nor set off the bomb outside the Murrah building: it was only later, when facing either death or life imprisonment, that he saw to it that he would be given sole credit for hoisting the black flag and slitting throats, to the rising fury of various 'militias' across the land who are currently outraged that he is getting sole credit for a revolutionary act organized, some say, by many others. At the end, if this scenario is correct, he and the detested Feds were of a single mind.

As Senator Danforth foresaw, the government would execute McVeigh as soon as possible (within ten days of Danforth's statement to *The Washington Post*) in order not to have to produce so quickly that mislaid box with documents which might suggest that others were involved in the bombing. The fact that McVeigh himself was eager to commit what he called 'federally assisted suicide' simply seemed a bizarre twist to a story that no matter how one tries to straighten it out never quite conforms to the Ur-plot of lone crazed killer (Oswald) killed by a second lone crazed killer (Ruby), who would die in stir with, he claimed, a tale to tell. Unlike Lee Harvey ('I'm the patsy') Oswald, our Henley hero found irresistible the role of lone warrior against a bad state. Where, in his first correspondence with me, he admits to nothing for the obvious reason his lawyers have him on appeal, in his last letter to me, April 20, 2001 – 'T. McVeigh 12076-064 POB 33 Terre Haute, In. 47808 (USA)' – he writes, 'Mr. Vidal, if you have read the recently published "American Terrorist", then you've probably realized that you hit the nail on the head with your article "The War at Home". Enclosed is supplemental material to add to that insight.' Among the documents he sent was an ABCNews.com chat transcript of a conversation with Timothy McVeigh's psychiatrist. The interview with Dr. John Smith was conducted by a moderator, March 29 of this year. Dr. Smith had had only one session with McVeigh, six years earlier. Apparently McVeigh had released him from his medical oath of confidentiality so that he could talk to Lou Michel and Dan Herbeck, authors of *American Terrorist*.

Moderator: You say that Timothy McVeigh 'was not deranged' and that he has 'no major mental illness'. So why, in your view, would he commit such a terrible crime?

Dr. John Smith: Well, I don't think he committed it because he was deranged or misinterpreting reality . . . He was overly sensitive, to the point of being a little paranoid, about the actions of the government. But he committed the act mostly out of revenge because of the Waco assault, but he also wanted to make a political statement about the role of the federal government and protest the use of force against the citizens. So to answer your original question, it was a conscious choice on his part, not because he was deranged, but because he was serious.

Dr. Smith then notes McVeigh's disappointment that the media had shied away from any dialogue 'about the misuse of power by the federal government.' Also, 'his statement to me, "I did not expect a revolution". Although he did go on to tell me that he had had discussions with some of the militias who lived in the hills around Kingman, AZ, about how easy it would be, with certain guns in the hills there, to cut interstate 40 in two and in that sense interfere with transportation from between the eastern and western part of the United States – a rather grandiose discussion.'

Grandiose but, I think, in character for those rebels who like to call themselves Patriots and see themselves as similar to the American colonists who separated from England. They are said to number from two to four million, of whom some 400,000 are activists in the militias. Although McVeigh never formally joined any group, for three years he drove all around the country, networking with like-minded gun-lovers and federal-government-haters; he also learned, according to *American Terrorist*, 'that the government was planning a massive raid on gun owners and members of the Patriot community in the spring of 1995.' This was all the trigger that McVeigh needed for what he would do – shuffle the deck, as it were.

The Turner Diaries is a racist daydream by a former physics teacher writing under the pseudonym Andrew Macdonald. Although McVeigh has no hang-ups about blacks, Jews, and all the other enemies of the various 'Aryan' white nations to be found in the Patriots' ranks, he shares the *Diaries'* obsession with guns and explosives and a final all-out war against the 'System.' Much has been made, rightly, of a description in the book of how to build a bomb like the one he used at Oklahoma City. When asked if McVeigh acknowledged copying this section from the novel, Dr. Smith said, 'Well, sort of. Tim wanted it made clear that, unlike *The Turner Diaries*, he was not a racist. He made that very clear. He did not hate homosexuals. He made that very clear.' As for the book as an influence, 'he's not going to share credit with anyone.' Asked to sum up, the good doctor said, simply, 'I have always said to myself that if there had not been a Waco, there would not have been an Oklahoma City.'

McVeigh also sent me a 1998 piece he had written for *Media Bypass*. He calls it 'Essay on Hypocrisy.'

The administration has said that Iraq has no right to stockpile chemical or biological weapons . . . mainly because they have used them in the past. Well, if that's the standard by which these matters are decided, then the U.S. is the nation that set the precedent. The U.S. has stockpiled these same weapons (and more) for over 40 years. The U.S. claims that this was done for the deterrent purposes during its 'Cold War' with the Soviet Union. Why, then, is it invalid for Iraq to claim the same reason (deterrence) – with respect to Iraq's (real) war with, and the continued threat of, its neighbor Iran? . . .

Yet when discussion shifts to Iraq, any day-care center in a government building instantly becomes 'a shield.' Think about it. (Actually, there is a difference here. The administration has admitted to knowledge of the presence of children in or near Iraqi government buildings, yet they still proceed with their plans to bomb – saying that they cannot be held responsible if children die. There is no such proof, however, that knowledge of the presence of children existed in relation to the Oklahoma City bombing.)

Thus, he denies any foreknowledge of the presence of children in the Murrah building, unlike the FBI, which knew that there were children in the Davidian compound, and managed to kill twenty-seven of them.

McVeigh quotes again from Justice Brandeis: 'Our government is the potent, the omnipresent teacher. For good or ill it teaches the whole people by its example.' He stops there. But Brandeis goes on to write in his dissent, 'Crime is contagious. If the government becomes the law breaker, it breeds contempt for laws; it invites every man to become a law unto himself.' Thus the straight-arrow model soldier unleashed his terrible swift sword and the innocent died. But then a lawless government, Brandeis writes, 'invites anarchy. To declare that in the administration of the criminal law the end justifies the means – to declare that the government may commit crimes in order to secure the conviction of a private criminal – would bring terrible retribution.'

One wonders if the Opus Dei plurality of the present Supreme Court's five-to-four majority has ever pondered these words so different from, let us say, one of its essential thinkers, Machiavelli, who insisted that, above all, the Prince must be feared.

Finally, McVeigh sent me three pages of longhand notes dated April 4, 2001, a few weeks before he was first scheduled to die. It is addressed to 'C.J.'(?), whose initials he has struck out.

I explain herein why I bombed the Murrah Federal
Building in Oklahoma City. I explain this not for publicity,
nor seeking to win an argument of right or wrong, I

explain so that the record is clear as to my thinking and
motivations in bombing a government installation.

I chose to bomb a Federal Building because such an
action served more purposes than other options. Foremost,
the bombing was a retaliatory strike: a counter-attack, for
the cumulative raids (and subsequent violence and
damage) that federal agents had participated in over the
preceding years (including, but not limited to, Waco).
From the formation of such units as the FBI's 'Hostage
Rescue' and other assault teams amongst federal agencies
during the 80s, culminating in the Waco incident, federal
actions grew increasingly militaristic and violent, to the
point where at Waco, our government – like the Chinese –
was deploying tanks against its own citizens.

. . . For all intents and purposes, federal agents had
become 'soldiers' (using military training, tactics,
techniques, equipment, language, dress, organization and
mindset) and they were escalating their behavior.
Therefore, this bombing was also meant as a pre-emptive
(or pro-active) strike against those forces and their
command and control centers within the federal building.
When an aggressor force continually launches attacks from
a particular base of operations, it is sound military strategy
to take the fight to the enemy. Additionally, borrowing a
page from U.S. foreign policy, I decided to send a message
to a government that was becoming increasingly hostile, by
bombing a government building and the government
employees within that building who represent that
government. Bombing the Murrah Federal Building was
morally and strategically equivalent to the U.S. hitting a
government building in Serbia, Iraq, or other nations.
Based on observations of the policies of my own

government, I viewed this action as an acceptable option. From this perspective what occurred in Oklahoma City was no different than what Americans rain on the heads of others all the time, and, subsequently, my mindset was and is one of clinical detachment. (The bombing of the Murrah Building was not personal no more than when Air Force, Army, Navy or Marine personnel bomb or launch cruise missiles against (foreign) government installations and their personnel.)

I hope this clarification amply addresses your question.
Sincerely,
T.M.
USP Terre Haute (In.)

There were many outraged press notes and letters when I said that McVeigh suffered from 'an exaggerated sense of justice.' I did not really need the adjective except that I knew that few Americans seriously believe that anyone is capable of doing anything except out of personal self-interest, while anyone who deliberately risks – and gives – his life to alert his fellow citizens to an onerous government is truly crazy. But the good Dr. Smith put that one in perspective: McVeigh is not deranged. He is serious.

It is June 16. It seems like five years rather than five days since the execution. The day before the execution, June 10, *The New York Times* discussed 'The Future of American Terrorism.' Apparently, terrorism has a real future; hence we must beware Nazi skinheads in the boondocks. The *Times* is, occasionally, right for the usual wrong reasons. For instance, their current wisdom is to dispel the illusion that 'McVeigh is merely a pawn in an expansive conspiracy led by a group of John Does that may even have had government involvement. But only a small fringe will cling to this theory for long.' Thank God: one had feared that rumors of a greater conspiracy would linger on and Old Glory herself would turn to fringe before our eyes. The *Times*, more in anger than in sorrow, feels that McVeigh blew martyrdom by first pleading not guilty and then by not using his trial to 'make a political statement about Ruby Ridge and Waco.' McVeigh agreed with the *Times*, and blamed his first lawyer, Stephen Jones, in unholy tandem with the judge, for selling him out. During his appeal, his new attorneys claimed that the serious sale took place when Jones, eager for publicity, met with the *Times*'s Pam Belluck. McVeigh's guilt was quietly conceded, thus explaining why the defense was so feeble. (Jones claims he did nothing improper.)

Actually, in the immediate wake of the bombing, the *Times* concedes, the militia movement skyrocketed from 220 antigovernment groups in 1995 to more than 850 by the end of '96. A factor in this growth was the belief circulating among militia groups 'that government agents had planted the bomb as a way to justify anti-terrorism legislation. No less than a retired Air Force general has promoted the theory that in addition to Mr. McVeigh's truck bomb, there were bombs inside the building.' Although the *Times* likes analogies to Nazi Germany, they are curiously reluctant to draw one between, let's say, the firing of the Reichstag in 1933 (Goering later took credit for this creative crime), which then allowed Hitler to invoke an Enabling Act that provided him with all sorts of dictatorial powers 'for protection of the people and the state' and so on to Auschwitz.

The canny *Portland Free Press* editor, Ace Hayes, noted that the one absolutely necessary dog in every terrorism case has yet to bark. The point to any terrorist act is that credit must be claimed so that fear will spread throughout the land. But no one took

credit until McVeigh did, *after* the trial, in which he was condemned to death as a result of circumstantial evidence produced
by the prosecution. Ace Hayes wrote, 'If the bombing was not terrorism then what was it? It was pseudo terrorism, perpetrated by
compartmentalized covert operators for the purposes of state police
power.' Apropos Hayes's conclusion, Adam Parfrey wrote in *Cult
Rapture*, '[The bombing] is not different from the bogus Viet
Cong units that were sent out to rape and murder Vietnamese to
discredit the National Liberation Front. It is not different from the
bogus "finds" of Commie weapons in El Salvador. It is not different from the bogus Symbionese Liberation Army created by the
CIA/FBI to discredit the real revolutionaries.' Evidence of a conspiracy? Edye Smith was interviewed by Gary Tuchman, May 23,
1995, on CNN. She duly noted that the ATF bureau, about seventeen people on the ninth floor, suffered no casualties. Indeed they
seemed not to have come to work that day. Jim Keith gives details
in *OKBOMB!*, while Smith observed on TV, 'Did the ATF have a
warning sign? I mean, did they think it might be a bad day to go
into the office? They had an option not to go to work that day, and
my kids didn't get that option.' She lost two children in the bombing. ATF has a number of explanations. The latest: five employees
were in the offices, unhurt.

Another lead not followed up: McVeigh's sister read a letter he
wrote her to the grand jury stating that he had become a member
of a 'Special Forces Group involved in criminal activity.'

In the end, McVeigh, already condemned to death, decided to
take full credit for the bombing. Was he being a good professional
soldier, covering up for others? Or did he, perhaps, now see himself in a historic role with his own private Harper's Ferry, and
though his ashes molder in the grave, his spirit is marching on? We
may know – one day.

As for 'the purposes of state police power,' after the bombing, Clinton signed into law orders allowing the police to commit all sorts of crimes against the Constitution in the interest of combating terrorism. On April 20, 1996 (Hitler's birthday of golden memory, at least for the producers of *The Producers*), President Clinton signed the Anti-Terrorism Act ('for the protection of the people and the state' – the emphasis, of course, is on the second noun), while, a month earlier, the mysterious Louis Freeh had informed Congress of his plans for expanded wiretapping by his secret police. Clinton described his Anti-Terrorism Act in familiar language (March 1, 1993, *USA Today*): 'We can't be so fixated on our desire to preserve the rights of ordinary Americans.' A year later (April 19, 1994, on MTV): 'A lot of people say there's too much personal freedom. When personal freedom's being abused, you have to move to limit it.' On that plangent note he graduated cum laude from the Newt Gingrich Academy.

In essence, Clinton's Anti-Terrorism Act would set up a national police force, over the long-dead bodies of the founders. Details are supplied by H.R. 97, a chimera born of Clinton, Reno, and the mysterious Mr. Freeh. A 2,500-man Rapid Deployment Strike Force would be organized, under the attorney general, with dictatorial powers. The chief of police of Windsor, Missouri, Joe Hendricks, spoke out against this supraconstitutional police force. Under this legislation, Hendricks said, 'an agent of the FBI could walk into my office and commandeer this police department. If you don't believe that, read the crime bill that Clinton signed into law in 1995. There is talk of the Feds taking over the Washington, D.C., police department. To me this sets a dangerous precedent.' But after a half-century of the Russians are coming, followed by terrorists from proliferating rogue states as well as the ongoing horrors of drug-related crime, there is little respite for a people so routinely – so fiercely – disinformed. Yet there is a native suspicion that seems to be a part of the individual American psyche – as demonstrated in polls, anyway. According to a Scripps Howard News Service poll, 40 percent of Americans think it quite likely that the FBI set the fires at Waco. Fifty-one percent believe federal officials killed Jack Kennedy (Oh, Oliver what hast thou wrought!). Eighty percent believe that the military is withholding evidence that Iraq used nerve gas or something as deadly in the Gulf. Unfortunately, the other side of this coin is troubling. After Oklahoma City, 58 percent of Americans, according to the *L.A. Times*, were willing to surrender some of their liberties to stop terrorism – including, one wonders, the sacred right to be misinformed by government?

Shortly after McVeigh's conviction, Director Freeh soothed the Senate Judiciary Committee: 'Most of the militia organizations around the country are not, in our view, threatening or dangerous.' But earlier, before the Senate Appropriations Committee, he had 'confessed' that his bureau was troubled by 'various individuals, as well as organizations, some having an ideology which suspects government of world-order conspiracies – individuals who have organized themselves against the United States.' In sum, this bureaucrat who does God's Work regards as a threat those 'individuals who espouse ideologies inconsistent with principles of Federal Government.' Oddly, for a former judge, Freeh seems not to recognize how chilling this last phrase is.

The C.I.A.'s former director William Colby is also made nervous by the disaffected. In a chat with Nebraska State Senator John DeCamp (shortly before the Oklahoma City bombing), he mused, 'I watched as the Anti-War movement rendered it impossible for this country to conduct or win the Viet Nam War . . . This Militia and Patriot movement . . . is far more significant and far more dangerous for Americans than the Anti-War movement ever was, if it is not intelligently dealt with . . . It is not because these people are armed that America need be concerned.' Colby continues, 'They are dangerous because there are so many of them. It is one thing to have a few nuts or dissidents. They can be dealt with, *justly or otherwise* [my emphasis], so that they do not pose a danger to the system. It is quite another situation when you have a true movement – millions of citizens believing something, particularly when the movement is made up of society's average, successful citizens.' Presumably one 'otherwise' way of handling such a movement is – when it elects a president by a half-million votes – to call in a like-minded Supreme Court majority to stop a state's recounts, create arbitrary deadlines, and invent delays until our ancient electoral system, by default, must give the presidency to the 'system's' candidate as opposed to the one the people voted for.

Many an 'expert' and many an expert believe that McVeigh neither built nor detonated the bomb that blew up a large part of the Murrah Federal Building on April 19, 1995. To start backward – rather the way the FBI conducted this case – if McVeigh was *not* guilty, why did he confess to the murderous deed? I am convinced from his correspondence and what one has learned about him in an ever lengthening row of books that, once found guilty due to what he felt was the slovenly defense of his principal lawyer, Stephen Jones, so unlike the brilliant defense of his 'co-conspirator' Terry Nichols's lawyer Michael Tigar, McVeigh believed that the only alternative to death by injection was a half-century or more of life in a box. There is another aspect of our prison system (considered one of the most barbaric in the First World) which was alluded to by the British writer John Sutherland in *The Guardian*. He quoted California's attorney general, Bill Lockyer, on the subject of the CEO of an electric utility, currently battening on California's failing energy supply. '"I would love to personally escort this CEO to an 8 by 10 cell that he could share with a tat-tooed dude who says – Hi, my name is Spike, Honey."' . . . The senior law official in the state was confirming (what we all sus-pected) that rape is penal policy. Go to prison and serving as a Hell's Angel sex slave is judged part of your sentence.' A couple of decades fending off Spike is not a Henley hero's idea of a good time. Better dead than Spiked. Hence, 'I bombed the Murrah building.'

Evidence, however, is overwhelming that there was a plot involving militia types and government infiltrators – who knows? – as prime movers to create panic in order to get Clinton to sign that infamous Anti-Terrorism Act. But if, as it now appears, there were many interested parties involved, a sort of unified-field theory is never apt to be found, but should there be one, Joel Dyer may be its Einstein. (Einstein, of course, never got his field quite together, either.) In 1998, I discussed Dyer's *Harvest of Rage* in these pages. Dyer was editor of the *Boulder Weekly*. He writes on the crisis of rural America due to the decline of the family farm, which also coincided with the formation of various militias and religious cults, some dangerous, some merely sad. In *Harvest of Rage*, Dyer made the case that McVeigh and Terry Nichols could not have acted alone in the Oklahoma City bombing. Now he has, after long investigation, written an epi-logue to the trials of the two co-conspirators. He lists leads not followed up by the FBI; some involved Iraqis – former Republican guards – re-established in Oklahoma City after the Gulf War.

It will be interesting to see if the FBI is sufficiently intrigued by what Joel Dyer has written to pursue the leads that he has so gen-erously given them.

Thus far, David Hoffman's *The Oklahoma City Bombing and the Politics of Terror* is the most thorough of a dozen or two accounts of what did and did not happen on that day in April. Hoffman begins his investigation with retired air force brigadier general Benton K. Partin's May 17, 1995, letter delivered to each member of the Senate and House of Representatives: 'When I first saw the pictures of the truck-bomb's asymmetrical damage to the Federal Building, my immediate reaction was that the pattern of damage would have been technically impossible without supplementing demolition charges at some of the reinforcing concrete column bases . . . For a simplistic blast truck-bomb, of the size and composition reported, to be able to reach out in the order of 60 feet and collapse a reinforced column base the size of column A-7 is beyond credulity.' In separate agreement was Samuel Cohen, father of the neutron bomb and formerly of the Manhattan Project, who wrote an Oklahoma state legislator, 'It would have been absolutely impossible and against the laws of nature for a truck full of fertilizer and fuel oil . . . no matter how much was used . . . to bring the building down.' One would think that McVeigh's defense lawyer, restlessly looking for a Middle East connection, could certainly have called these acknowledged experts to testify, but a search of Jones's account of the case, *Others Unknown*, reveals neither name.

In the March 20, 1996, issue of *Strategic Investment* newsletter, it was reported that Pentagon analysts tended to agree with General Partin. 'A classified report prepared by two independent Pentagon experts has concluded that the destruction of the Federal building in Oklahoma City last April was caused by five separate bombs . . . Sources close to the study say Timothy McVeigh did play a role in the bombing but "peripherally," as a "useful idiot."' Finally, inevitably – this is wartime, after all – 'the multiple bombings have a Middle Eastern "signature," pointing to either Iraqi or Syrian involvement.'

As it turned out, Partin's and Cohen's pro bono efforts to

examine the ruins were in vain. Sixteen days after the bombing, the search for victims stopped. In another letter to Congress, Partin stated that the building should not be destroyed until an independent forensic team was brought in to investigate the damage. 'It is also easy to cover up crucial evidence as was apparently done in Waco . . . Why rush to destroy the evidence?' Trigger words: the Feds demolished the ruins six days later. They offered the same excuse that they had used at Waco, 'health hazards.' Partin: 'It's a classic cover-up.'

Partin suspected a Communist plot. Well, nobody's perfect.

'So what's the take-away?' was the question often asked by TV producers in the so-called golden age of live television plays. This meant: what is the audience supposed to think when the play is over? The McVeigh story presents us with several take-aways. If McVeigh is simply a 'useful idiot,' a tool of what might be a very large conspiracy, involving various homegrown militias working, some think, with Middle Eastern helpers, then the FBI's refusal to follow up so many promising leads goes quite beyond its ordinary incompetence and smacks of treason. If McVeigh was the unlikely sole mover and begetter of the bombing, then his 'inhumane' (the Unabomber's adjective) destruction of so many lives will have served no purpose at all unless we take it seriously as what it is, a wake-up call to a federal government deeply hated, it would seem, by millions. (Remember that the popular Ronald Reagan always ran *against* the federal government, though often for the wrong reasons.) Final far-fetched take-away: McVeigh did not make nor deliver nor detonate the bomb but, once arrested on another charge, seized all 'glory' for himself and so gave up his life. That's not a story for W. E. Henley so much as for one of his young men, Rudyard Kipling, author of *The Man Who Would Be King*.

Finally, the fact that the McVeigh-Nichols scenario makes no sense at all suggests that, yet again, we are confronted with a 'perfect' crime – thus far.

After I published 'The Meaning of Timothy McVeigh' I received a letter from Eric F. Magnuson, Director of The World Liberation Order. Mr Magnuson on May 21 2001, wrote to McVeigh on Death Row asking him what changes he would make, if he could, in the way the US administers itself. McVeigh duly responded with ten additions to the ten Amendments that comprise our Bill of Rights. Herewith, thanks to Mr Magnuson, are McVeigh's last thoughts on how to correct our system. Mr Magnuson has also asked me to reprint his own position on the matter.

3:06 PM June 20, 2001. It should be stressed here that the WLO does not necessarily agree with any of Timothy McVeigh's ideas just because we reproduce them here. Our writings are entirely separate from his. We certainly do not advocate or condone the blowing up of large buildings filled with people that one doesn't even know. You might kill a future Libertarian. We do believe, however, that we cannot prevent these tragic things from happening in the future unless we are willing to take a clear and honest look at why they have happened in the past. We are confident that all right-thinking people agree with this very basic principle. Those who disagree are those who prefer fantasy to truth. Such people are the problem, not any part of the solution. The fact that Timothy McVeigh did a desperate and destructive thing does not conveniently negate the fact that government in America has become too big and oppressive, it simply underscores it.

Eric F. Magnuson

Tim's Bill of Rights

1.) Neither Speech, Press, Religion, nor Assembly shall be infringed, nor shall such be forced upon any person by the government of the United States.

2.) There shall be no standing military force during peacetime, (this) to include large bodies of federal law enforcers or coalitions of these officers that would constitute a military force, with the exception of sea-based maritime forces.

3.) The Executive Office shall hold no power to unilaterally alter Constitutional rights.

4.) No person shall be subjected to any form of direct taxation or wage withholdings by the Federal government.

5.) No person's life or liberty shall be taken without due process. Any government employee circumventing due process rights shall be punished with imprisonment. Citizens shall not be subjected to invasions of their homes or property by employees of the Federal government. Property or other assets of United States citizens shall not be subject to forfeiture to the Federal government.

6.) Personal activities that do not infringe upon the rights or property of another shall not be charged, prosecuted, or punished by the United States government. Any crime alleged will be prosecuted by the jurisdiction most local to the alleged crime, respectively. No person shall be twice tried for an offense alleged and adjudicated in another jurisdiction. No person shall be subjected to cruel and unusual punishment, nor shall the Federal government hold power to execute any individual as punishment for a crime convicted, or contract to another entity for this purpose. No person shall be held to account for the actions of another, unless proven by more than one witness to be the principal figure.

7.) All currency shall be redeemable in a globally recognized material of intrinsic value, such as silver.

8.) Legislative members shall earn no more than twice the current poverty level and shall not be subject to any additional pay, bonuses, rewards gifts, entitlements, or other such privileges, as holding such office is meant to serve the people and should not be looked upon as a capitalist career opportunity.

9.) Where non-violent checks and balances fail to remedy government abuse or tyranny, the common people reserve the right to rebellion. Inherent with this right, the common people maintain the absolute right to own and possess those weapons which are used by any level of government for domestic policing.

10.) Any rights not enumerated here belong inherently to the people or the states respectively, and shall not be assumed by omission (to be) delegated to the jurisdiction of the Federal government.

Timothy J. McVeigh
28 May, 2001

A version of this essay was published in *Vanity Fair*, September 2001.

Black Tuesday

1

According to the Koran, it was on a Tuesday that Allah created darkness. Last September 11 when suicide-pilots were crashing commercial airliners into crowded American buildings, I did not have to look to the calendar to see what day it was: Dark Tuesday was casting its long shadow across Manhattan and along the Potomac River. I was also not surprised that despite the seven or so trillion dollars we have spent since 1950 on what is euphemistically called 'Defense', there would have been no advance warning from the FBI or CIA or Defense Intelligence Agency.

While the Bushites have been eagerly preparing for the last war but two – missiles from North Korea, clearly marked with flags, would rain down on Portland, Oregon, only to be intercepted by our missile-shield balloons, the foxy Osama bin Laden knew that all *he* needed for his holy war on the infidel were fliers willing to kill themselves along with those random passengers who happened to be aboard hijacked airliners. Also, like so many of those born to wealth, Osama is not one to throw money about. Apparently, the airline tickets of the nineteen known dead hijackers were paid through a credit card. I suspect that United and American Airlines will never be reimbursed by American Express, whose New York offices Osama – inadvertently? – hit.

On the plane that crashed in Pennsylvania, a passenger telephoned out to say that he and a dozen or so other men – several of them athletes – were going to attack the hijackers. 'Let's roll!' he shouted. A scuffle. A scream. Silence. But the plane, allegedly aimed at the White House, ended up in a field near Pittsburgh. We have always had wise and brave civilians. It is the military and the politicians and the media that one frets about. After all, we have not encountered suicide bombers since the kamikazes, as we called them in the Pacific where I was idly a soldier in the Second World War. Japan was the enemy then. Now, bin Laden . . . The Moslems . . . The Pakistanis . . . Step in line.

The telephone rings. A distraught voice from the United States. 'Berry Berenson's dead. She was on Flight . . .' The world was getting surreal. Arabs. Plastic knives. The beautiful Berry. What on earth did any of these elements have in common other than an unexpected appointment in Samarra with that restless traveler Death?

The telephone keeps ringing. In summer I live south of Naples, Italy. Italian newspapers, TV, radio, want comment. So do I. I have written lately about Pearl Harbor. Now I get the same question over and over: Isn't this exactly like Sunday morning, December 7,1941? No, it's not, I say. As far as we *now* know, we had no warning of last Tuesday's attack. Of course, our government has many, many secrets which our enemies always seem to know about in advance but our people are not told of until years later, if at all. President Roosevelt provoked the Japanese to attack us at Pearl Harbor. I describe the various steps he took in a book, *The Golden Age*. We now know what was on his mind: coming to England's aid against Japan's ally, Hitler, a virtuous plot that ended triumphantly for the human race. But what was – is – on bin Laden's mind?

For several decades there has been an unrelenting demonization of the Moslem world in the American media. Since I am a loyal American, I am not supposed to tell you *why* this has taken place but then it is not usual for us to examine why *anything* happens other than to accuse others of motiveless malignity. 'We are good,' announced a deep-thinker on American television. 'They are evil,' which wraps that one up in a neat package. But it was Bush himself who put, as it were, the bow on the package in an address to a joint session of Congress where he shared with them – as well as all of us somewhere over the Beltway – his profound knowledge of Islam's wiles and ways: 'They hate what they see right here in this chamber.' A million Americans nodded in front of their TV sets. 'Their leaders are self-appointed. They hate our freedoms, our freedom of religion, our freedom of speech, our freedom to vote and assemble and disagree with each other.' At this plangent moment what American's gorge did not rise like a Florida chad to the bait?

Should the forty-four-year-old Saudi-Arabian bin Laden be the prime mover, we know surprisingly little about him. We can assume that he favors the Palestinians in their uprising against the European- and American-born Israelis, intent, many of them, on establishing a theocratic state in what was to have been a common holy land for Jews, Moslems and Christians. But if Osama ever wept tears for Arafat, they have left little trace. So why do he and millions of other Moslems hate us?

Let us deal first with the six-foot-seven-inch Osama who enters history in 1979 as a guerrilla warrior working alongside the CIA to defend Afghanistan against the invading Soviets. Was he anti-Communist? Irrelevant question. He is anti-Infidel in the land of the Prophet. Described as fabulously wealthy, Osama is worth 'only' a few million dollars, according to a relative. It was his father who created a fabulous fortune with a construction company that specialized in building palaces for the Saudi royal family. That company is now worth several billion dollars, presumably shared by Osama's fifty-four brothers and sisters. Although he speaks perfect English, he was entirely educated at the Saudi capital, Jidda, and he has never traveled outside the Arabian Peninsula. Several siblings live in the Boston area and give large sums to Harvard. We are told that much of his family appears to have disowned him while many of his assets in the Saudi kingdom have been frozen.

Where does Osama's money now come from? He is a superb fund-raiser for Allah but only within the Arab world; contrary to legend, he has taken no CIA money. He is also a superb organizer within Afghanistan. In 1998, he warned the Saudi King that Saddam Hussein was going to invade Kuwait. Osama assumed that after his own victories as a guerrilla against the Russians, he and his organization would be used by the Saudis to stop the Iraqis. To Osama's horror, King Fahd sent for the Americans: thus were infidels established on the sacred sands of Mohammed. 'This was,' he said, 'the most shocking moment of my life.' 'Infidel,' in his sense, does not mean anything of great moral consequence – like cheating sexually on your partner; rather it means lack of faith in Allah, the one God, and in his Prophet.

Osama persuaded 4,000 Saudis to go to Afghanistan for military training by his group. In 1991, Osama moved on to Sudan. In 1994, when the Saudis withdrew his citizenship, Osama was already a legendary figure in the Islamic world and so, like Shakespeare's Coriolanus, he could tell the royal Saudis,

'I banish you. There is a world elsewhere.' Unfortunately, that world is us.

In a twelve-page 'declaration of war,' Osama presented himself as potential liberator of the Moslem world from the great Satan of modern corruption, the United States.

When Clinton lobbed a missile at a Sudanese aspirin factory, Osama blew up two of our embassies in Africa, put a hole in the side of an American war-ship off Yemen, and so on to the events of Tuesday, September 11. Now President George W. Bush, in retaliation, has promised us not only a 'new war' but a secret war. That is, not secret to Osama but only to us who pay for and fight it. 'This administration will not talk about any plans we may or may not have,' said Bush. 'We're going to find these evil-doers . . . and we're going to hold them accountable' along with the other devils who have given Osama shelter in order to teach them the one lesson that we ourselves have never been able to learn: In history, as in physics, there is no action without re-action. Or, as Edward S. Herman puts it, 'One of the most durable features of the U.S. culture is the inability or refusal to recognize U.S. crimes.'

When Osama was four years old, I arrived in Cairo for a con-versation with Nasser to appear in *Look* magazine. I was received by Mohammed Hekal, Nasser's chief adviser. Nasser himself was not to be seen. He was at the Barricade, his retreat on the Nile. Later, I found out that a plot to murder him had just failed and he was in well-guarded seclusion. Hekal spoke perfect English; he was sardonic, cynical. 'We are studying the Koran for hints on birth control.' He sighed.

'Not helpful?'

'Not very. But we keep looking for a text.' We talked off and on for a week. Nasser wanted to modernize Egypt. But there was a reactionary, religious element . . . Another sigh. Then a surprise.

'We've found something very odd, the young village boys — the bright ones that we are educating to be engineers, chemists and so on — are turning religious on us.'

'Right wing?'

'Very.' Hekal was a spiritual son of our eighteenth-century Enlightenment. I thought of Hekal on Dark Tuesday when one of his modernized Arab generation had, in the name of Islam, struck at what had been, forty years earlier, Nasser's model for a modern state. Yet Osama seemed, from all accounts, no more than a practicing, as opposed to zealous, Moslem. Ironically, he was trained as an engineer. Understandably, he dislikes the United States as symbol and as fact. But when our clients, the Saudi royal family, allowed American troops to occupy the Prophet's holy land, Osama named the fundamental enemy 'the Crusader Zionist Alliance.' Thus, in a phrase, he defined himself and reminded his critics that he is a Wahhabi Moslem, a Puritan activist not unlike our Falwell Robertson zanies, only serious. He would go to war against the United States, 'the head of the serpent.' Even more ambitiously, he would rid all the Moslem states of their Western-supported regimes, starting with that of his native land. The word 'Crusader' was the give-away. In the eyes of many Moslems, the Christian West, currently in alliance with Zionism, has for a thousand years tried to dominate the lands of the Umma — the true believers. That is why Osama is seen by so many simple folk as the true heir to Saladin, the great warrior king who defeated Richard of England and the Western Crusaders.

Who was Saladin? Dates 1138–93. He was an Armenian Kurd. In the century before his birth, western Christians had established a kingdom at Jerusalem, to the horror of the Islamic Faithful. Much as the United States used the Gulf War as pretext for our current occupation of Saudi Arabia, Saladin raised armies to drive out the Crusaders. He conquered Egypt, annexed Syria, and finally smashed the Kingdom of Jerusalem in a religious war that pitted Mohammedan against Christian. He united and 'purified' the Moslem world and, though Richard Lion-heart was the better general, in the end he gave up and went home. As one historian put it, Saladin 'typified the Mohammedan utter self surrender to a sacred cause.' But he left no government behind him, no political system because, as he himself said, 'My troops will do nothing save when I ride at their head . . .' Now his spirit has returned with a vengeance.

2

The Bush administration, though eerily inept in all but its principal task, which is to exempt the rich from taxes, has casually torn up most of the treaties to which civilized nations subscribe like the Kyoto Accords or the nuclear missile agreement with Russia. As the Bushites go about their relentless plundering of the Treasury and now, thanks to Osama, Social Security (a supposedly untouchable trust fund) which, like Lucky Strike green has gone to war, they have also allowed the FBI and CIA either to run amok – or not budge at all, leaving us, the very first 'indispensable' and at popular request last global empire, rather like the Wizard of Oz doing his odd pretend-magic tricks while hoping not to be found out. Latest Bushism to the world, 'Either you are with us or you are with the terrorists.' That's known as asking for it.

To be fair, one cannot entirely blame the current Oval One for our incoherence. Though his predecessors have generally had rather higher IQs than his, they, too, assiduously served the 1 percent that owns the country while allowing everyone else to drift. Particularly culpable was Bill Clinton. Although the most able chief executive since FDR, Clinton in his frantic pursuit of election victories set in place the trigger for a police state which his successor is now happily squeezing.

Police state? What's that all about? In April 1996, one year after the Oklahoma City bombing, President Clinton signed into law the Anti-Terrorist and Effective Death Penalty Act, a so-called 'conference bill' in which many grubby hands played a part, including the bill's co-sponsor, Senate majority leader Dole. Although Clinton, in order to win elections, did many unwise and opportunistic things, he seldom, like Charles II, ever said an unwise one. But faced with opposition to anti-terrorism legislation which not only gives the attorney general the power to use the armed services against the civilian population, neatly nullifying the Posse Comitatus Act of 1878, it also, selectively, suspends habeas corpus, the heart of Anglo-American liberty. Clinton attacked his critics as 'unpatriotic.' Then, wrapped in the flag, he spoke from the throne: 'There is nothing patriotic about our pretending that you can love your country but despise your government.' This is breathtaking since it includes, at one time or another, most of us. Put another way, was a German in 1939 who said that he detested the Nazi dictatorship unpatriotic?

There have been ominous signs that our fragile liberties have been dramatically at risk since the 1970s when the white-shirt-and-tie FBI reinvented itself from a corps of 'generalists,' trained in law and accounting, into a confrontational 'Special Weapons and Tactics' (aka SWAT) green beret-style army of warriors who like to dress up in camouflage or black ninja clothing and, depending on the caper, the odd ski mask. In the early Eighties an FBI super-SWAT team, the Hostage 270 Rescue Team, was formed. As so often happens in United States-speak, this group specialized not in freeing hostages or saving lives but in murderous attacks on groups that offended them, like the Branch Davidians – evangelical Christians who were living peaceably in their own compound at Waco, Texas, until an FBI SWAT team, illegally using army tanks, killed eighty-two of them, including twenty-seven children. This was 1993.

Post-Tuesday, SWAT teams can now be used to go after suspect Arab-Americans or, indeed, anyone who might be guilty of terrorism, a word without legal definition (how can you fight terrorism by suspending habeas corpus since those who want their corpor released from prison are already locked up?). But in the post-Oklahoma City trauma, Clinton said that those who did not support his draconian legislation were terrorist co-conspirators who wanted to turn 'America into a safe house for terrorists.' If the cool Clinton could so froth what are we to expect from the over-heated Bush post-Tuesday?

Incidentally, those who were shocked by Bush the Younger's shout that we are now 'at war' with Osama and that those parts of the Moslem world that support him should have quickly put on their collective thinking caps. Since a nation can only be at war with another nation-state, why did our smoldering if not yet Burning Bush come up with such a phrase? Think hard. This will count against your final grade. Give up? Well, most insurance companies have a rider that they need not pay for damage done by 'an act of war.' Although the men and women around Bush know nothing of war and less of our Constitution, they understand fund-raising. For this wartime exclusion, Hartford Life would soon be breaking open its piggy bank to finance Republicans for years to come. But it was the mean-spirited *Washington Post* that pointed out, under U.S. case law, *only* a sovereign nation, not a bunch of radicals, can commit an 'act of war.' Good try, W. This now means that *We the People*, with our tax money, will be allowed to bail out the insurance companies, a rare privilege not afforded to just any old generation.

Although the American people have no direct means of influencing their government, their 'opinions' are occasionally sampled through polls. According to a November 1995 CNN-*Time* poll, 55 percent of the people believe 'the federal government has become so powerful that it poses a threat to the rights of ordinary citizens.' Three days after Dark Tuesday, 74 percent said they thought 'It would be necessary for Americans to give up some of their personal freedoms.' Eighty-six percent favored guards and metal detectors at public buildings and events. Thus, as the police state settles comfortably in place, one can imagine Cheney and Rumsfield studying these figures, transfixed with joy. 'It's what they always wanted, Dick.'

'And to think we never knew, Don.'

'Thanks to those liberals, Dick.'

'We'll get those bastards now, Don.'

It seems forgotten by our amnesiac media that we once energetically supported Saddam Hussein in Iraq's war against Iran and so he thought, not unnaturally, that we wouldn't mind his taking over Kuwait's filling stations. Overnight our employee became Satan – and so remains, as we torment his people in the hope that they will rise up and overthrow him, as the Cubans were supposed, in their U.S.-imposed poverty, to dismiss Castro a half-century ago whose only crime was refusal to allow the Kennedy brothers to murder him in their so-called Operation Mongoose. Our imperial disdain for the lesser breeds did not go unnoticed by the latest educated generation of Saudi Arabians, and by their evolving leader, Osama bin Laden, whose moment came in 2001 when a weak American president took office in questionable circumstances.

The New York Times is the principal dispenser of opinion received from corporate America. It generally stands tall, or tries to. Even so, as of September 13, the *NYT*'s editorial columns were all slightly off-key.

Under the heading 'Demands of Leadership' the *NYT* was upbeat, sort of. It's going to be OK if you work hard and keep your eye on the ball, Mr. President. Apparently Bush is 'facing multiple challenges, but his most important job is a simple matter of leadership.' Thank God. Not only is that *all* it takes, but it's *simple*, too! For a moment . . . The *NYT* then slips into the way things look as opposed to the way they ought to look. 'The Administration spent much of yesterday trying to overcome the impression that Mr. Bush showed weakness when he did not return to Washington after the terrorists struck.' But from what I could tell no one cared, while some of us felt marginally safer that the national silly-billy was trapped in his Nebraska bunker. Patiently, the *NYT* spells it out for Bush and for us, too. 'In the days ahead, Mr. Bush may be asking the nation to support military actions that many citizens, particularly those with relations in the services will find alarming. He must show that he knows what he is doing.' Well, that's a bull's eye. If only FDR had got letters like that from Arthur Krock at the old *NYT*.

Finally, Anthony Lewis thinks it wise to eschew Bushite unilateralism in favor of cooperation with other nations in order to contain Tuesday's darkness by *understanding its origin* while ceasing our provocations of cultures opposed to us and our arrangements. Lewis, unusually for a *New York Times* writer, favors peace now. So do I. But then we are old and have been to the wars and value our fast-diminishing freedoms, unlike those jingoes now beating their tom-toms in Times Square in favor of an all-out war for other Americans to fight.

As usual, the political columnist who has made the most sense of all this is William Pfaff in *The International Herald Tribune* (September 17, 2001). Unlike the provincial war-lovers at *The*

New York Times, he is appalled by the spectacle of an American president who declined to serve his country in Vietnam howling for war against not a nation or even a religion but one man and his accomplices, a category that will ever widen.

Pfaff: 'The riposte of a civilized nation: one that believes in good, in human society and does oppose evil, has to be narrowly focused and, above all, intelligent.

'Missiles are blunt weapons. Those terrorists are smart enough to make others bear the price for what they have done, and to exploit the results.

'A maddened U.S. response that hurts still others is what they want: It will fuel the hatred that already fires the self-righteousness about their criminal acts against the innocent.

'What the United States needs is cold reconsideration of how it has arrived at this pass. It needs, even more, to foresee disasters that might lie in the future.'

War is the no-win, all-lose option. The time has come to put the good Kofi Annan to use. As glorious as total revenge will be for our war-lovers, a truce between Saladin and the Crusader Zionists is in the interest of the entire human race. Long before the dread monotheists got their hands on history's neck, we had been taught how to handle feuds by none other than the god Apollo as dramatized by Aeschylus in *The Eumenides* (a polite Greek term for the Furies who keep us daily company on CNN). Orestes, for the sin of matricide, cannot rid himself of the Furies who hound him wherever he goes. He appeals to the god Apollo who tells him to go to the UN – also known as the Citizens' Assembly at Athens – which he does and is acquitted on the ground that blood feuds must be ended or they will smolder forever, generation after generation, and great towers shall turn to flame and incinerate us all until 'the thirsty dust shall never more suck up the darkly steaming blood . . . and vengeance crying death for death! But man with man and state with state shall vow the pledge of common hate and common friendship, that for man has oft made blessing out of ban, be ours until all time.' Let Annan mediate between East and West before there is nothing left of either of us to salvage.

The awesome physical damage Osama and company did us on Dark Tuesday is as nothing compared to the knockout blow to our vanishing liberties – the Anti-Terrorism Act of 1991 combined with the recent request to Congress for additional special powers to wiretap without judicial order; to deport lawful permanent residents, visitors and undocumented immigrants without due process, and so on. Even that loyal company-town paper *The Washington Post* is alarmed '. . . Justice Department is making extraordinary use of its powers to arrest and detain individuals, taking the unusual step of jailing hundreds of people on minor . . . violations. The lawyers and legal scholars . . . said they could not recall a time when so many people had been arrested and held without bond on charges – particularly minor charges – related to the case at hand.'

This is from a pre-Osama 'Restrictions on personal liberty, on the right of free expression of opinion, including freedom of the press; on the rights of assembly and associations; and violations of the privacy of postal, telegraphic and telephonic communications and warrants for house searches, orders for confiscations as well as restrictions on property, are also permissible beyond the legal limits otherwise prescribed.' The tone is familiar. It is from Hitler's 1933 speech calling for 'an Enabling Act' for 'the protection of the People and the State' after the catastrophic Reichstag fire that the Nazis had secretly lit.

Only one congresswoman, Barbara Lee of California, voted against the additional powers granted the President.

Meanwhile, a *New York Times*-CBS poll notes that only 6 percent now oppose military action while a substantial majority favor war 'even if many thousands of innocent civilians are killed.' Most of this majority are far too young to recall World War II, Korea, even Vietnam. Simultaneously, Bush's approval rating has soared from the 50s to 91 percent. Traditionally, in war, the president is totemic like the flag. When Kennedy got his highest rating after the débâcle of the Bay of Pigs he observed, characteristically, 'It would seem that the worse you fuck up in this job the more popular you get.' Bush, father and son, may yet make it to Mount Rushmore, though it might be cheaper to redo the handsome Barbara Bush's look-alike, George Washington, by adding two strings of Teclas to his limestone neck, in memoriam, as it were.

Since V-J Day 1945 ('Victory over Japan' and the end of World War II), we have been engaged in what the great historian Charles A. Beard called 'perpetual war for perpetual peace.' I have occasionally referred to our Enemy of the Month Club: each month a new horrendous enemy at whom we must strike before he destroys us. I have been accused of exaggeration, so here's the scoreboard from Kosovo (1999) to Berlin Airlift (1948–49). You will note that the compilers, the Federation of American Scientists, record a number of our wars as 'ongoing', even though many of us have forgotten about them. We are given, under 'Name', many fanciful Defense Department titles like Urgent Fury, which was Reagan's attack on the island of Grenada, a month-long caper which General Haig disloyally said could have been handled more briefly by the Provincetown police department.

Current Operations

Name	Locale	Dates		US Forces involved
Joint Guardian	Kosovo	11 June 1999	TDB 200?	
Allied Force/Noble Anvil		23 Mar 1999	10 Jun 1999	
Determined Force	Kosovo	08 Oct 1998	23 Mar 1999	
Cobalt Flash				
Shining Hope				
Sustain Hope/Allied Harbour				
Provide Refuge	Kosovo	05 April 1999	Fall 1999	
Open Arms				
Eagle Eye	Kosovo	16 Oct 1998	24 Mar 1999	
Determined Falcon		15 Jun 1998	16 Jun 1998	
Determined Effort	Kosovo & Albania	Jul 1995	Dec 1995	
Joint Endeavor		Dec 1995	Dec 1996	
Joint Guard	Bosnia-Herzegovina	Dec 1996	20 Jun 98	
Joint Forge		20 Jun 98	Present	6,900
Deliberate Force	Bosnian Serbs	29 Aug 1995	21 Sep 1995	
Quick Lift	Croatia	03 Jul 1995	11 Aug 1995	
Nomad Vigil	Albania	01 Jul 1995	05 Nov 1996	
Nomad Endeavor	Taszar, Hungary	Mar 1996	Present	
Able Sentry	Serbia-Macedonia	05 Jul 1994	Present	
Deny Flight		12 Apr 1993	20 Dec 1995	
Decisive Endeavor/ Decisive Edge		Jan 1996	Dec 1996	2,000
Decisive Guard/ Deliberate Guard	Bosnia-Herzegovina	Dec 1996	20 Jun 1998	
Deliberate Force		20 Jun 1998	Present	
Sky Monitor	Bosnia-Herzegovina	16 Oct 1992	Present	
Maritime Monitor	Adriatic Sea	16 Jul 1992	22 Nov 1992	
Maritime Guard		22 Nov 1992	15 Jun 1993	
Sharp Guard		15 Jun 1993	Dec 1995	11,700
Decisive Enhancement		Dec 1995	19 Jun 1996	
Determined Guard		Dec 1996	Present	
Provide Promise	Bosnia	03 Jul 1992	Mar 1996	1,000

Southwest Asia

Name	Locale	Dates		US Forces involved
[none] (air strike)		26 Jun 1992	13 Jan 1993	
[none] (cruise missile strike)		13 Jan 1993	17 Jan 1993	
[none] (cruise missile strike)		17 Jan 1993	26 Jun 1993	
Desert Strike	Iraq	03 Sep 1996	04 Sep 1996	
Desert Thunder		Feb 1998	16 Dec 1998	
Desert Fox		16 Dec 1998	20 Dec 1998	
Shining Presence	Israel	Dec 1998	Dec 1998	
Phoenix Scorpion IV	Iraq	Dec 1998	Dec 1998	
Phoenix Scorpion III		Nov 1998	Nov 1998	
Phoenix Scorpion II		Feb 1998	Feb 1998	
Phoenix Scorpion I		Nov 1997	Nov 1997	
Desert Focus	Saudi Arabia	Jul 1996	Present	
Vigilant Warrior		Oct 1994	Nov 1994	
Vigilant Sentinel	Kuwait	Aug 1995	15 Feb 1997	
Intrinsic Action		01 Dec 1995	01 Oct 1999	
Desert Spring		01 Oct 1999	Present	
Iris Gold	Southwest Asia	?? 1993	Present	
Pacific Haven/ Quick Transit	Iraq > Guam	15 Sep 1996	16 Dec 1996	
Provide Comfort		05 Apr 1991	Dec 1994	42,500
Provide Comfort I	Kurdistan	24 July 1991	31 Dec 1996	
Northern Watch		31 Dec 1996	Present	1,100
Southern Watch	Southwest Asia/Iraq	1991	Present	14,000
Desert Falcon	Saudi Arabia	1991	Present	

Other Operations

Name	Locale	Dates		US Forces involved
Korea	Korea	ongoing	ongoing	
New Horizons	Central America	ongoing	ongoing	
Sierra Leone NEO	Sierra Leone	May 2000	ongoing	

Other Operations – *continued*

Name	Locale	Dates		US Forces involved
MONUC [UN PKO]	DR Congo	Feb 2000	ongoing	
Resolute Response	Africa	Aug 1998	Present	
Gatekeeper	California			
Hold-the-Line	Texas	1995	Present	
Safeguard	Arizona			
Golden Pheasant	Honduras	Mar 1998	Present	
Alliance	US southern border	1986	Present	
Provide Hope I		10 Feb 1992	26 Feb 1992	
Provide Hope II		15 Apr 1992	29 Jul 1992	
Provide Hope III	Former Soviet Union	1993	1993	
Provide Hope IV		10 Jan 1994	19 Dec 1994	
Provide Hope V		06 Nov 1998	10 May 1999	

Counterdrug Operations

Name	Locale	Dates		US Forces involved
Coronet Nighthawk	Central/South America	1991	Present	
Coronet Oak		Oct 1997	17 Feb 1999	
Selva Verde	Colombia	1995	Present	
Badge	Kentucky	1990	Present?	
Ghost Dancer	Oregon	1990	Present?	
Greensweep	California	Jul 1990	Aug 1990	
Grizzly		1990	Present?	
Wipeout	Hawaii	1990	Present	
Ghost Zone	Bolivia	Mar 1990	1993?	
Constant Vigil	Bolivia	199?	?	
Support Justice		1991	1994	
Steady State		1994	Apr 1996	
Green Clover	South America	199?	199?	
Laser Strike		Apr 1996	Present	
Agate Path	Puerto Rico	1989	?	
Enhanced Ops			Present	

Completed Operations

Name	Locale	Dates		US Forces involved
Silent Promise	Mozambique/ South Africa	Feb 2000	? Apr 2000	
Fundamental Response	Venezuela	20 Dec 1999	early 2000	
Stabilize	Timor	11 Sep 1999	Nov 1999	
Avid Response	Turkey	18 Aug 1999	Sep 1999	
Strong Support [Fuerte Apoyo]	Central America	Oct 1998	10 Feb 1999	5,700
Infinite Reach	Sudan/Afghanistan	20 Aug 1998	20 Aug 1998	
Shepherd Venture	Guinea-Bissau	10 Jun 1998	17 Jun 1998	130
[none]	Asmara, Eritrea NEO	05 Jun 1998	06 Jun 1998	130
Noble Response	Kenya	21 Jan 1998	25 Mar 1998	
Bevel Edge	Cambodia	Jul 1997	Jul 1997	
Noble Obelisk	Sierra Leone	May 1997	Jun 1997	
Guardian Retrieval	Congo (formerly Zaire)	Mar 1997	Jun 1997	
Silver Wake	Albania	14 Mar 1997	26 Mar 1997	
Guardian Assistance	Zaire/Rwanda/ Uganda	15 Nov 1996	27 Dec 1996	
Assurance/Phoenix Tusk				
Quick Response	Central African Republic	May 1996	Aug 1996	
Assured Response	Liberia	Apr 1996	Aug 1996	
Zorro II	Mexico	Dec 1995	02 May 1996	
Third Taiwan Straits Crisis	Taiwan Strait	21 Jul 1995	23 Mar 1996	
Safe Border	Peru/Ecuador	1995	30 Jun 1999	
United Shield	Somalia	03 Jan 1995	25 Mar 1995	4,000
Uphold/Restore Democracy	Haiti	19 Sep 1994	31 Mar 1995	21,000
Quiet Resolve / Support Hope	Rwanda	22 Jul 1994	30 Sep 1994	2,592
Safe Haven/Safe Passage	Cuba > Panama	06 Sep 1994	01 Mar 1995	

Completed Operations – *continued*

Name	Locale	Dates		US Forces involved
Sea Signal/JTF-160	Haiti > Guantanamo, Cuba	18 May 1994	Feb 1996	
Distant Runner	Rwanda NEO	09 Apr 1994	15 Apr 1994	
Korean Nuclear Crisis	North Korea	10 Feb 1993	Jun 1994	
[none]	Liberia NEO	22 Oct 1992	25 Oct 1992	
Provide Relief	Somalia	14 Aug 1992	08 Dec 1992	
Restore Hope		04 Dec 1992	04 May 1993	26,000
Continue Hope		04 May 1993	Dec 1993	
Provide Transition	Angola	03 Aug 1992	09 Oct 1992	
Garden Plot	Los Angeles, CA	May 1992		4,500
Silver Anvil	Sierra Leone NEO	02 May 1992	05 May 1992	
GTMO	Haiti > Guantanamo, Cuba	23 Nov 1991		
Safe Harbor		1992		
Quick Lift	Zaire	24 Sep 1991	07 Oct 1991	
Victor Squared	Haiti NEO	Sep 1991		
Fiery Vigil	Philippines NEO	Jun 1991		
Productive Effort/ Sea Angel	Bangladesh	May 1991	Jun 1991	
Eastern Exit	Somalia	02 Jan 1991	11 Jan 1991	
Desert Shield	Southwest Asia	02 Aug 1990	17 Jan 1991	
Imminent Thunder		Nov 1990	Nov 1990	
Proven Force		17 Jan 1991	28 Feb 1991	
Desert Storm		17 Jan 1991	28 Feb 1991	550,000
Desert Sword/Desert Sabre		24 Feb 1991	28 Feb 1991	
Desert Calm		01 Mar 1991	01 Jan 1992	
Desert Farewell		01 Jan 1992	1992?	
Steel Box/Golden Python	Johnston Island	26 Jul 1990	18 Nov 1990	
Sharp Edge	Liberia	May 1990	08 Jan 1991	

Cold War Era

Name	Locale	Dates		US Forces involved
Classic Resolve	Philippines	Nov 1989	Dec 1989	
Hawkeye	St. Croix, U.S. Virgin Islands	20 Sep 1989	17 Nov 1989	
Nimrod Dancer		May 1989	20 Dec 1989	
Just Cause	Panama	20 Dec 1989	31 Jan 1990	
Promote Liberty		31 Jan 1990	?	
Ernest Will	Persian Gulf	24 Jul 1987	02 Aug 1990	
Praying Mantis		17 Apr 1988	19 Apr 1988	
Blast Furnace	Bolivia	Jul 1986	Nov 1986	
El Dorado Canyon	Libya	12 Apr 1986	17 Apr 1986	
Attain Document	Libya	26 Jan 1986	29 Mar 1986	
Achille Lauro	Mediterranean	07 Oct 1985	11 Oct 1985	
Intense Look	Red Sea/Gulf of Suez	Jul 1984	Jul 1984	
Urgent Fury	Grenada	23 Oct 1983	21 Nov 1983	
Arid Farmer	Chad/Sudan	Aug 1983	Aug 1983	
Early Call	Egypt/Sudan	18 Mar 1983	Aug 1983	
US Multinational Force	Lebanon	25 Aug 1982	01 Dec 1987	
Bright Star	Egypt	06 Oct 1981	Nov 1981	
Gulf of Sidra	Libya/Mediterranean	18 Aug 1981	18 Aug 1981	
Rocky Mountain Transfer	Colorado	Aug 1981	Sep 1981	
Central America	El Salvador/Nicaragua	01 Jan 1981	01 Feb 1992	
Creek Sentry	Poland	Dec 1980	1981	
SETCON II	Colorado	May 1980	Jun 1980	
Eagle Claw/Desert One	Iran	25 Apr 1980		
ROK Park Succession Crisis	Korea	26 Oct 1979	28 Jun 1980	
Elf One	Saudi Arabia	Mar 1979	15 Apr 1989	
Yemen	Iran/Yemen/Indian Ocean	06 Dec 1978	06 Jan 1979	
Red Bean	Zaire	May 1978	Jun 1978	

Cold War Era – *continued*

Name	Locale	Dates		US Forces involved
Ogaden Crisis	Somalia/Ethiopia	Feb 1978	23 Mar 1978	
SETCON I	Colorado	1978	1978	
Paul Bunyan/Tree Incident	Korea	18 Aug 1976	21 Aug 1976	
Mayaguez Operation	Cambodia	15 May 1975		
New Life	Vietnam NEO	Apr 1975		
Frequent Wind	Evacuation of Saigon	29 Apr 1975	30 Apr 1975	
Eagle Pull	Cambodia	11 Apr 1975	13 Apr 1975	
Nickel Grass	Middle East	06 Oct 1973	17 Nov 1973	
Garden Plot	U.S.A. Domestic	30 Apr 1972	04 May 1972	
Red Hat	Johnston Island	Jan 1971	Sep 1971	
Ivory Coast/Kingpin	Son Tay, Vietnam	20 Nov 1970	21 Nov 1970	
Graphic Hand	U.S. Domestic	1970	1970	
Red Fox [Pueblo incident]	Korea theater	23 Jan 1968	05 Feb 1969	
Six Day War	Middle East	13 May 1967	10 Jun 1967	
CHASE	various	1967	1970	
Powerpack	Dominican Republic	28 Apr 1965	21 Sep 1966	
Red Dragon	Congo	23 Nov 1964	27 Nov 1964	
[none]	Chinese nuclear facilities	15 Oct 1963	Oct 1964	
Cuban Missile Crisis	Cuba, worldwide	24 Oct 1962	01 Jun 1963	
Vietnam War	Vietnam	15 Mar 1962	28 Jan 1973	
Operation Ranch Hand	Vietnam	Jan 1962	1971	
Operation Rolling Thunder	Vietnam	24 Feb 1965	Oct 1968	
Operation Arc Light	Southeast Asia	18 Jun 1965	Apr 1970	
Operation Freedom Train	North Vietnam	06 Apr 1972	10 May 1972	
Operation Pocket Money	North Vietnam	09 May 1972	23 Oct 1972	
Operation Linebacker I	North Vietnam	10 May 1972	23 Oct 1972	

Cold War Era – *continued*

Name	Locale	Dates		US Forces involved
Operation Linebacker II	North Vietnam	18 Dec 1972	29 Dec 1972	
Operation Endsweep	North Vietnam	27 Jan 1972	27 Jul 1973	
Operation Ivory Coast/Kingpin	North Vietnam	21 Nov 1970	21 Nov 1970	
Operation Tailwind	Laos	1970	1970	
Berlin	Berlin	14 Aug 1961	01 Jun 1963	
Laos	Laos	19 Apr 1961	07 Oct 1962	
Congo	Congo	14 Jul 1960	01 Sep 1962	
Taiwan Straits	Taiwan Straits	23 Aug 1958	01 Jan 1959	
Quemoy and Matsu Islands		23 Aug 1958	01 Jun 1963	
Blue Bat	Lebanon	15 July 1958	20 Oct 1958	
Suez Crisis	Egypt	26 Jul 1956	15 Nov 1956	
Taiwan Straits	Taiwan Straits	11 Aug 1954	01 May 1955	
Korean War	Korea	27 Jun 1950	27 July 1953	
Berlin Airlift	Berlin	26 Jun 1948	30 Sep 1949	

In these several hundred wars against Communism, terrorism, drugs, or sometimes nothing much, between Pearl Harbor and Tuesday September 11, 2001, we always struck the first blow.

THE ESSENTIAL GORE VIDAL

Gore Vidal

'It is Vidal himself who is essential. Hail to the chief'
Victoria Glendinning, *Daily Telegraph*

The range and size of Gore Vidal's literary achievement is
remarkable. He is a master of the historical novel, the novel
of ideas, theatre, satire and science fiction, and is an essayist
of deserved distinction. He is at once a contrarian, a wise
man and a romantic, wickedly funny, and often outrageous.

The Essential Gore Vidal is both a place to start reading
Vidal and a place to return for refreshment. It contains two
complete long works – the novel *Myra Breckinridge* and the
play *The Best Man* – selections from his other fiction and
twenty-five essays on subjects from philosophy to
politics to sex.

'There is no one quite like him, and if you
do not know his work you should'
Erica Wagner, *The Times*

'Gore Vidal is the most elegant, erudite and
eclectic writer of his generation'
Roy Hattersley, *Guardian*

'A figure whose vibrant verbal presence
has itself been an essential of American
cultural life for the past fifty-odd years'
Sylvia Brownrigg, *TLS*

Abacus
0 349 11267 3

PALIMPSEST

A Memoir

Gore Vidal

'*Palimpsest* is not only one of the best first
person accounts of this century we are likely
to get but also a kind of love story'
Sunday Times

'Wonderfully entertaining.
You want high-level political gossip? You get it here.
There is no one who was anyone whom he has not met
and although some receive magisterial putdowns, he is
generous to more, including rivals like Mailer . . . [readers]
will be richly rewarded, for it offers all the zing of a Dry
Martini without the danger of getting drunk'
Allan Massie, *Daily Telegraph*

'*Palimpsest* reads at times like a turbo-charged
gossip column where all the anecdotes are funny
or endearing, and the sycophancy of the journalist is
replaced by a robust directness. A storyteller of great timing
and burnished phrase, Vidal achieves the wit of fine
conversation . . . The result is a book that is far more
than a memoir; bawdy catalogue, family saga, political
history, elegy. And one of the year's best books'
Guy Reynolds, *Evening Standard*

'An engrossing and beguiling read.
Admirably candid, refreshingly indiscreet, intelligent
and full of wit, it is also startlingly original in form
and structure. An unequivocal triumph'
William Boyd

Abacus
0 349 10800 5

<u>UNITED STATES:</u>
<u>ESSAYS 1952–1992</u>

Gore Vidal

'All the Vidals are on display in this glittering showcase . . .
Long may he continue to nip and bite at the flanks of the
corrupt, the powerful, the moronic and the self-serving'
Guardian

'The arc and span of Vidal's erudition and intelligence are
prodigious . . . For forty years it has been Vidal's vocation
to restore a witty and classically literate sense of memory
and historical continuity to a country he calls "Amnesia"'
Independent on Sunday

'Vidal is the outstanding literary radical of America'
Melvyn Bragg

'He can express in a phrase what a more solemn
essayist would be hard pressed to put in a paragraph'
Peter Ackroyd

'Unique; masterly; an indispensible book' *Time Out*

'Every reader of sense should hurry to acquire
Gore Vidal's brilliant offering' *Daily Telegraph*

'He is a great historian. America needs his intelligence, and
we should not be averse to it. This volume has a very
considerable importance' Anthony Burgess, *Observer*

'Gloriously funny' Jonathan Raban

Abacus
0 349 10524 3

A VIEW FROM THE DINERS CLUB

Gore Vidal

The most elegant, incisive and caustic American writer
today, Gore Vidal here brings his fascinated attention to
bear on a wide variety of subjects from H. L. Mencken to
Oscar Wilde, Ford Madox Ford and Somerset Maugham.
He has much fun with the letters exchanged by Henry
Miller and Lawrence Durrell, deals unsparingly with
Colonel Oliver North and remembers with fondness
and wit his old friend Orson Welles.

A gadfly and a great phrase-maker, Vidal is as concerned
with politics and 'the unloved American empire' as
he is with literature; he can never be ignored.

'Stylish' *Sunday Telegraph*

'A characteristically enjoyable and stimulating collection'
Evening Standard

'He can express in a phrase what a more solemn
essayist would be hard pressed to put in a paragraph . . .
an astringent and necessary corrective to the rubbish
that is always being written about rubbish'
Peter Ackroyd

'Entertaining . . . funny, shrewd and intelligent' *Guardian*

'Sparkling . . . There are no weak lines in this
enjoyable, often brilliant collection'
Sebastian Faulks, *Independent*

Abacus
0 349 104 76 X

Now you can order superb titles directly from Abacus

☐	The Essential Gore Vidal	Gore Vidal	£12.99
☐	Palimpsest: A Memoir	Gore Vidal	£10.99
☐	United States: Essays 1952–1992	Gore Vidal	£14.99
☐	A View From The Diners Club	Gore Vidal	£7.99

The prices shown above are correct at time of going to press. However, the publishers reserve the right to increase prices on covers from those previously advertised, without further notice.

───────────────── ⬭ ABACUS ─────────────────

Please allow for postage and packing: **Free UK delivery.**
Europe: add 25% of retail price; Rest of World: 45% of retail price.

To order any of the above or any other Abacus titles, please call our credit card orderline or fill in this coupon and send/fax it to:

Abacus, PO Box 121, Kettering, Northants NN14 4ZQ
Fax: 01832 733076   Tel: 01832 737527
Email: aspenhouse@FSBDial.co.uk

☐ I enclose a UK bank cheque made payable to Abacus for £ . . . .
☐ Please charge £ . . . . . . to my Visa/Access/Mastercard/Eurocard

Expiry Date ☐☐☐☐   Switch Issue No. ☐☐

NAME (BLOCK LETTERS please) . . . .

ADDRESS . . . .

. . . .

. . . .

Postcode . . . . Telephone . . . .

Signature . . . .

Please allow 28 days for delivery within the UK. Offer subject to price and availability.

Please do not send any further mailings from companies carefully selected by Abacus ☐